T0224840

Learning VMware Workstation for Windows

Implementing and Managing VMware's Desktop Hypervisor Solution

Peter von Oven

Apress®

Learning VMware Workstation for Windows: Implementing and Managing VMware's Desktop Hypervisor Solution

Peter von Oven
Gloucestershire, UK

ISBN-13 (pbk): 978-1-4842-9968-5   ISBN-13 (electronic): 978-1-4842-9969-2
https://doi.org/10.1007/978-1-4842-9969-2

Managing Director, Apress Media LLC: Welmoed Spahr
Acquisitions Editor: Aditee Mirashi
Development Editor: James Markham
Coordinating Editor: Aditee Mirashi

Cover image by Freepik

Distributed to the book trade worldwide by Apress Media, LLC, 1 New York Plaza, New York, NY 10004, U.S.A. Phone 1-800-SPRINGER, fax (201) 348-4505, e-mail orders-ny@springer-sbm.com, or visit www.springeronline.com. Apress Media, LLC is a California LLC and the sole member (owner) is Springer Science + Business Media Finance Inc (SSBM Finance Inc). SSBM Finance Inc is a **Delaware** corporation.

For information on translations, please e-mail booktranslations@springernature.com; for reprint, paperback, or audio rights, please e-mail bookpermissions@springernature.com.

Apress titles may be purchased in bulk for academic, corporate, or promotional use. eBook versions and licenses are also available for most titles. For more information, reference our Print and eBook Bulk Sales web page at http://www.apress.com/bulk-sales.

Any source code or other supplementary material referenced by the author in this book is available to readers on GitHub (https://github.com/Apress). For more detailed information, please visit https://www.apress.com/gp/services/source-code.

Paper in this product is recyclable

This book is dedicated to my family. Without their ongoing support, I would never be able to continue writing.

Table of Contents

About the Author

Peter von Oven is an experienced technical consultant working closely with customers, partners, and vendors in designing technology solutions to meet business needs and deliver outcomes. During his career, Peter has presented at key IT events such as VMworld, IP EXPO, and various VMUG and CCUG events across the UK. He has also worked in senior presales roles and presales management roles for Fujitsu, HP, Citrix, and VMware and has been awarded VMware vExpert for the last nine years in a row and vExpert EUC for the last three consecutive years. In 2021, Peter added the vExpert Desktop Hypervisor award to his portfolio of awards. In 2016, Peter founded his own company specializing in application delivery. Today, he works with partners and vendors helping drive and deliver innovative technology solutions. He is also an avid author, having now written 18 books and made numerous videos about VMware end-user computing solutions. In his spare time, Peter volunteers as a STEM Ambassador, working with schools and colleges, helping the next generation develop the skills and confidence in building careers in technology. He is also a serving Royal Air Force Reservist currently working as an instructor with the Air Cadet organization.

About the Technical Reviewers

Iwan Hoogendoorn started his IT career in 1999 as a helpdesk agent.

Soon after this, Iwan started to learn Microsoft products that resulted in his MCP, MCSA, MCDBA, and MCSE certification.

While working as a Microsoft Systems Engineer, Iwan gained an excellent basis to develop additional skills and knowledge in computer networking. Networking became a passion of his life. This passion resulted in learning networking with Cisco products.

He got the opportunity to work for VMware in 2016 as a Senior NSX PSO Consultant. In his time at VMware, he gained more knowledge on private and public clouds and the related products that VMware developed to build the software-defined data center (SDDC). As new technology is growing at a very high pace (especially within VMware and the VMware Cloud Space), Iwan is playing catch-up all the time and is trying to keep up with the new VMware solutions. After working for four years as a Senior NSX PSO Consultant (primarily with VMware NSX-v and NSX-T), Iwan got promoted to a Staff SDDC Consultant focusing on the full SDDC stack including Hyperscaler offerings on the main public clouds like AWS (VMC on AWS), Microsoft (Azure VMware Solution), and Google (Google Cloud VMware Engine).

Iwan is certified on multiple VMware products, including NSX, and he is actively working together with VMware certification to develop network-related exams for VMware. Next to his VMware certifications, Iwan is also AWS and TOGAF certified.

Shank Mohan is a VMware Virtual Cloud Networking (VCN) Specialist Solutions Engineer. He brings over a decade of experience in IT infrastructure and architecture, with a specialization in networking, VCN, and VMware Cloud Foundation (VCF).

Shank is a VMware Certified Implementation Expert in Network Virtualization, a vExpert in NSX, Security, and NSX Advanced Load Balancer (AVI), and is CISCO and AWS certified.

Shank was born and raised in Sydney, Australia, but now prefers the calm and cold capital city, Canberra. Between firmware upgrades and breaking his home lab, he makes time for weightlifting, gardening, and most importantly, his family.

Shank has spent many hours giving back to the VMware community with his blog LAB2PROD (`https://lab2prod.com.au`) and YouTube channel LAB2PROD. He has also written a book, *NSX-T Logical Routing*.

Introduction

The VMware Workstation Pro solution is a type 2 desktop hypervisor solution that enables you to run virtual machines, containers, and Kubernetes clusters on your local PC or laptop. It provides the ideal solution for building and testing virtual machines locally before moving them into production.

This book will focus on how to get started with VMware Workstation Pro and how to install it, configure it, and start to build virtual machines and even virtual infrastructure.

Throughout this book, we will work through the Workstation Pro solution to enable you to build and manage virtual machines locally, using step-by-step instructions with real-life screenshots to demonstrate each key feature and how it works.

We start with a high-level overview of VMware Workstation Pro, introducing you to hypervisors and how CPU, storage, and memory resources work when it comes to building virtual machines and the associated virtual hardware. Armed with this knowledge, we then move on to how this applies to the Workstation Pro solution.

Next, the book moves on to explaining how to install Workstation Pro and configure the various settings and preferences, using actual screenshots as you work through the various configuration steps. Once installed, the next step is to understand how to "drive" the user interface ready to start building virtual machines.

With virtual machines built, the next step of the book will walk you through working with these virtual machines and managing them, configuring additional virtual hardware and other features.

Finally, the book will focus on how to upgrade to a new version of Workstation Pro and how to upgrade existing virtual machines to reflect the upgrade and any new available features.

Throughout the chapters in this book, you will be given hints and tips, along with best practices, all seen from the eyes of somebody who works with this technology day in, day out, and in many different types of environments and scenarios. By the end of this book, you will have acquired the skills to build a Workstation Pro environment for building and configuring virtual machines and virtual environments for development and testing purposes.

The following are some key topics we will cover in this book:

- Learn how VMware Workstation Pro can help with the development and testing of virtual machines and virtual environments.

- Install, configure, and deploy Workstation Pro ready to start building virtual machines for testing and development.

- Build a nested vSphere environment for testing ESXi, vCenter, and VSAN for training and development purposes.

- Build Windows virtual machines.

- Connect to remote virtual infrastructure.

- Learn how virtual hardware is configured and how it compares to physical hardware.

I hope that you enjoy reading this book and that the content helps you learn all about VMware Workstation Pro and how to deploy and manage the solution along with the virtual machines you build and configure.

CHAPTER 1

Introduction to Hypervisors

In this first chapter, although this book focuses on VMware Workstation, we are going to set the scene and first introduce you to hypervisors.

Before we start to get into the details of any VMware Workstation product specifics, we are first going to take a step back and describe what a hypervisor is and what role it plays. This will help define and explain what VMware Workstation is about and the fundamentals as to how it works given that VMware Workstation is described as a desktop hypervisor solution.

Let us start at the beginning and describe what a hypervisor is and how it works and then go on to talk about the different types of hypervisors and containers and why they are different to hypervisors, and then finally, touch on some of the other forms of virtualization techniques we will talk about in this book.

What Is a Hypervisor?

A hypervisor is a type of emulator that enables you to create and run virtual machines. It is a software solution that provides a layer of abstraction, or separation, between the software running on the machine and the machine's physical hardware resources.

Using a hypervisor allows you to create virtual machines, called guest machines. These guests are called virtual machines because they do not physically exist in terms of hardware. They only exist in software and share the hardware resources of the physical machine that they all run on; this machine being called the host.

These resources are presented back to the virtual machines by the hypervisor, as emulated instances such as CPU, memory, disk, and networking to name a few of the core components.

© Peter von Oven 2023
P. von Oven, *Learning VMware Workstation for Windows*, https://doi.org/10.1007/978-1-4842-9969-2_1

Because of the shared resources approach, you now can make better use of the host's machine resources. Before hypervisors came into being, deploying machines took a very siloed approach. By that I mean that you would deploy one physical machine, install the operating system, and then install the application or service. For each application, you would install another machine, another OS, then the app, and so on. You would end up with potentially a lot of physical machines and those machines not making the best use of the available resources.

Figure 1-1 illustrates the pre-virtualization siloed approach to deploying machines and applications.

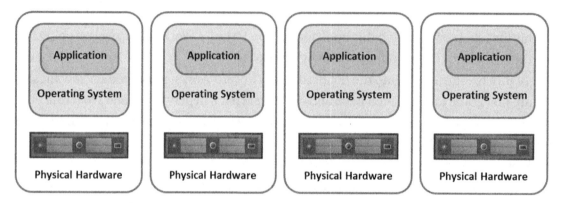

Figure 1-1. *Siloed approach to deploying applications*

As we mentioned previously, there is also the question of resource utilization. For example, if the operating system and the application running on an individual machine only consumes 10% of the machine's overall resources, then the remaining 90% would just sit there unused and would not be available for anything else to be able to use it. As a result, the physical machine resources would potentially be underutilized.

Now, if that very same machine was deployed as a virtual machine that was hosted on the same physical machine and only consumed 10% of the total resources of that physical machine, then there are a couple of things that you could do differently.

First off, as you have additional resource capacity on the physical machine, you could deploy more than one virtual machine on the same physical host. As host machines have grown in terms of resources (CPU and memory capacity), they can host more and more virtual machines. In virtualization terms this is often referred to as the consolidation ratio and results in less physical hardware being required; therefore, less power and cooling requirements too.

But a hypervisor is more intelligent than just allowing multiple virtual machines to run on a single host server. It can share the resources of the physical machine with the virtual machines that it is hosting, enabled by means of its advanced scheduling feature. This means that should a particular virtual machine be running idle and consuming very little in the way of resources, then the hypervisor can temporarily move those currently unused resources to another virtual machine that does require them. When the original virtual machine needs them back, then they are switched again. Using this technique allows you to overprovision resources when you configure your virtual machines.

There is a lot more science behind how hypervisors work and how to configure them which is out of the scope of this book. The objective of this chapter is to set the scene in describing what a hypervisor delivers before we look at the different types and, in particular, the type of hypervisor used with VMware Workstation.

Type 1 Hypervisors

A type 1 hypervisor, often called a bare metal hypervisor, is installed directly onto the physical hardware, just as you would when installing the operating system. In fact, the hypervisor in this case is basically a lightweight operating system in its own right, designed specifically to run, host, and manage virtual machines.

Figure 1-2 illustrates a type 1 hypervisor.

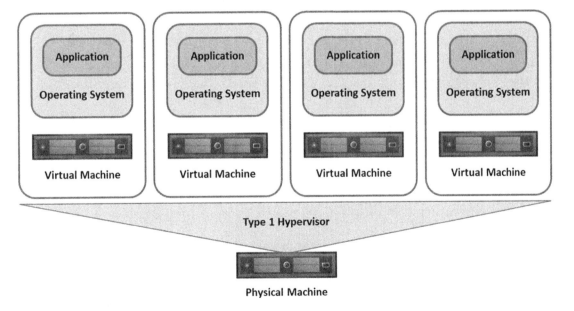

Figure 1-2. *Type 1 hypervisor*

It would typically have a basic text-based user interface to enable you to get the hypervisor running and connected to the network, and once connected to the network, you would manage it remotely using some form of hypervisor management software that would enable you to not only build, deploy, and manage virtual machines but to also implement the advanced features such as live migration or high availability.

If we take VMware vSphere as an example, VMware ESXi is the hypervisor platform, and VMware vCenter delivers advanced management capabilities.

You would find a type 1 hypervisor running on a server in a datacenter or as the virtualization layer of a cloud platform. It would be used to host multiple operating system instances, typically a mixture of both Windows and Linux based, which in turn run the applications within the environment.

Examples of type 1 hypervisors include VMware ESXi, Citrix Hypervisor (formerly XenServer), and Microsoft Hyper-V.

Type 2 Hypervisors

In contrast to the type 1 hypervisor, a type 2 hypervisor does not run on the bare metal, or in other words it does not install and run directly on the physical machine as shown in Figure 1-3.

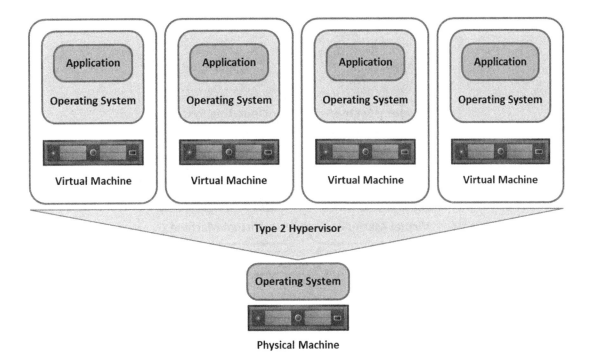

Figure 1-3. *Type 2 hypervisor*

Instead, a type 2 hypervisor runs as an application and is installed on the operating system that is already running on the physical machine.

VMware Workstation, the subject of this book, is a type 2 hypervisor. It installs as an application on your existing Windows operating system and allows you to build your virtual machines on top of that.

Just to add some complexity around the running of virtual machines on a type 2 hypervisor, you can in fact install and run a type 1 hypervisor as a virtual machine on your type 2 hypervisor! This is a form of what is called nesting or nested hypervisors as shown in Figure 1-4.

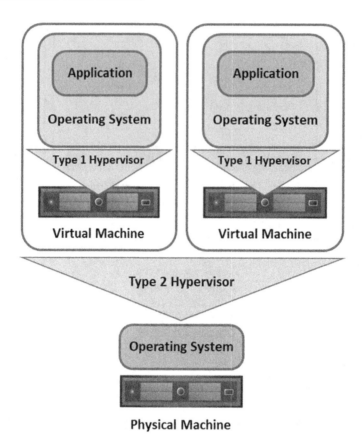

Figure 1-4. *Nested hypervisor*

Why would you do this, you ask? It is a great way to quickly build a lab environment without having to purchase massive amounts of physical hardware.

In fact, many of the step-by-step instructions in my previous books for building VMware infrastructure have been done using VMware Workstation hosting VMware ESXi and vCenter.

Containers

A question that often gets asked is "so how is a container different to a virtual machine or hypervisor-based solution?"

In this section of Chapter 1, although a container is not a hypervisor, we are going to briefly describe why that is the case and what are the differences between a hypervisor and a container.

As we have already discussed, a virtual machine runs a guest operating system instance that shares the physical resources of the host server on which it runs. It is a guest on the host's hardware.

In contrast, a container is an environment that runs an application that is not dependent on a guest operating system. Instead, it isolates just the application by bundling the application's code together with the related configuration files and libraries, and with the dependencies that the application requires for it to run.

Figure 1-5 shows the comparison between a hypervisor-based VM solution and a containerized environment.

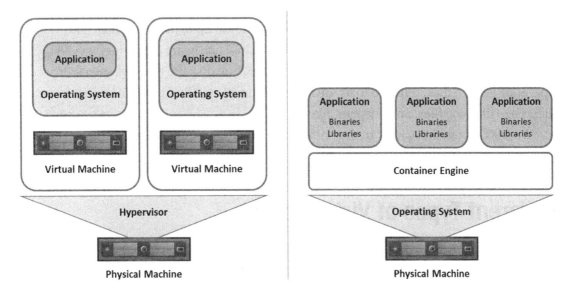

Figure 1-5. *Comparison between a hypervisor and a container*

This bundling is where the container name originates from. To give you an analogy, think about the process of moving house where you would use a shipping container into which you place all your belongings. Putting everything into a container makes it easy to move everything around in on go, rather than each item separately. It is the same for applications. Using this analogy now substitute your household belongings for the application run times, config files and libraries, and there you have your containerized apps, ready to run across any environment.

Containers provide a straightforward way to build, test, deploy, and redeploy applications on multiple environments either from a developer's local machine to an on-premises data center and to the cloud.

Examples of container engines are Docker and Kubernetes.

We will revisit containers in Chapter 13 of this book when we will look at how VMware Workstation enables you to work with containerized environments.

Virtual Machines

In the previous sections, we have talked about the hypervisor which is used to host and run virtual machines. But what is a virtual machine exactly?

A virtual machine is, on the face of it, the same as any other physical computer. It has the same basic makeup in that it has a CPU, memory, hard disk, and network connection. However, while a physical computer uses physical hardware, that is, a physical CPU, physical memory, etc., a virtual machine creates all these components in software and refers to these as virtual CPUs, virtual memory, and so on. This is often referred to as being software-defined.

A software-defined virtual machine is typically made up of just a few files, the key files being configuration files that define the virtual hardware components (CPU, memory, disk size, network connections) and the virtual disk file that represents the operating system disk, referred to as the image. You will also find other files such as swap files, page files, log files, and suspend files.

We will discuss these later in the book when we start to build virtual machines and look at what files are created.

Different Types of Virtualization

So far in this book, we have discussed hypervisors and creating virtual machines. We also touched on the makeup of a virtual machine and its software-defined components.

But it is not just the hypervisor and the virtual machines that are the focus for virtualization. There are other types of virtualization too. The key work here when talking about virtualization is abstraction.

In this section we are going to call out the key virtualization types.

Hardware Virtualization

We have already discussed hardware virtualization in this chapter. At a basic level this is the process of creating virtual machines and hosting them on a hypervisor. In doing this we have enabled the virtual machines to share the underlying hardware of the physical machine hosting them.

In this case we are talking about taking physical x86 server hardware and sharing CPU, memory, network, and storage resources with the virtual machines it runs. For example, the CPU could be "sliced" and shared with a number of virtual machines.

Storage Virtualization

With storage virtualization, you can consolidate physical storage devices and present them back as a single storage device. For example, VMware vSAN allows you to create a cluster of host servers, each one configured with its own storage resources, and present that storage as one big storage array.

The virtual machines using the storage just see a disk or storage. They do not see where the disk is physically located as they do not need to. The disks from all the hosts get pooled together and presented as one.

This approach to delivering storage enables higher availability and disaster recovery along with simplified management and lower cost.

Network Virtualization

Building virtual networks enables you to create multiple sub-networks using the same physical network. Once the physical network is cabled and connected to external physical switches, it is then extremely easy to create virtual switches, virtual routers, virtual firewalls, and other virtual networks with just a click of a mouse.

Network virtualization can also divide the available network bandwidth into multiple, independent channels, which you can then assign to virtual machines in real time, again, with the click of a mouse.

If you take a solution such as VMware NSX, this not only allows you to create all of your network components in software, but it also enables higher levels of security with features such as micro segmentation, allowing you to define the traffic flow around your network.

Being able to define network rules and policies also allows for error-free scalability and automation.

Server Virtualization

Server virtualization describes the process of creating a virtual machine that is running a server-based operating system. So, the server OS in this example is abstracted from the underlying physical hardware.

In this case the server virtual machine exists as several files and shares resources with the physical hardware on which it is hosted.

Desktop Virtualization

Desktop virtualization uses the same approach as server virtualization does to abstract a server-based OS from the physical hardware. However, the operating systems deployed are desktop operating systems such as Windows 10.

This approach separates the desktop environment from the physical device and creates a virtual desktop on host servers in the datacenter. The end user then logs on to their virtual desktop, using some form of connection broker, from anywhere and using any device using some form of remote display protocol.

In addition to easy accessibility, benefits of virtual desktops include better data security, cost savings on software licenses and updates, and ease of management as well as enabling remote and home working and BYOD.

Application Virtualization

Application virtualization is the next level up in terms of abstraction. Where desktop and server virtualization abstracts the OS from the physical hardware, application virtualization abstracts the individual application from the operating system.

This approach enables applications to become portable. Typically, solutions such as VMware ThinApp will package all the files the application needs to run such as .exe and .dll and creates a container that also includes all the elements of the operating system that are also required by the application.

The application is then wrapped up into a single executable file, and as it has its own operating system dependencies [packaged with it, it can run on different versions of the operating system.

Summary

In this chapter we have introduced you to hypervisors and discussed the two different types and how they work.

We also looked at how hypervisors and virtual machines differ from containers.

Finally, we discussed the key different types of virtualization and their use case.

In the next chapter, we are going to introduce you to VMware Workstation, a type 2 hypervisor solution for running virtual machines on your Windows PCs and laptops.

CHAPTER 2

Introduction to VMware Workstation Pro

Before we start to get into the technical details of the solution, in this second chapter we are going to introduce you to VMware Workstation Pro for Windows, VMware's desktop (type 2) hypervisor solution. Given that this was the first product that VMware released, it has a significant place in the overall history of VMware and deserves that extra bit of focus on how it all started for VMware and not just this particular solution.

It is probably worth noting that there is also a Linux version of Workstation Pro, and if you are an Apple Mac user, then there is equivalent desktop hypervisor for that platform too, in the form of VMware Fusion.

We are going to start this chapter with a quick glimpse into the history of VMware Workstation Pro. This product was the first VMware solution to be released and was generally available two years before VMware ESX was available.

A Brief History of VMware Workstation

VMware Version 1.0

Version 1.0 of VMware Workstation was just simply called VMware 1.0 as this was the very first product release by VMware.

It installed and ran on an Intel Pentium II desktop PC running Windows NT or Windows 2000 as the host operating system and enabled users to create virtual machines with the following guest operating systems: MS-DOS 6, Windows 95, Windows 98, Windows NT, Red Hat 5.0, SuSE Linux 5.3, and FreeBSD 2.2.8, 3.0, and 3.1.

Each virtual machine could support up to 2GB of virtual memory.

© Peter von Oven 2023
P. von Oven, *Learning VMware Workstation for Windows*, https://doi.org/10.1007/978-1-4842-9969-2_2

Figure 2-1 shows the splash screen for VMware 1.0.

Figure 2-1. *VMware 1.0 splash screen*

As you can see from the date on the splash screen, VMware 1.0 was released in 1999. To be exact it was the 15th of May 1999. In September of 1999, the name was extended to include the host OS platform, so in this case VMware 1.0 for Windows. This name change occurred prior to the release of the Linux version.

The Linux version of Workstation was released in October later that year. The first version to be released was version 1.1; notice it did not start at version 1.0.

VMware Version 2.0

Released in March 2000, version 2.0 added support for enabling virtual machines to be suspended in their current state and then restored instantly by allowing the virtual machines to be saved to disk. This enabled the virtual machines to be instantly restored to their prior state without the need for booting or rebooting.

It also added the ability to shrink virtual disks and enabled additional network features that allowed the virtual machine to be connected to the network using bridged or host-only networking modes.

There were five releases from v2.0 through to v2.0.4, which was released in May 2001.

VMware Workstation 3.0

The first thing to note about version 3.0, released in November 2001, was the change in name. The solution was renamed to VMware Workstation x.y. This was due to VMware releasing other products in 2001, specifically VMware ESX (a type 1 hypervisor solution) that ran on bare metal and VMware GSX (a type 2 hosted hypervisor solution for server virtualization).

Version 3.0 also saw the introduction of a repeatable resume feature that allowed a VM to be resumed from a specific point from which it was suspended. Another new feature added support for remote desktop which enabled you to connect a host to remotely manage VMs. Aside from the new features, the support for guest operating systems was expanded to now include Windows XP, Windows 2000, Novell Netware 6.0, and newer Linux OS versions.

VMware Workstation 4.0

In April 2003 VMware Workstation 4.0 was released with the key feature being the support of PAE (Physical Address Extension) for both the host OS and the VM's running as guest OS's. PAE is a memory management feature designed for x86 hardware that enables the processor to access more than 4 GB of memory.

Version 4.0 also saw the addition of USB 2.0 support as well as the ability to take snapshots of powered on, powered off, or suspended virtual machines. The final feature of note was a feature that allows you to drag and drop files that enabled file transfer to shared folders.

VMware Workstation 5.0

The core features of the VMware Workstation 5.0 released in April 2005 were focused on snapshots and cloning VMs. With the snapshot feature, you can now take an unlimited number of snapshots of running VMs.

The new cloning features allowed users to copy virtual machines and share them, as well as adding support for full or linked clones of virtual machines.

A 5.5 version was released in November of 2005 which added support of Intel VT-x/AMD-V virtualization instructions. These instructions were an integrated part of the Intel and AMD CPUs, which also enabled x86-64 bit and multiprocessor virtual machines.

VMware Workstation 6.0

Version 6.0 was released in May 2007; the end-user experience was enhanced to include support for multiple monitors. This release also allowed for VMs to run in the background.

Another feature that was added was the Converter Import wizard that was found in the VMware Converter solution. Using this tool allowed you to convert your physical Windows machines into Windows VMs.

Workstation 6.5 was released in September 2008 and included features, one of which enabled Visual Studio developers, using C/C++, to help find and diagnose bugs by replaying recordings of programs running in virtual machines.

VMware Workstation 7.0

As the Windows OS was enhanced, particularly around graphics and its user interface, Workstation was refined to add in support for these new features. Version 7.0 which was released in October 2009 added a new Windows Display Driver Model (WDDM). This display driver enabled use of the Windows Aero user interface, OpenGL 1.4, and Shader Model 3.0 within VMs.

To support these more advanced or resource hungry machines, support was added by allowing you to configure VMs with up to 4 vCPUs and 32 GB of memory.

Another significant addition was the ability to run type 1 hypervisors in the form of VMware vSphere 4.0 and ESX. These run in a "nested" environment within Workstation. There were also improvements to the replay debugging feature.

VMware Workstation 8.0

Workstation version 8.0, released in September 2011, was the first version that required a 64-bit CPU.

Features also added included support for USB 3.0 connected peripherals and the ability to automatically start VMs in the background. Finally, there was a remote connection feature that gives you the ability to connect to remote hosts running either Workstation or ESX 4.

There was also a feature removed in version 8.0, and that was the replay debugging feature.

VMware Workstation 9.0

In August 2012 Workstation 9.0 was released along with a new feature called WSX. WSX added a web interface that enabled end users to access shared virtual machines using a web browser.

This version also included enhancements for nested virtualization, meaning that you could run a type 1 hypervisor in the form of VMware ESX as a guest OS. While on the subject of hypervisors, this version also added experimental support for Microsoft Hyper-V.

There were also some hardware focuses updated with USB 3.0 support being added for Linux and Windows 8 guests, along with an improved graphics subsystem that also provided support for OpenGL in Linux guests.

Finally, additional support was added for the following OS versions Ubuntu 12.04, Microsoft Windows 8, and Microsoft Windows Server 2012.

VMware Workstation 10.0

VMware Workstation 10.0, released in September 2013, saw numerous improvements and additions with regard to virtual hardware, with VMware hardware version 10 being added. This meant that a virtual machine could now support 16 vCPUs and 8 TB virtual disks.

Also introduced were tablet sensors, a virtual accelerometer, gyroscope, compass, and ambient light sensor.

The addition of a new SSD pass-through feature allowed the guest OS to detect when the virtual machine disk file was stored on an SSD drive. If an SSD drive is being used, then the OS was able to perform virtual machine-based optimizations to increase disk performance.

The final hardware-related updates included a new virtual SATA hard disk controller and VMware KVM (keyboard, video, mouse). VMware KVM mode allows virtual machines to be run in full screen without launching the Workstation user interface and provides an alternative way to run virtual machines only in full screen. It then allows you to switch between virtual machines.

As well as an update to WSX with WSX version 1.1, the final additions included support for new guest OS versions with Microsoft Windows 8.1, Microsoft Windows Server 2012 R2, and Ubuntu 13.10 all being added.

There were several bug fix releases during the lifetime of Workstation Version 10.0, all the way up to version 10.0.7 in July 2015. This release was the last version to include support for Microsoft Windows Vista and Windows XP.

VMware Workstation 11

The key features added to Workstation 11.0, released in December 2014, focused on support for new guest operating systems. These included the following:

- Windows 10

- Ubuntu 14.10

- RHEL 7

- CentOS 7

- Fedora 20

- Debian 7.6

There was also an upgrade to the VMware hardware version, from version 10 to version 11. This added support for high resolution displays such as QHD+ displays running at a resolution of 3200x1800. As part of this support for higher display resolution, the amount of video memory support was increased to 2GB of video memory.

As cloud options continued to become more prevalent, vCloud Air was integrated that meant virtual machines could be scaled to an external cloud.

VMware Workstation 12 Pro

The first thing to note about Workstation 12.0 was the change in name. The product was renamed to Workstation 12.0 Pro and was released in August of 2015.

As with most new versions of Workstation, Workstation 12.0 Pro added several new supported guest operating systems. These included support for

- Ubuntu 15.04

- Fedora 22

- CentOS 7.1

- RHEL 7.1

- Oracle Linux 7.1

- VMware Project Photon

New hardware-based features were also added with graphics support for DirectX 10 and OpenGL 3.3, along with support for 4K monitors.

The other key feature of the release was support for IPv6 NAT networking.

The 12.5 release, released in September 2016, was really a version 13 release. However, there was no release version containing the number 13, or called version 13, as after this release VMware went straight to version 14.

As well as containing several bug fixes, it also added support for Windows 10 Anniversary Update and Microsoft Windows Server 2016.

The official release notes can be found using the following link:

```
https://docs.vmware.com/en/VMware-Workstation-Pro/12.0/rn/
workstation-125-release-notes.html
```

Workstation 14 Pro

Workstation 14.0 Pro added several new supported guest operating systems when it was released in September 2017. These included support for

- Windows 10 Creators Update support

- Ubuntu 17.04

- Fedora 26

- CentOS 7.4

- RHEL 7.4

- Debian 9.1

- Oracle Linux 7.4

- SLE 12 SP3

- OpenSUSE 42.3

A new security feature, Guest VBS Support, provides virtualization-based security features when running Windows 10 and Windows Server 2016 as guest operating systems. This allowed users to take advantage of features such as Device Guard and Credential Guard within the guest operating system. However, VBS support is only available when the host machine had an Intel-based CPU.

Another new security feature in the form of a Virtual TPM (TPM 2.0) or virtual Trusted Platform Module was also added to enable advanced security and encryption technologies, such as BitLocker. Finally, secure boot was introduced that enabled virtual machines to only trust code loaded by the UEFI firmware prior to the OS "handoff" process.

When it comes to hardware with Workstation 14 Pro, VMware Hardware Version 14 was introduced with new CPU enablement, for CPUs such as Intel Skylake and AMD Ryzen.

Virtual NVMe support was also added in the form of a new virtual NVMe storage controller. This provides improved guest operating system performance when using SSD drives in the host machine. An important use case for this feature is that it supports testing VMware vSAN.

Workstation 14 Pro also added several advanced networking features. The first of these was the ability to rename virtual networks, along with a network latency simulation that can introduce packet loss and bandwidth caps. These networking controls for introducing incoming and outgoing Latency can be configured on a per-NIC basis.

This release also included the ability to display a VM's IP and MAC address on the VM console. To enable this feature, a minimum of VMware Tools version 10.1.15 needed to be installed on the virtual machine.

An earlier release of Workstation allowed ESXi to be deployed as a VM; this release brought in several enhancements to the integration and management of ESXi power operations. Capabilities such as shutdown, restart, and enter/exit Maintenance Mode.

Coupled with the ESXi enhancements, via its improved OVF/OVA support, enables you to deploy a VMware VCSA (vCenter Server Appliance) OVA package for testing. Both VCSA version 6.0 and version 6.5 are supported.

Workstation 14 Pro allowed users to refresh their VM inventory by scanning for VMs. VMs can be located in local folders, shared network storage, and USB drives.

Finally, a feature was introduced for the automatic cleanup of Windows VM disk space. Disk cleanups could be automated while the VM was powered off.

The official release notes can be found using the following link:

```
https://docs.vmware.com/en/VMware-Workstation-Pro/14/rn/workstation-14-
release-notes.html
```

Workstation 15 Pro

In September 2018 Workstation 15 Pro was released with added support for the following guest operating systems:

- Windows 10 1803

- Ubuntu 18.04

- Fedora 28

- RHEL 7.5

- CentOS 7.5

- Debian 9.5

- OpenSuse Leap 15.0

- FreeBSD 11.2

- vSphere 6.7 support (ESXi 6.7 and VCSA 6.7)

With the added vSphere 6.7 support, users could upload or download virtual machines running on ESXi or locally. VCSA could also be deployed as an OVA package. Two new views were added in vSphere, A hosts and clusters and VM's view.

Hardware version 16 was introduced with this release and added support for DirectX 10.1 coupled with the ability to configure up to 3 GB of graphics memory.

The REST API can be used with Workstation to automate some of the more common VM tasks. The API uses standard JSON over HTTP or HTTPS and can support the following:

- Virtual machine inventory management

- Virtual machine power management

- Virtual machine clone

- Networking management

Another new feature was support for high DPI that required the host and virtual machine to both be running a minimum version of Windows 10 (1703). With this new feature, the Workstation interface auto detects the host level DPI change and auto adjusts the layout to meet the new DPI. If the DPI changes on the host side, then the guest OS adjusts its DPI to match the host DPI. To take advantage of this feature, you need to be running VMware Tools version 10.3.2.

A new useful feature is the USB auto connect feature. This allows USB devices to be automatically connected to a powered on VM. You simply configure a rule to remember the connection.

If you run Linux VMs on Workstation 15 Pro, then you can now access these VMs using SSH provided by Workstation 15 Pro; this was supported on host machines that are running Windows 10 version 1803 or later.

This release added a number of user experience enhancements. The stretch guest display feature allowed the display of the guest virtual machine to be resized. In addition, the Keep Aspect Ratio Stretch feature is used to stretch the VM display while maintaining the user interface aspect ratio. You can also use the Free Stretch feature to stretch the VM display to fill the user interface.

In September 2019 Workstation 15.5 Pro was released which had several new features including added support for the following guest OS's:

- Windows 10 19H2

- Debian 10.0/10.1

- Debian 9.11

- Oracle Linux 8.0

- SLE 15 SP1

- FreeBSD 12.0

- PhotonOS 3.0

There were a couple of network enhancements introduced as part of this release. The first of these was the addition of jumbo frame support which allows virtual networks to be configured with an MTU size of up to 9000 bytes. The second network related feature was the Preserve Network Configuration feature which meant that network settings were preserved after upgrades as well as allowing you to import and export network configurations.

The end-user experience was further enhanced with the addition of the multiple display shortcut key that enables you to quickly adjust the VM display layout using a keyboard shortcut.

Finally, a PVSCSI adapter was officially supported by Workstation, providing enhanced compatibility for migrating VMs between Workstation and vSphere.

The official release notes can be found using the following link:

https://docs.vmware.com/en/VMware-Workstation-Pro/15/rn/workstation-15-release-notes.html

Workstation 16 Pro

Workstation 16 Pro, released in September 2020, included additional support for the following OS's:

- RHEL 8.2

- Debian 10.5

- Fedora 32

- CentOS 8.2

- SLE 15 SP2 GA

- FreeBSD 11.4

- ESXi 7.0 (connect to, upload, and download VMs)

New to this version is support for containers and Kubernetes (also supports KIND Kubernetes clusters using the VTCL command line). This enables you to build, run, pull, and push container images on host machines that are running Windows 10 (1809) or higher.

This version also saw several graphics-based enhancements such as VM support for DirectX 11 and OpenGL 4.1. To take advantage of this new feature, you will need a GPU that supports DirectX 11.0. In addition to the GPU requirement, the host needs to be running a minimum of Windows 8 (64-bit), and the guest OS needs to be running a minimum of Windows 7.

The other graphics-based feature enhanced VM security by removing graphics render from vmx and running it as a separate sandbox process.

Workstation 16 Pro now supports USB 3.1. The other new hardware-based features deliver increased VM configurations, with the maximum configurations supported as

- 32 virtual CPUs (requires host and guest OS both support 32 logical processors)

- 128 GB virtual memory

- 8 GB virtual graphics memory

The end-user experience was also improved with the addition of a new dark mode supported on hosts running a minimum version of Windows 10 1809.

Other end-user experience improvements came in the form of performance enhancements. These included an improvement with drag and drop, copy and paste transfers, faster VM shutdown times, and better virtual NVMe storage performance.

The official release notes can be found using the following link:

```
https://docs.vmware.com/en/VMware-Workstation-Pro/16/rn/VMware-
Workstation-16-Pro-Release-Notes.html
```

How Does VMware Workstation Work?

As we have discussed throughout this book so far, VMware Workstation Pro is a type 2 hypervisor, or a hosted hypervisor that simply installs as an application onto a Windows host in the same way you would install a word processing or spreadsheet application.

This means that you can easily switch between VMware Workstation and your virtual machines and any other application running on your host machine as shown in Figure 2-2.

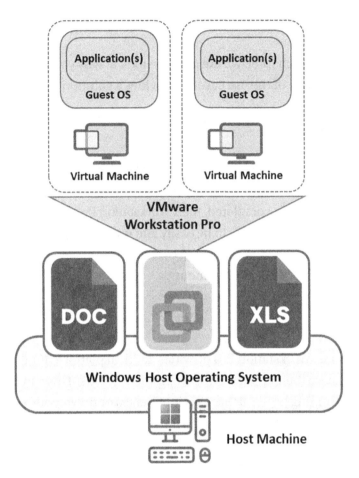

Figure 2-2. *High-level overview of VMware Workstation*

Once installed and configured, Installing Workstation Pro will be discussed in Chapter 7, you can simply create a virtual machine and configure its virtual hardware and networking as needed. The virtual hardware is shared with the host machine; therefore, the number of CPUs, memory, and storage is limited by the resources available in the host system. Resource configuration and the networking options will be discussed in more detail in the next few chapters.

The last point to touch on is the portability aspects of running a virtual machine. As we have already discussed, a virtual machine is simply made up of a set of files that can easily be copied from one machine to another. We will cover this in more detail later in this book.

Use Cases

In the final section of this chapter, we are going to look at why you would need VMware Workstation Pro and some of the use cases it provides a solution for.

IT Administrators

Workstation Pro enables IT professionals to run and test applications locally on their device. This could be to test a new version or to test OS compatibility.

Once application tests are completed, then Workstation Pro can connect to the vSphere infrastructure and allow the new VMs to be easily and quickly be promoted to production.

With its integrated advanced networking control features, an IT admin can design and test full datacenter network environments.

Developers

As with the IT admins, Workstation Pro provides an ideal platform for developers to build, test, and share their application development efforts. This can be from downloading and running pre-built application images or downloading applications from a shared or production environment, which can then be run locally.

This enables developers to quickly deploy virtual environments on an as-needed basis, without impacting the production environment.

Business Users

For traditional end users, or business users, those that are not IT professionals or developers, Workstation Pro provides a platform to deliver a standard corporate desktop environment. That could be for end users to work anywhere or to allow them to run a different and older operating system to provide access to legacy applications.

Summary

In this chapter we have introduced you to the VMware Workstation Pro solution.

After taking a brief history lesson on the evolution of the solution, from inception to where we are today, we then went on to talk about how Workstation Pro works and some of the use cases that it delivers against.

CHAPTER 3

Configuring CPU Resources

In this third chapter, we are going to focus our attention on the central processing unit, or CPU, and in the virtual world how this works and how to configure this resource within VMware Workstation Pro.

We are going to look at the terminology that is used to describe the different elements of a CPU. We will then define what a virtual central processing unit, or vCPU, is, before looking at how the two relate to each other. By this we mean looking at calculating the ratio of physical CPUs to virtual CPUs. This is a typical question that comes up when discussing CPU resources on virtual machines and how many vCPUS can be allocated to a physical CPU.

We will then look at some of the more specific features that relate to specific platforms and how hardware acceleration plays a part in compatibility and performance for both the host machine and the VMs running the guest OS's.

Understanding CPU Terminology

To start, we are going to briefly outline some of the CPU terminology to help better understand the roles of the different elements to CPUs and vCPUs.

Socket

A socket is a physical component and basically relates to the physical CPU chip itself as shown in Figure 3-1.

© Peter von Oven 2023
P. von Oven, *Learning VMware Workstation for Windows*, https://doi.org/10.1007/978-1-4842-9969-2_3

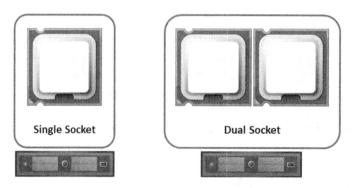

Figure 3-1. *CPU sockets*

Socket refers to the plugging in of the CPU into the motherboard of the host device.

Physical Cores

While on the theme of physical components, a physical core is essentially a CPU or the processing engine (brain) of a system. If we go back in time then, a CPU was made up of just a single core, or just one processing engine if you like.

Thanks to the ability to squeeze even more transistors onto modern silicon, a single physical CPU can now contain multiple cores, or multiple processing engines as shown in Figure 3-2.

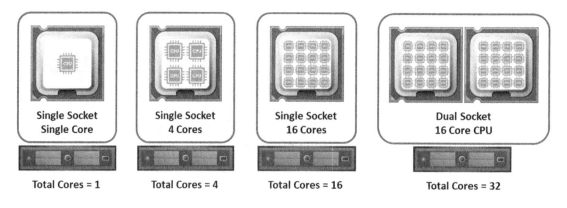

Figure 3-2. *Physical cores*

In the first example, shown on the left in the preceding figure, it depicts a single host machine with a single CPU or socket, that is, a single chip or socket. That CPU has just a single core.

The second example has a single CPU or socket; however, it contains four processing engines or cores, so the total CPU cores available is four.

In the third example, there is again a single CPU or socket; however, this single CPU has 16 cores.

Finally, in the last example, it depicts a host machine configured with two sockets, or two CPUs with each of the CPUs having 16 cores. This means that the host machine in this example has a total of 32 cores.

In the previous examples, we have looked at different CPU configurations based on the number of cores and the number of sockets. So, why do CPUs have multiple cores? The answer is simply so that they can perform multiple tasks. Each core can only execute a single task at a time, so the more cores you have the more tasks the CPU can complete simultaneously. Referring to the example in Figure 3-2, the single core example can only carry out one task at a time, whereas the 32-core system can carry out 32 tasks at a time.

However, if the CPU does not have enough cores to be able to process the tasks that are being sent for processing, then it will experience a performance penalty. This penalty is called the Context Switch Overhead. This switching means that for a core to process another task, then a task needs to be removed. Once the task is removed, then the next task can be loaded. The performance overhead is because the CPU is spending more time switching than it is processing the tasks.

The final piece we are going to discuss, on the subject of cores, is the speed at which the cores run. This is called the clock speed and defines the frequency at which processes are executed. To further define the clock speed, it is the frequency of the number of calculations per second that the CPU can execute measured in Gigahertz or GHz. 1GHz is 1,000,000,000 calculations per second.

You would think that this defines the overall performance of the CPU; however, there are several contributing factors as to why this is not the case, things such as the memory capability of the processor, known as cache, which can hold instructions ready for execution. This means that they get to the CPU much quicker. Different CPUs have different amounts and different types of cache that will affect performance. Other factors such as disk speeds and network speeds also affect how quickly the information is sent to the CPU for processing.

The final part of our CPU tour is going to discuss threading, hyperthreading, and logical CPU cores and what the difference is.

Threading, Hyperthreading, and Logical Processors

Let's start by defining what a thread is in its basic terms. A thread is essentially data that gets sent to the CPU for the CPU to action and process. As such, a thread is not actually a physical part of the CPU. It is just the amount of data streams the CPU can handle.

As we discussed previously, there is a performance overhead on the CPU if it spends time context switching due to there not being enough cores available to complete the calculation processes requested. To help with this threading and to increase the number of threads a CPU can handle, multi-threading is used to create an additional virtual core from each CPU core. This results in each CPU core having two virtual cores (threads) or the ability to appear to be able to process two threads at the same time.

This ability to process more than one thread or multi-threads is called hyperthreading (Intel CPUs). It is called simultaneous multi-threading or SMT on AMD-based CPUs. Figure 3-3 shows the CPU architecture for multi-threading.

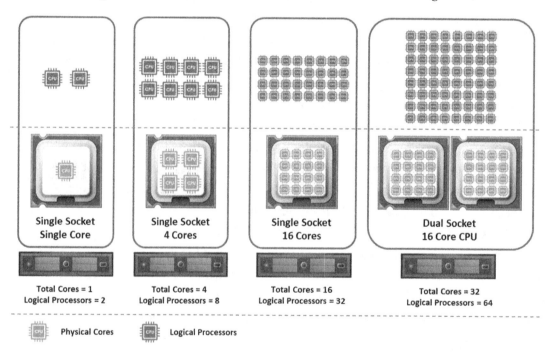

Figure 3-3. CPU architecture for multi-threading

In the previous statement, we stated that the thread *appears* to be able to process two threads simultaneously. However, what happens with multi-threading is that the CPU cores are not simultaneously processing two threads using one physical core. Instead, multi-threading is a way of efficiently scheduling the threads to be executed by the core without delay or performance hit. It does this by readying a thread to be processed while one thread is being readied, another thread can be executed by the CPU core.

So far, we have mainly discussed what happens at the CPU side, with the sockets, cores, and threads. But what does the operating system see? and how are these then allocated to virtual machines? These are called logical processors.

This is where virtualization is first introduced. However, we are still talking at the silicon level here and not at the VMware hypervisor level.

A logical processor is a virtualized processor (at the silicon level) that is then presented to the operating system. From there the operating system can address each logical processor as if it were an actual processor or core.

For example, if I look at the Task Manager on my laptop as shown in Figure 3-4.

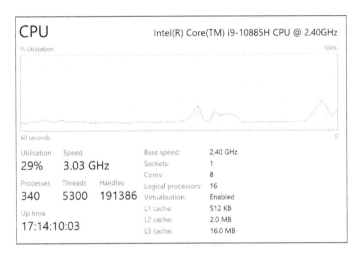

Figure 3-4. *CPU view of Task Manager*

you can see that it has a single socket with eight physical cores and with hyperthreading enabled (this is an Intel i9 CPU); you can see that there are 16 logical processors.

If you were to open the Device Manager, you would see that there are 16 logical processors listed and therefore available to the operating system (Figure 3-5).

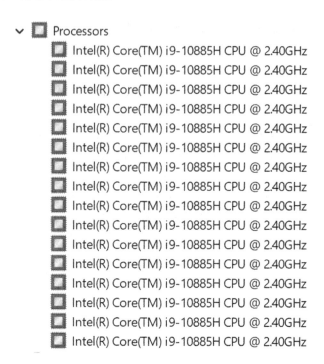

Figure 3-5. *Device Manager view of logical processors*

Now that we have discussed the physical CPU; in the next section, we are going to move on to virtual CPUs taking on board what we have learned about CPUs previously.

What Is a Virtual CPU (vCPU)?

Now that you understand the constructs of a physical CPU, its cores, and logical processors; in this section, we are going to take this knowledge and map it into the virtual world.

A virtual CPU or vCPU is basically a virtual machine being scheduled time or sharing time on the physical CPU to complete its execution of tasks. That scheduling is the responsibility of the hypervisor. It manages the relationship between the number of CPUs configured in the virtual machine and the actual physical CPUs in the host system. This concept of time sharing is how you can host multiple virtual machines on a single host. Obviously, this is dependent on the physical CPU resources the host can deliver.

You may see this described as the vCPU to physical CPU ratio.

So how does a vCPU work? As we just said, it is the job of the hypervisor to schedule CPU time by allocating a portion of the physical CPU resources and mapping that to a vCPU. In turn vCPUs are assigned to a virtual machine.

The next question is how you calculate that ratio and work out how many vCPUs you can configure per physical CPU.

Previously, calculations were very simple and were just a case of calculating the number of vCPUs available using the figure of eight vCPUs per physical CPU cores available in the host machine. However, the physical CPU technology has evolved with larger number of cores and larger number of threads. This means that that figure of eight vCPUs per physical core is somewhat on the conservative side and doesn't really make use of the total CPU resources available.

Therefore, that calculation has been updated by now taking into account the number of threads available per core and multiplying the number of occupied sockets. To calculate the number of vCPUs available, you can use the following equation:

(Threads x Cores) x Physical CPU = Number vCPUs

However, having said all that, this is the calculated or theoretical values, and what you need to bear in mind is the actual workload profile of the virtual machines themselves. By that I mean you need to understand what the VMs are doing with regard to consuming CPU resource.

For example, do apps regularly run at 100% utilization, or do they sometimes peak at 100% or run at 100% continually? Basically, this means understanding whether apps burst the CPU requirement. Or are there periods, such as out of office hours, where they require next to no CPU resource?

Where I am going with this is to understand how many VMs the host can comfortably accommodate. Maybe not quite so critical when running VMware Workstation Pro as the VMs are likely for test and development; however, what you do need to do is ensure your host has enough resources to run everything else, including its own operating system. It is all about the overall end-user experience and not making the host machine run slowly.

The key takeaway is not to over provision CPU resource. It is very easy to get carried away when building VMs and to configure more CPU resource than is needed. Don't forget the underlying hardware needs to be able to service that demand. While this is probably more relevant to building virtual datacenters and ensuring resources are correctly configured, it is still important for VMware Workstation Pro as misconfiguring could slow the entire machine, both VMs and locally running apps.

For example, if you have VMs that typically use very little CPU resource, then you will be able to run more VMs. On the flip side, if your VMs need more or a greater amount of CPU resource, then you will end up with less VMs running on the host.

CPU Hardware Acceleration

We are not going to discuss hardware acceleration in any detail in this section; however, we will touch on the concept, so you get an understanding of the capabilities of some of the new CPU technologies that enable better performance and compatibility when running virtual environments.

One of the latest x86 CPU-based technologies is a hardware-based solution that helps the performance of CPU resources using hardware-assisted virtualization at the CPU level.

In the Intel world, this technology is called Intel VT or Intel Virtualization Technology, and in the AMD world, this technology is called AMD-V. Both can be enabled in the BIOS of the host machine if they are not already enabled by default. So how does CPU hardware-assisted virtualization work?

An x86 CPU typically runs in protected mode. Protected mode allows the software running on the host machine to have access to features such as virtual memory, paging, and safe multi-tasking. These features are all designed to not only increase the control over the applications that the OS has over them, but to also provide an enhanced level of security as well as to increase the overall stability of the system. Without these additional features, it would mean that it would be significantly more difficult for the OS to function correctly or even impossible without this level of hardware support.

In protected mode the operating system kernel runs at a higher privilege level enabling it to have access to everything. This privilege level is called ring 0. There are four levels, or rings, for different privilege levels:

- **Ring 0** – Kernel (highest privilege level)
- **Ring 1** – Device drivers
- **Ring 2** – Device drivers
- **Ring 3** – Applications (lowest privilege level)

Applications, however, run in a lower privilege level, ring 3. As software-based virtualization solutions effectively act as the operating system, it will have direct access to underlying hardware in the host. The guest virtual machines running on that host, however, are deemed to be applications and, therefore, behave like applications and have limited access to the underlying hardware.

One approach to get over this issue when running on x86 software-based virtualization is called ring deprivileging. This simply allows a guest operating system or virtual machine to run at a higher privilege ring level such as ring 2, where it would have direct access to some of the device drivers running on the host machine. There are a few key elements that enable protected mode to be virtualized:

- Binary translation is used to rewrite certain ring 0 instructions into ring 3 instructions. An example of this is the CPU interrupt flag that is used to decide whether the CPU will respond immediately to maskable hardware interrupts. This flag can only be modified by the kernel and therefore only with a ring 0 privilege. In normal operation trying to execute this at any other ring privilege level would cause it to fail. This would make trap-and-emulate virtualization impossible.

- **Shadow page tables** – Several of the key data structures used by a CPU need to be shadowed. This is down to operating systems using paged virtual memory to operate correctly. If you give the guest OS direct access to the memory management unit (MMU), it could potentially result in the loss of control by the virtualization manager. Therefore, the shadow page table feature comes into play where some of the work of the x86 MMU is duplicated in software so that the guest OS can access it. It does this by denying the guest OS access to the "real" page table entries by trapping the access attempts and then emulating them.

- I/O device emulation allows unsupported devices running on the guest OS to be emulated by a device emulator running on the host.

In this section we have just focused on the enhanced CPU features and functionality designed specifically for running virtual environments. However, there are also similar techniques that apply to accelerating things like GPU (graphics processing unit) to enable hardware accelerated graphics in virtual desktop solutions.

Hyper-V Enabled Hosts

Just to finish up on the theme of the last section, and the hardware acceleration features that can now be found integrated at the CPU hardware level, it is not just a unique feature that VMware virtualization solutions can take advantage of. As this technology is at the host's physical CPU level, that means that other technologies can also take advantage of CPU virtualization features. The question is can these all be used together or is it more binary?

If we take VMware Workstation Pro, for example, as this is the subject of this book, it relies on having direct access to the CPU in order to take advantage of these new integrated virtualization features such as Intel VT or AMD-V. As we mentioned previously, these features being at the hardware level are not exclusive to VMware Workstation Pro, and as you are running VMware Workstation Pro as an application on a Windows host machine, then this host machine and host OS are likely to be using the Microsoft Hyper-V feature built into the latest version of Windows.

As Hyper-V is also a software-based virtualization solution, it too needs access to these virtualization features built into the CPU. For example, one of the features of the Windows OS is virtualization-based security (VBS) that is built on Hyper-V. Therefore, to enable VBS you need Hyper-V and then the CPU virtualization features. This means that VMware Workstation Pro could not have access to the CPU virtualization features, and therefore, you would not be able to power on any virtual machines unless Hyper-V was disabled.

The reason for this is that the VMware Workstation Pro Virtual Machine Monitor (VMM) runs in privileged mode so therefore needs direct access to the CPU and the virtualization features of that CPU. But when the Windows host running VMware Workstation Pro enables VBS, the Windows OS creates a Hyper-V hypervisor layer V between the hardware and the Windows OS. Therefore, when the VMware VMM tries to launch a virtual machine, it will fail simply because Hyper-V has abstracted the hardware from the OS itself, meaning the VMware VMM cannot see or access it. The result is no virtualization features available and no VMs can power on.

Luckily, this issue has now been resolved as of VMware Workstation Pro version 15.5.5 when VMware and Microsoft collaborated and developed a project that adopts Microsoft Windows Hypervisor Platform (WHP) APIs which are available in Windows from the April 2018 update.

To fix this VMware redeveloped their VMM to allow it to now run at the user level and not in privileged mode as it did before. It also allowed the VMM to use the WHP APIs to manage the execution of a guest instead of using the underlying hardware directly. It's like allowing the VMware VMM and Hyper-V to work together to deliver resources. The result is that you no longer need to disable Hyper-V on your Windows host machine if you want to run VMware Workstation Pro.

Just remember you will need to be running Windows 10 20H1 build 19041.264 or newer and VMware Workstation Pro 15.5.5 to take advantage of this feature. If neither of these versions are being used, then you will need to disable Hyper-V on your Windows host OS to be able to power on VMs.

Summary

In this chapter we have discussed, in detail, the CPU and how it works in a virtualized environment. We started by describing the different terminologies and the architecture of a physical CPU when it comes to sockets, cores, and threads. Next, we looked at virtual CPUs and how to calculate how many vCPUs you can configure for each physical CPU in your host machine. Finally, we looked at CPU acceleration and how to configure Hyper-V when running Workstation Pro.

CHAPTER 4

Configuring Storage Resources

In this chapter, we are going to turn our attention to virtual storage and how this works when virtualized and particularly for use in VMware Workstation Pro.

The first part of this chapter is going to describe the overall concept of what a virtual hard disk is, what it is used for, the different types of provisioning methods, and the different formats for the different vendor solutions. We will, of course, focus on the VMware virtual disk configuration used in VMware Workstation Pro.

We will then look at some of the features and benefits of virtual hard disks such as the snapshot functionality. Finally, we are going to look at the different disk formats used by VMware, focusing on VMware's own VMDK virtual hard disk format, open formats such as OVF, and raw disks.

Virtual Hard Disks

The first thing we are going to discuss is what defines a virtual hard disk and how a virtual hard disk compares with a physical hard disk.

At the basic level, a virtual hard disk file is a container file that acts in a similar way to how a physical hard disk would behave in that it contains a disk image file format for storing the entire contents of a computer's hard drive. It replicates the physical hard disk including its structure, such as the file system.

Like a physical hard disk, a virtual hard disk file contains a file system, and therefore it can then host an operating system, applications, and any other data that would normally be stored on a hard disk.

As a virtual hard disk is basically a file, using its own virtual disk and file system, it can then be attached or mounted to virtual machines (VMs), to provide the same functionality as a physical hard disk for storing the OS, apps, and data. In some cases,

© Peter von Oven 2023
P. von Oven, *Learning VMware Workstation for Windows*, https://doi.org/10.1007/978-1-4842-9969-2_4

virtual hard disk files are also used for archival purposes as they are portable and potentially don't use as much space as a physical disk. This means they can be stored on non-production storage systems.

In the previous paragraph, we touched on the ability of the virtual hard disk to be mounted to a virtual machine to provide the virtual machine with its operating system disk.

You can also mount virtual hard disks to the operating system. For example, the virtual machine OS would use a VMware VMDK format, and you can then mount a VHD or VHDX format virtual hard disk to the operating system as an additional hard disk. It is similar to the way that you attach any other type of removable media to a computer. That is, you plug it in, and the OS has access to it. Or, as we described, if it is the OS disk itself, it is mounted before the machine boots and delivers the C:\ disk on which the OS and associated boot files reside.

Virtual Hard Disk Formats

We touched on a specific format (VHD and VHDX) in the previous section; however, there are several different types of virtual hard disk file formats. It's usually possible to differentiate between the different virtual hard disk types and therefore which vendor solution they are used for, by looking at the filename extension.

Don't forget, at the end of the day, the virtual hard disk is just a file.

Some of the more common types of virtual hard disk format include

- Virtual Disk Image (VDI), used by Oracle VirtualBox

- Virtual Machine Disk (VMDK), used by VMware

- Virtual Hard Disk (VHD), used by Microsoft and Citrix

- Virtual Hard Disk (VHDX), used by Microsoft

Some virtual hard disk file formats are supported by multiple vendor products. For example, VDI, VMDK, and VHD are all supported by Oracle VirtualBox.

Virtual Hard Disk Classifications

There are three main classifications of virtual hard disk files. A classification defines how the virtual hard disk stores its data and ultimately how much disk space it is going to consume.

The three types we are going to describe are

- Fixed

- Dynamic

- Differencing

Fixed Virtual Hard Disks

A fixed virtual hard disk file, as the name suggests, creates a virtual hard disk with a fixed size. This size is configured at the time the virtual hard disk is created.

As the size is configured when you create the virtual hard disk, then the virtual hard disk allocates 100% of the configured size at creation time.

For example, if you create a fixed virtual hard disk of 250GB, then the full 250GB will be fixed at that size, and also 250GB will be allocated from the underlying physical storage layer as shown in Figure 4-1.

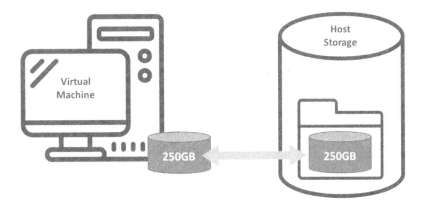

Figure 4-1. *Fixed virtual hard disks*

As this is the least efficient method of creating virtual hard disks, it is likely that this classification would only be used where you needed to guarantee the amount of storage required and you know all that disk space is going to actually be used.

Dynamic Virtual Hard Disks

A dynamic virtual hard disk is, like the fixed disk, configured to be a specific size; however, that configured size is not fully allocated on creation. Instead, it is set as a maximum to which the virtual hard disk can grow to if required.

For example, take the 250GB virtual hard disk example used in the previous example. On creation, the virtual hard disk is presented to the virtual machine as a 250GB virtual hard disk; however, not all that capacity is required from day one, and so the disk grows as the data being stored on it grows.

Typically, this will start off with a minimal amount of data, maybe just a few megabytes or gigabytes, until it reaches its maximum capacity of 250GB. It may be that it never reaches its maximum capacity, and typically virtual machines don't, but it is there if it is required. This is shown in Figure 4-2.

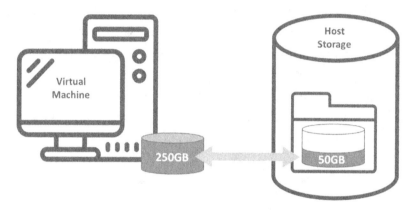

Figure 4-2. *Dynamic virtual hard disks*

This mode of operation is also referred to as thin provisioning, meaning that only a "thin" amount of data is stored rather than allocating the entire capacity when creating the virtual hard disk.

Thin provisioning is the most common way in that virtual hard disks are created given that it makes best utilization of the physical storage resources available.

Differencing Virtual Hard Disks

A differencing virtual hard disk is a virtual hard disk that has a link to another virtual disk or physical disk. Instead of making a new and unique copy of the original virtual hard disk, a differencing disk, as the name suggests, just stores the differences, or changes that are made to the original disk.

The easiest way to explain this is with a couple of examples, the first one being the snapshot feature.

Snapshots are a point-in-time representation of a virtual hard disk file. The hypervisor management tools track any changes made to the original or parent virtual hard disk file with these changes being stored on a separate virtual hard disk file. We will talk about snapshots later in this chapter.

The other example of differencing disks is when using cloning technologies designed for rapid deployment of virtual machines at scale. If you take a virtual desktop solution such as VMware Horizon, there used to be a feature called Linked Clones. Linked Clones basically took a parent gold image of the desktop OS and created multiple copies as each virtual desktop machine was created and powered on. These copies of the virtual hard disk files stored the changes that each new virtual desktop made and were linked back to the original parent image to read any new data required. Figure 4-3 shows differencing virtual hard disks.

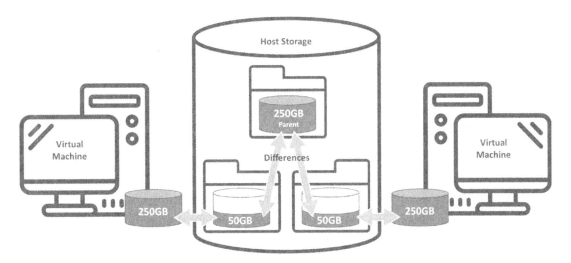

Figure 4-3. *Differencing virtual hard disks*

This feature has now been superseded by instant clones which create on-demand copies of virtual machines, again using snapshot technology.

Virtual Hard Disk Advantages

Obviously with virtual machines, you need virtual hard disks, but there are also additional advantages with virtual hard disks other than them being used by virtual machines to store OS, applications, and data.

Backup and Restore

Virtual hard disks are also often used by backup applications and data archive solutions that use the snapshot feature to efficiently create backups without using large amounts of physical capacity.

This also allows for instant recovery in some cases and depending on the backup solution. Even the virtualization platform itself can manage multiple snapshots; however, these are designed more for development work and provide the ability to roll back in the event of a failed update for example.

Security and Privacy

Virtual hard disks can be formatted using the same file systems as used with physical hard disks which means that they can be encrypted using standard encryption tools.

For example, if you are creating Windows virtual machines, then you could use BitLocker to encrypt virtual hard disks.

Portability

Virtual hard disks are portable, but not in the same way a physical hard disk is. It is easy to create a new virtual hard disk or to delete one, but as a virtual hard disk is basically a file, it can easily be mounted to different virtual machines, meaning it is easy to move between virtual machines. This provides an ideal solution for delivering DR as the virtual hard disk files can be replicated to other storage platforms, such as a lower tier of storage or be ready in the event of a failure of the primary site.

Virtual Storage Controllers

As with physical machines, a hard disk controller, in this case a virtual hard disk controller, is required to control and provide access to the virtual hard disks and any other multi-media devices such as DVD drives that you want to connect to your virtual machines.

When configured, a virtual storage controller appears to a virtual machine as a type of block-based controller which can be either a SCSI or SAS controller with the following controller types available in VMware Workstation:

- BusLogic

- LSI Logic

- LSI Logic SAS

- Paravirtual SCSI

The following sections explain in more detail these different types of virtual hard disk and storage controllers and their use cases.

BusLogic Parallel

BusLogic was one of the first virtual storage controller types that was emulated on virtual machines hosted on the VMware vSphere platform.

One of the reasons for using BusLogic was due to the fact that at the time the Windows OS provided a driver for this controller by default and, for that reason, this controller can still be used when configuring virtual machines running older versions of the Windows OS, but ultimately this particular virtual storage controller is now considered to be legacy.

As an older virtual storage controller, it has limitations in what it can support. For example, you cannot create a virtual machine with a virtual hard disk that is bigger than 2 TB in size. It is also not as performant as newer virtual storage controllers give that it only supports a disk queue depth of 1.

LSI Logic Parallel

Like the BusLogic virtual storage controller discussed in the previous section, the LSI Logic storage controller has also been available since the first versions of the VMware virtualization platform.

As with the virtual storage controller, the LSI Logic Parallel SCSI controller also has support for many different operating systems including some legacy operating systems as again, by default, they contain the driver for this controller.

However, the LSI Logic controller supports a queue depth of 32 which made it a better choice if you need better performance and basically the reason why it became the default selection when creating virtual machines. For example, this controller is selected as the default controller when you create a Windows Server 2003 virtual machine. Not only because of the increased queue depth but also because the LSI Logic controller supports SCSI2 commands.

LSI Logic SAS

The LSI Logic SAS storage controller is the new and updated version of the LSI Logic Parallel and therefore will be the default selected controller when building and creating Windows Server 2008. The core reason for this being that this controller supports SCSI3 commands and which the newer versions of the Windows operating systems support.

VMware Paravirtual SCSI

The VMware Paravirtual SCSI is different from the previously described controllers as it is virtualization-aware and supports high throughput. This means that a lot of the processing is offloaded from the CPU in comparison to the other controllers that use emulation. It also means that this controller can deliver high IOPS performance.

As this storage controller is purely virtualization-based, there is no hardware equivalent. This means that several operating systems will not support this controller by default and won't be included in the standard drivers that ship with the OS. This is especially true when it comes to older OS versions.

To fix this then, the driver will need to be installed manually on the OS to make it work. This controller is adopted for high IOPS performance (input/output operations per second).

If there are snapshots for virtual disks that are connected to a paravirtual SCSI controller, or if memory is overcommitted on a host, then performance may be lower than expected when using this storage controller type for a VM.

Configuration of Storage Controllers and Storage Devices

When you create a virtual machine, the first hard disk, which will be disk 0, is assigned to the default controller, controller 0. You will see this displayed as 0:0 as shown in Figure 4-4.

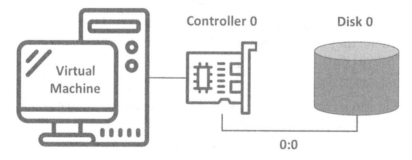

Figure 4-4. *Single controller with single disk - (0:0)*

When you add more storage controllers, then they will be numbered sequentially, so the next one will be 2, then 4, and so on up to the maximum number of controllers supported. This is shown in Figure 4-5.

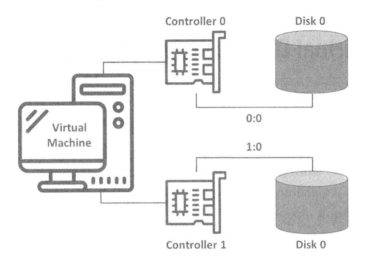

Figure 4-5. *Two controllers each with a single disk*

If you continue to add new hard disks, or other storage devices, either at the time of creation or once the virtual machine has been created, then the new device is assigned to the first available virtual device node on the default controller as shown in Figure 4-6.

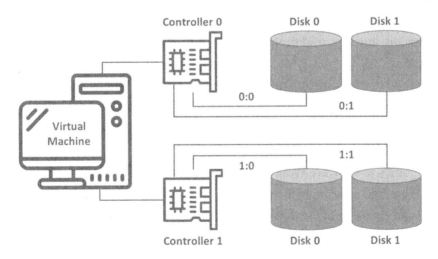

Figure 4-6. *Two controllers each with two disks*

For example, if you add a second virtual hard disk to the default controller, it will be displayed as 0:1, and if you add a second virtual hard disk to the second controller, then it will be displayed as 1:1 as shown in the example graphic in Figure 4-6.

VMware Virtual Disk Files (VMDK)

In the previous sections, we have talked about the virtual disks and virtual controllers and have stated that a virtual hard disk is essentially a file that gets created on your host machine. But what sort of file is it?

A VMware Virtual Machine Disk file, or a VMDK file for short, is a format specification used for storing files created by virtual machines and is a complete and independent virtual machine as it contains all files whether OS, apps, file system, or data that make up an entire virtual machine.

This is how virtual machines are portable between platforms and as such can be moved across them. That could be a simple migration between two hosts or copying a virtual machine from a type 1 hypervisor such as ESXi to a type 2 hypervisor such as VMware Workstation Pro.

However, it's worth mentioning that virtual machines that have been created on an ESXi host server have a slightly different format when it comes to the virtual disk file or VMDK file. With ESXi host servers, you will see that there are two separate files, a descriptor file that defines the structure of the virtual disk, virtual disk geometry, virtual hardware version, and IDs, and then the actual virtual disk file itself that will store the raw data.

If you browse to the datastore on the ESXi host, you will see the two files as follows:

- **<vm_name>. vmdk** - contains the descriptor

- **<vm_name>-flat. vmdk** - contains the raw data

When it comes to VMware Workstation and its use of the VMDK disk format, the virtual disk is created as a single file with the name **<vm_name>.vmdk**. This monolithic sparse disk is an extent data file that contains an embedded virtual disk descriptor as well as the raw data all in that single VMDK file.

The VMDK virtual hard disk format was originally developed by VMware, but is now an open file format that can be used by other hypervisors.

It is worth mentioning that Microsoft's virtual hard disk format VHD and VHDX are not compatible with VMDK files. You can make use of third-party conversion tools if you need to convert virtual disk files that have been created using a different hypervisor platform. You won't need these third-party tools to move between VMware ESXi and VMware Workstation Pro, even though the formats are slightly different. At the end of the day, they both use the VMDK file format for virtual hard disks.

Disk Mode Settings

So far in the virtual hard disk discussions, we have talked about disk classification, controllers, and the virtual disk file format used by VMware.

In this section we are going to talk about the different disk modes that virtual hard disks operate with. There are three different disk modes that you can choose from:

- Dependent

- Independent persistent

- Independent non-persistent

In the following sections, we are going to describe each of these different disk mode settings and their use case.

It is worth noting that disk modes have a direct relationship with snapshots and define the behavior of a VMDK file when a virtual machine snapshot is taken.

Dependent

Dependent disk mode is the default option, and every new virtual hard disk created, unless changed, will be configured as dependent.

The word dependent, used in this disk mode, refers to the fact that when a snapshot of the virtual machine is created, then this disk is included in that snapshot.

When you configure a disk mode, then it applies to each individual VMDK file and not the all the disks configured on the virtual machine. Therefore, you could in theory configure different modes for each disk attached to any one virtual machine.

Independent Persistent

In contrast to dependent disk mode, independent means that any snapshot created of this virtual machine is not included with the disk. Think of the word "independent" referring to the fact that the disk operates independently of any snapshots.

When you take a snapshot of a virtual machine with an independent persistent disk mode configured, you will see that there is no delta file associated with this disk when the snapshot is taken. The VMDK will carry on as if no snapshot is being taken which means that it will continue to write to the virtual hard disk rather than these changes being written to the delta file. Remember, there is no delta file in this mode. This mode of operation describes the independent element, but what about persistency?

This disk mode is persistent due to the fact that any changes made to the disk are preserved even when the snapshot gets deleted. On that note of deleting the snapshot, you need to bear in mind that as all the changes are committed to the disk, you will not be able to roll back as you can with the dependent disk mode.

Independent Non-persistent

Like the independent persistent disk mode, snapshots that get created for this virtual machine are not included with the disk.

But in non-persistent mode, rather than write any changes directly to the disk, instead a redo log file is created and is used to capture these changes, leaving the original disk as is, and unchanged.

When you then come to power off the virtual machine, this redo log file that has captured the changes is deleted. This is also true if you delete the snapshot too. As the name suggests, changes are non-persistent, that is, they are discarded.

Disk Mode Setting Use Case Examples

To complete the disk mode settings section, we are going to look at a use case for the different mode settings.

In this example you have a Windows virtual machine that is configured with two virtual hard disks demonstrating that each virtual hard disk can be configured with a different disk mode. Virtual hard disk #1 contains the OS and therefore is configured as the default dependent disk mode.

Virtual hard disk #2 is used for the Windows swap file and so is configured for independent non-persistent mode. As Windows swap files do not need to be kept, then these will be deleted when the virtual machine is powered off. This saves disk space by not allowing the swap file to potentially grow to consume more disk space than is necessary.

Another use case could be for classroom-based virtual machines configured with independent non-persistent disk mode. All the time they are in class accessing the virtual machine, they can make changes and do whatever they need, but when they leave class, and the virtual machine is powered off, then any changes they have made are discarded. Then, when the next student comes to use the same virtual machine, it is effectively reset back to where it started from, with a clean OS.

Snapshots

In the previous section, when discussing disk modes, we stated that snapshots have a direct link to the disk mode, but what is a snapshot?

A snapshot in VMware terminology is a copy of a virtual machine's disk file at a given point in time. That point in time being when the snapshot is created. By having this copy of the disk file at a specific time then, it allows you to roll a virtual machine back to that specific point in time should you need to.

Not only does it take a copy of the disk file at the given point in time, but the snapshot also preserves the state of a virtual machine such as whether it is powered-on, powered-off, or suspended.

It's not just data from the virtual hard disk that is included in the snapshot. All the elements that make up the virtual machine are also included, so CPU, disks, memory, and any other devices attached to the virtual machine at the time the snapshot is created. This state is captured and stored in a separate file which will have the VMSS file extension. It is these two files, the VMDK and VMSS files, that define the current state of the virtual machine. This is shown in Figure 4-7.

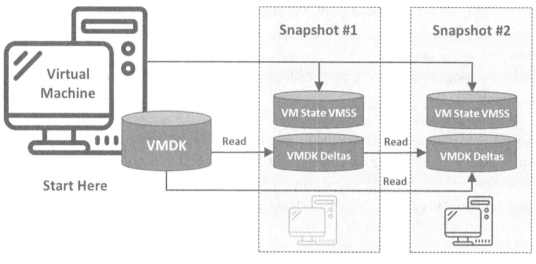

Figure 4-7. *Architecture of a snapshot*

When the snapshot is taken, the VMDK file effectively becomes frozen and can only be read from. If any of the files are changed, then these are written back to a delta disk that gets created as well.

An example use case for snapshots is for applying a patch update to a virtual machine. Before you apply the patch, you take a snapshot. You then apply the patch and during testing realize that the patch has broken something. You can then simply roll back to the snapshot taken before you applied the patch taking the virtual machine back to its known working state. Think of snapshots as a quick and simple "get out of jail free" card.

Having just defined what a snapshot is, it is equally as important to define what a snapshot is not! Often snapshots get described as a backup based on their ability to restore the virtual machine to a previously known working state. Snapshots are not backups and should not be relied on as such.

It is against VMware best practice to consider snapshots as a backup solution for virtual machines.

The key reason for snapshots to not be considered as backups of virtual machines is, primarily, they do not meet the criteria for what an effective backup and recovery point should deliver.

A backup should be a completely independent copy of the original virtual machine. However, a snapshot is stored on the same disk as its parent virtual machine. That means should the parent virtual machine fail due to an infrastructure outage, either due to a failed host server or even the storage subsystem failing and you losing data, don't forget a virtual hard disk is just a file at the end of the day, then the snapshot will also be lost.

If you have a true backup, then this backup will be stored on a separate storage platform, or cloud service, independent of the virtual infrastructure. Therefore, the backed-up data is unaffected by any outage and so can be used to restore the failed virtual machine's virtual hard disk.

The other reason for not using snapshots for backup is the fact that they consume a lot of disk space and will continue to grow. Not only that, having a large number of snapshots all stored on the same storage platform will result in poor performance as they each need to reference each other and the parent.

Snapshots are designed for the short-term and as such should be deleted and not kept longer than necessary. So, for example, once you have completed your update for which you created the snapshot for, and everything works, then delete the snapshot.

OVF Disk Format

Open Virtualization Format, or OVF, is an open-source standard for the packaging and distributing of software applications and services used by virtual machines.

It provides an open standard that enables not only the portability of virtual machines but also a way to distribute virtual machines between the different hypervisor platforms.

One thing to remember is that OVF is a standard and not a type of virtual hard disk format. It merely represents the metadata used by a virtual machine. This means that will contain the VM name, its RAM configuration, and its CPU configuration along with other settings such as storage, networking, and graphics.

As it is a standard, OVF is specified by the Distributed Management Task Force and published by the International Organization for Standardization as an ISO. In this case ISO 1720. As we have already mentioned, as OVF is a standard, it is independent of any hardware platform or hypervisor architecture. Using the DMTF's Common Information Model (CIM), the OVF open standard can be used to map and interpret the metadata to create virtual machines.

In the context of VMware Workstation Pro, you can import OVF files and deploy the virtual machines as per the configuration contained in the metadata. We will cover this in more detail in Chapter 11.

Summary

In this chapter we have discussed virtual machine storage. We defined what a virtual disk is and what it is made up of and the different formats, focusing on the VMware VMDK format used by Workstation Pro.

Next, we looked at the different disk mode settings and then what a snapshot is and how snapshots work. Finally, we looked at OVF file formats and what they are used for.

CHAPTER 5

Virtual Network Resources

In this chapter we are going to focus on virtual networking and how virtual machines can communicate with each other as well as communicate with external machines and services such as the Internet when running as virtual machines hosted by VMware Workstation Pro.

We are going to start by describing how virtual networking works along with an overview of the core components that make up a virtual network.

Next, we are going to look at some of the networking types that are used by VMware Workstation Pro to enable communication between virtual machines and external networks.

Finally, we are going to take a closer look at some of the additional networking features included with VMware Workstation Pro, such as Network Condition Simulation and the Virtual Network Editor.

Virtual Networking Overview

A virtual network emulates a physical network by taking the hardware components and the software components that you find in physical network resources and creating a single administrative unit; this is defined in software alone.

As with a physical network, virtual networking components that are defined in software include virtual switches, virtual network adapters, and in the case of VMware Workstation Pro virtual networking, a virtual DHCP server and a NAT device.

We will describe the use case for each of these components used in Workstation Pro in the coming sections.

© Peter von Oven 2023
P. von Oven, *Learning VMware Workstation for Windows*, https://doi.org/10.1007/978-1-4842-9969-2_5

Virtual Switches

A virtual switch, or vSwitch, is the core and central component in any virtual network. The same as it would be in any physical network, a virtual switch connects networking components together and enables them to communicate with each other.

As such a virtual switch performs the tasks as any other network switch; however, it is now done in software. Tasks such as forwarding and virtual local area network (VLAN) segmentation are all now done in software.

There are some Workstation Pro-specific networking elements to be aware of and that's with regard to virtual switches. In Workstation Pro virtual switches are called virtual networks. Unlike ESXi, you don't create virtual switches or distributed virtual switches and then provide uplinks and port groups, etc. In Workstation Pro you just connect the virtual machine to the appropriate network, and in turn that either connects directly to the network or via the host machine depending on your configuration. You can also connect a private network that has no external connections.

If you create a new network, then as part of the creation process of the new network, a virtual switch will be created as well. For example, if you create VMnet5, as this is not one of the existing networks, then the switch will be created for this network. You then configure the connections.

Workstation Pro is able to create up to 20 virtual switches or virtual networks for connecting to. These are labelled VMnet0 through to VMnet19.

As per the preceding note regarding Workstation Pro networks, although 20 virtual switches are created, some of them are already mapped to specific networks by default. These networks are as follows:

- **VMnet0** – Bridged connections

- **VMnet1** – Host only connections

- **VMnet8** – NAT connections

You can connect an unlimited number of virtual network devices to a virtual switch on a Windows host system.

In the next section we are going to look at how virtual machines connect to the virtual switches and networks by means of a virtual network adapter.

Virtual Network Adapters

As with the virtual switches, a virtual network adapter, more commonly called a virtual network interface card (vNIC), recreates the functions of a physical adapter and defines that functionality in software.

When you create a new virtual machine in Workstation Pro, then as part of that configuration, a virtual network adapter will be added to the virtual machine configuration. Unlike with virtual network adapters, you might be used to, in ESXi, you don't get to choose the type of network card that gets configured. The virtual network adapter model is defined based on the guest operating system of the virtual machine.

For example, it may appear as an AMD PCNET PCI adapter, Intel Pro/1000 MT Server Adapter, or an Intel 82574L Gigabit Network Connection. In Windows 10 it will be listed as the latter, the Intel 82574L Gigabit Network Adapter.

Newer versions of Workstation Pro, version 6.x and later, support up to 10 virtual network adapters.

Virtual DHCP Server

Workstation Pro has its own integrated Dynamic Host Configuration Protocol or DHCP server. This is used to provide IP addresses to virtual machines that are not connected directly to an external network such as when using host-only mode and NAT-based network configurations.

NAT Device

The final network component in Workstation Pro is the Network Address Translation, or NAT device. When you configure the NAT option for networking, the NAT device is responsible for passing network data between virtual machines and the external network. As part of this job, it identifies incoming data packets destined for the virtual machines and ensures that the data gets sent to the correct destination.

We will discuss the NAT networking option in more detail in the Network Configuration Options section of this chapter.

Network Configuration Options

In this section of the chapter, we are going to discuss the different network configuration options that Workstation Pro uses to communicate with virtual machines and external networks.

There are three different configuration options:

- Bridged (VMnet0)

- NAT (VMnet8)

- Host-Only (VMnet1)

During the installation, you will have seen network adapters for VMnet1 and VMnet8 added as devices on the host machine. If you open the Device Manager on your host machine, you will see the following entries for VMware Virtual Ethernet Adapters along with your other network adapters as shown in Figure 5-1.

Figure 5-1. *VMware virtual network adapters in Device Manager*

In the next sections, we are going to discuss these networking options in more detail.

Bridged Networking

When you select the bridged networking option, then the virtual machines will be visible and accessible from the external network. If the host machine is already configured and connected to a network, then bridged networking is often the easiest way to give the virtual machine access to that network.

This works by the host machine sharing its network connection with the virtual machines. The virtual machines will appear as any other machine would appear that is connected to your network and, therefore, will be visible and accessible to everyone on that network for them to connect to or interact with. This is shown in Figure 5-2.

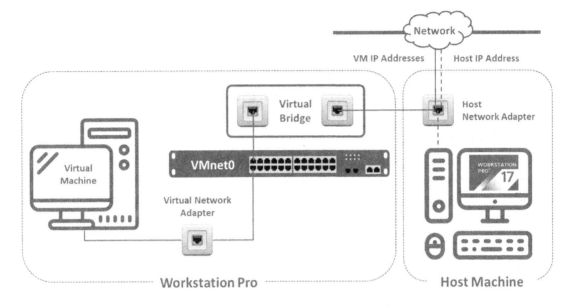

Figure 5-2. *Bridged network connections*

With bridged networking, the virtual network adapter in the virtual machine connects to a physical network adapter in the host system. The host network adapter enables the virtual machine to connect to the same network used by the host machine via either a physical wired connection or a wireless connection if the host has a wireless network adapter installed. This is shown in Figure 5-2 with one virtual machine IP address. However, you will need a separate connection and IP address for each virtual machine.

When you configure a bridged network, then the switch, named VMnet0 and reserved for bridged network connections, is automatically created and configured as part of the network configuration and provides the virtual machine with a unique identity on the network. This unique identity is the MAC address of the virtual machine and is separate from and completely unrelated to the network identity used by the host machine.

That means that the virtual machine appears as any other network connected machine and has access to other resources on the same network given that it will also have an IP address on that network either delivered by DHCP from your infrastructure, or if you have given it a static IP address. IP addresses, by the way, are configured as you would normally configure them in the guest operating system.

However, if security is a concern for your virtual machines, then you can use NAT which we will cover in the next section of this chapter.

NAT Configuration

Unlike bridged network connections, NAT shares the host machines network connection by assigning the virtual machines with an IP address delivered from a private network. In this case the IP address is delivered by a virtual DHCP server integrated into Workstation Pro.

This IP address of the virtual machine on the private network is not visible on the external network and translates network requests from the virtual machine to the host machine. This means that the host machine appears as a single machine on the network, whereas with bridged connections, virtual machines all appear individually with unique IP addresses.

When you configure a NAT network connection, then the switch, named VMnet8 and reserved for NAT network connections, is automatically created and configured as part of the network configuration and provides a gateway to the network for the virtual machines. These virtual machines are not visible on the network and only appear visible to the host machine. Effectively the virtual machines are on a separate network.

This means that the virtual machines and the host machine are sharing a single network identity that is not visible on the external network. NAT works by translating the IP addresses of the virtual machines on the private network to the IP address used by the host machine. When a virtual machine sends a request to access a network resource, the request appears to be coming from the host machine and its IP address. This is shown in Figure 5-3.

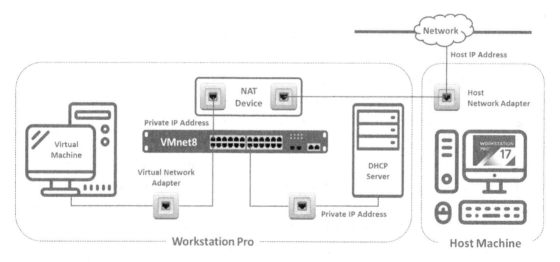

Figure 5-3. *NAT network connections*

It does this by configuring a virtual network adapter on the NAT network that is used by the host machine. This virtual network adapter enables the host machine to communicate with the virtual machines. The NAT device passes network data between one or more virtual machines and the external network. It also identifies the incoming data packets destined for each virtual machine and ensures they are sent to the correct destination.

The final network configuration is the host only network option.

Host Only

When you configure a host-only network, the virtual machines and the host virtual network adapter are connected to a private network.

This private network is completely self-contained within the host machine and is not visible externally.

When you configure a host-only network connection, then the switch, named VMnet1, is automatically created and configured as part of the network configuration as shown in Figure 5-4.

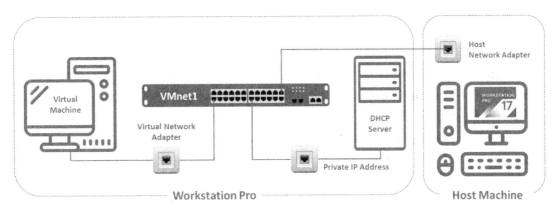

Figure 5-4. *Host-only network connections*

The network connection between the virtual machine and the host system is provided by a virtual network adapter that is visible on the host operating system. The virtual DHCP server provides IP addresses on the host-only network.

As this network is a host-only network and has no direct connection to an external network, then with the default configuration, virtual machines are unable to connect to the Internet. If you install routing or proxy software on the host machine, you could configure that to connect between the host virtual network adapter and the physical network adapter. The other option is to use the Windows Internet Connection Sharing feature and configure that to use either the dial-up networking adapter or any other Internet connection available on the host machine.

Network Condition Simulation

Network Condition Simulation is a feature that was introduced with VMware Workstation Pro 14.

It is designed to allow you to configure the incoming and outgoing network so that you can simulate different network characteristics such as helping developers who are building applications to understand how that application behaves under certain network conditions that are different to the network they are currently connected to. Maybe they have limited bandwidth or a high-latency connection.

You can control and configure the following network characteristics:

- Bandwidth

- Latency

- Packet Loss

We will cover this feature in more detail in Chapter 10, Configuring Virtual Machine Options as this is configured on a per virtual machines basis rather than as a global settings that applies to all virtual machines.

The final option we are going to touch on in this chapter is the Virtual Network Editor feature that allows you to configure the network connection and the DHCP functionality of Workstation Pro.

Virtual Network Editor

We have mentioned, in the host-only and NAT networking sections, the use of a DHCP server that is integrated in Workstation Pro that delivers IP addresses to virtual machines when configured with NAT and host-only network configurations.

However, where does the DHCP server get its addresses from in the first place, and can you configure those addresses to use your own IP address range rather than use the default ones.

As this is a global setting, then we are going to cover this in more detail in this section.

To configure the different network connection options, Workstation Pro has the **Virtual Network Editor**. To configure virtual networking, follow the steps described:

1. From the menu, click **Edit** and select **Virtual Network Editor...** as shown in the following screenshot in Figure 5-5.

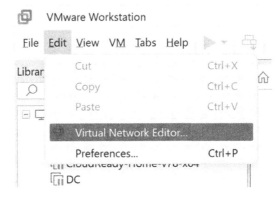

Figure 5-5. *Launching the Virtual Network Editor*

2. Once launched, you will see the following screenshot in Figure 5-6 showing the host-only and NAT network options and the default assigned subnet addresses.

Figure 5-6. *Virtual Network Editor*

3. The first thing to do if you want to edit any of these settings is to click the **Change Settings** button which you will find next to the **Administrator privileges are required to modify the network configuration** warning message.

4. When you click the button, you will see a UAC warning message. Click **Yes** to continue.

5. You will now return to the Virtual Network Editor screen where you will now see that you are able to edit all the settings as the bridged network connection is now visible to configure.

We are going to look at the configuration options starting with the VMnet0 network used for the bridged network connections. If you click on the entry for **VMnet0** in the list at the top, you will see it becomes highlighted and that the radio button option for **Bridged** in the **VMnet Information** box is highlighted as shown in Figure 5-7 in the following screenshot.

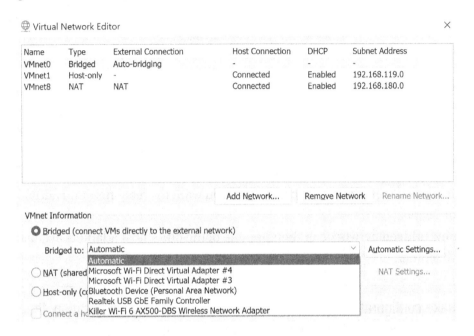

Figure 5-7. *Virtual Network Editor for bridged connections*

VMnet0 is the default network used in the configuration for auto-bridging mode. This includes bridging to all the active network adapters configured in the host machine.

You can then configure which physical network connection or connections you want to use by clicking on the drop-down menu for **Bridged to**.

As you can see from the list, you can select just one of the individual physical network adapters that is present in the host machine to be used, or you can select the option for **Automatic**.

If you click the **Automatic Settings...** button, you will see the following screenshot in Figure 5-8.

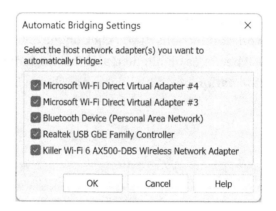

***Figure 5-8.** Virtual Network Editor for automatic bridged connections*

Check the box for each of the adapters you want to be made available automatically. If you deselect any of them, then they will not be part of the automatic selection which frees them up to be selected in the case where you want to create new and additional bridged networks.

The new bridged network can then use one of the other host adapters available in the host machine.

If you make configuration changes to the bridged network configuration, then these changes will affect all the virtual machines that are currently configured to use the bridged network connection on the host machine.

It is also worth noting that if you reassign a host network adapter to a different virtual network, the virtual machines using that virtual network will lose their network connection as that host network adapter will no longer be available to them. To ensure continued connectivity, you will need to change the setting for each virtual machine network adapter individually.

There is also another issue to be aware of should you change host adapters, especially if the host machine only has a single physical network adapter installed in it.

If you change the configuration and now assign the physical adapter to another virtual network other than VMnet0, even though the virtual network appears to be correctly bridged to a host adapter that is selected automatically, the only adapter it can use is assigned to a different virtual network.

It is also worth adding, and it goes without saying, the bridged and NAT options have a 1:1 relationship. That means if you want to add additional NAT or bridged connections, then you will need to make sure you have the additional host network adapters to support this.

Next, we are going to look at the options for changing the configuration for VMnet1 or the host-only network.

If you click on the entry for **VMnet1** in the list at the top, you will see it becomes highlighted and that the radio button option for **Host-only** in the **VMnet Information** box is highlighted as shown in Figure 5-9 in the following screenshot.

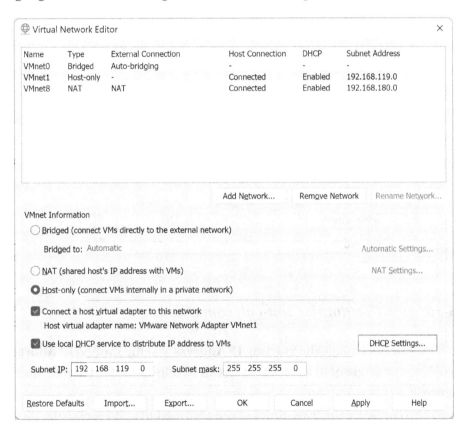

Figure 5-9. *Virtual Network Editor for host-only connections*

You then have two options, both enabled by default, and selected or deselected by checking or unchecking the corresponding check box.

The first option is for **Connect a host virtual adapter to this network**. This enables the connection to the virtual network adapter in the host machine and therefore allows you to connect a physical network from the host machine to this network.

The second option is for **Use local DHCP service to distribute IP address to VMs**. Enabling this means that the integrated DHCP feature of Workstation Pro will provide the virtual machines on this network with IP addresses allocated from the range set. The **Subnet IP** and the **Subnet mask** of the currently configured scope is displayed below this setting.

You can, if required, reconfigure this from the current default settings. To do this click on the **DHCP Settings...** button. You will now see the DHCP Settings screen as shown in the following screenshot in Figure 5-10.

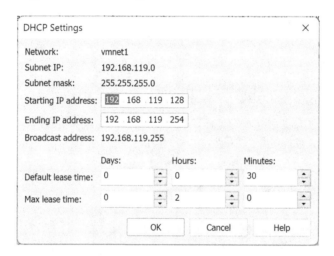

Figure 5-10. *DHCP Settings for host-only connections*

From here you can change the **Starting IP Address** and the **Ending IP Address** to configure a range or scope of IP addresses that can be allocated to the virtual machines on this network.

You can also configure the lease times of the allocated IP addresses using the **Default lease time** and **Max lease time** configuration fields.

Click **OK** once you have made your configuration changes, and then once you return to the Virtual Network Editor screen, ensure you click Apply to save and make these changes active.

If you have changed IP address ranges, you may need to update the virtual machines too so that they pick up any new IP addresses.

There are a couple of use cases for reconfiguring the host-only network or creating additional host-only networks.

The first is just purely because you want separate and isolated networks. Maybe this is for testing virtual machines for two separate projects.

Another is where you want to test routing between multiple networks to simulate having different networks that need to communicate with each other.

Perhaps, you have a requirement whereby a machine has more than one connection to more than one network using a network adapter for each network connection. In this case you can create a virtual machine with multiple network adapters and simulate the different networks. This is a more cost-effective way of doing this rather than having to buy additional hardware just for testing.

The final option is the NAT configuration as shown in Figure 5-11.

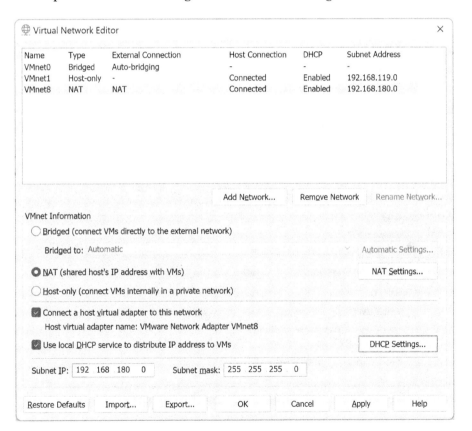

Figure 5-11. *Virtual Network Editor for NAT connections*

If you click on the entry for **VMnet8** in the list at the top, you will see it becomes highlighted and that the radio button option for **NAT** in the **VMnet Information** box is highlighted as shown in the previous screenshot.

The first two configurable options are the same as we described for the host-only connection and that is for **Connect a host virtual adapter to this network** and **Use local DHCP service to distribute IP address to VMs**.

As before these can be configured to provide the same functionality as already described, along with the ability to change the DHCP settings if you need to.

The other option for NAT is to change the settings of how NAT works within Workstation Pro. To configure this, click the **NAT Settings...** button. You will see the following screenshot in Figure 5-12.

Figure 5-12. *Virtual Network Editor for NAT settings*

The first thing you can change is the **Gateway IP** address for this network. Simply type in the IP address you want to use if you need to reconfigure this.

The next option is to configure port forwarding. With port forwarding, any incoming TCP or UDP requests are sent to a specific virtual machine on the virtual network that is served by the NAT device.

By default, there are no ports forwarded, but if you want to add port forwarding for a particular port, then in the **Port Forwarding** section, click the **Add...** button. You will see the **Map Incoming Port** box as shown in the following screenshot in Figure 5-13.

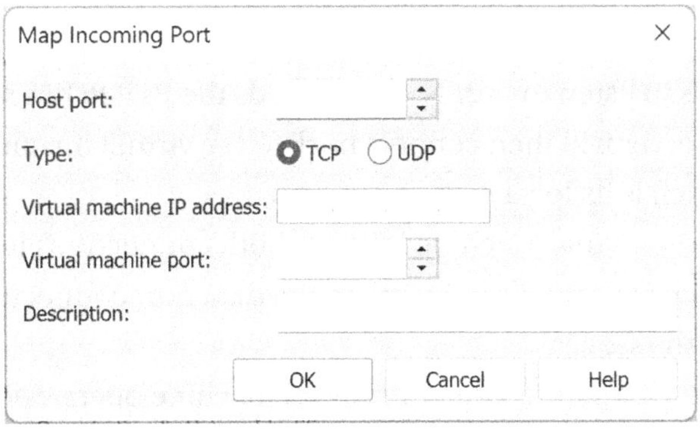

Figure 5-13. *Configuring Port Forwarding for NAT network*

The first thing to configure is the Host port. This is the port on which the incoming request is received from the host machine. In the **Host port** field, you can either use the up and down arrows to select a port number or you can type it in directly.

Next, you can choose whether this is a **TCP** or **UDP** host port. To select the port, click the radio button in the **Type** field and select the type of port for the incoming request.

In the **Virtual machine IP address** field, type in the IP address of the virtual machine to which the incoming requests should be forwarded to. In the **Virtual machine port field**, you can also enter a port number used by the virtual machine for these requests.

Then finally, in the **Description** field, you can optionally enter text to describe this port mapping rule.

Once configured, click **OK**.

If you already have some existing port forwarding rules setup, then to edit these you would simply click and highlight the mapping you wanted to edit from the **Port Forwarding** box and then click the **Properties** button. That will show the Map Incoming Port box again with the already configured settings shown which you can now update or change.

Similarly, if you wanted to completely remove a port forwarding rule, then click to highlight it and then click the **Remove** button.

Next, you have the **Advanced** section of the NAT Settings screen shown in Figure 5-12.

The first option in **Advanced** settings is the **Allow active FTP** setting. The file transfer protocol, or FTP, is an application-layer protocol used for transferring files over TCP networks. FTP supports two modes, active and passive, with each mode requiring different connection mechanisms.

With active mode the virtual machine makes a connection from a random unprivileged port to port 21 on the FTP server. This is the command port. Then, the virtual machine starts to listen to port N+1 and sends the FTP PORT N+1 command to the FTP server. The server will then connect back to the virtual machine's specified data port from port 20 which is its local data port.

In passive mode the virtual machine initiates both connections to the server. This solves the issue of firewalls that filter the incoming data port connection between the virtual machine and the server.

When opening an FTP connection, the virtual machine opens two random unprivileged ports locally. The first port contacts the server on port 21, but then instead of issuing a PORT command and allowing the server to connect back to its data port, the virtual machine issues the PASV command. PASV is how this mode got its name. The result of this is that the server then opens a random unprivileged port and sends P back to the virtual machine in response to the PASV command. The virtual machine then initiates the connection from port N+1 to port P on the server so that data can be transferred.

The next setting is for **Allow any Organizationally Unique Identifier**. This setting is used if you change the organizationally unique identifier, or OUI, part of the virtual machine's MAC address. The OUI is the part of the MAC address that identifies the vendor of the network adapter and is identified by the first three bytes (first 24 bits) of the six-byte field. This would mean you could not use NAT with the virtual machine if you changed the OUI unless you enable this feature by checking the box.

The **UDP Timeout** option allows to configure the number of minutes that the UDP mapping for the NAT is kept for before timing out.

Config port should not be changed unless otherwise directed to do so by the VMware technical support team, so do not change this setting.

Finally, there are two options relating to the configuration of IPv6. The first is the **Enable IPv6** check box. Checking the box switches IPv6 on which is followed by the IPv6 prefix field that allows you to enter the IPv6 prefix used by the NAT device when you enable IPv6.

You will also see two buttons at the bottom of the NAT Settings box. The first of these is the **DNS Settings...** button. This enables you to configure the DNS servers for the virtual NAT device to use.

If you click this button, you will see the **Domain Name Server (DNS)** box as shown in Figure 5-14.

Figure 5-14. *Configuring DNS*

The first option is the **Auto detect available DNS servers**. To enable this, ensure the box is checked. This means that DNS servers will be automatically detected and added. If you uncheck the box, then you can manually add DNS servers in the **DNS Servers** section which is no longer grayed out when you uncheck the auto detect box.

Next is the Policy option. This is used for when you have multiple DNS servers in your environment. If you click the drop-down, you will see that there are three options:

- **Order** - Sends DNS requests one at a time in order of the name of the DNS servers that are available

- **Rotate** - Sends DNS requests one at a time rotating through the DNS servers that are available

- **Burst** - Sends DNS requests to all servers listed simultaneously and then waits for the first server to respond to the request

The **Timeout (sec)** option, which is the next option on the list, allows you to set the number of seconds to keep trying the DNS requests if the NAT device cannot connect to the DNS server. After that period of time has lapsed, then the requests are no longer sent.

Along with the timeout, the final option is for Retries. This simply allows you to set the number of times you want to retry sending the request.

With the default settings, then each request is sent to the DNS servers in order, and if no response is received within two seconds, then it will retry the operation three times before stopping.

The last button on the Nat Settings screen is for NetBIOS settings. If you click the **NetBIOS Settings...** button, you will see the **NetBIOS Settings** box as shown in the following screenshot in Figure 5-15.

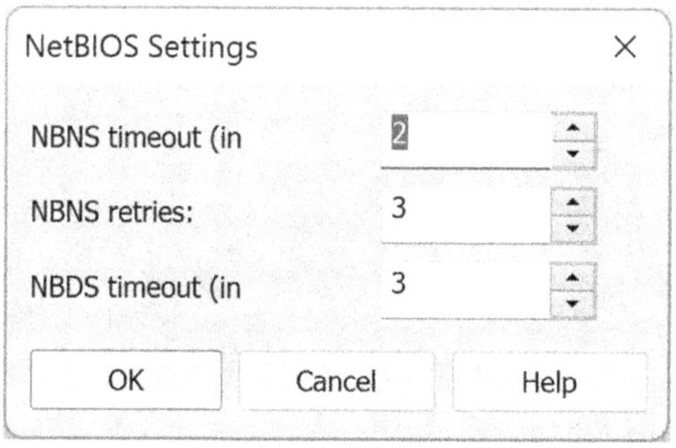

Figure 5-15. *NetBIOS Settings*

NetBIOS is a non-routable OSI Session Layer 5 Protocol. It allows applications running on computers to be able to communicate with other computers and devices over a local area network or LAN. In this case we are talking about both virtual machines and physical machines and devices on the network.

The first two settings relate to the NBNS (NetBIOS Name Service) which is part of the NetBIOS-over-TCP/IP protocol suite. It enables legacy computer applications relying on the NetBIOS Application Programming Interface (API) to be used on a TCP/IP network. It provides a name lookup service for legacy rather than DNS.

For the NBNS you can configure the **NBNS timeout** and the **NBNS retries**. These work in a similar way as those configured for DNS in that timeout specifies a time period to keep trying for and retired specifies the number of time to try that period for.

Finally, you have the option for NBDS (NetBIOS Datagram Service). The NetBIOS datagram service provides a connectionless, unreliable transport used for unicast, multicast, and broadcast messages or datagrams and is rarely used today. However, if you need it for legacy, then you have the option to set the **NBDS timeout** setting.

Finally, in this section we are going to touch on the other buttons at the bottom of the Virtual Network Editor screen. These are as follows:

- **Restore Defaults** - Resets all the values to the default values

- **Import** - Allows you to import an existing network configuration file

- **Export** - Allows you to export the current network configuration as a file

Next, we are going to look at adding a new network.

Adding a Network

The last thing we are going to look at is how to add a new network.

If you want to add a new network, it is a simple case of clicking the **Add Network...** button. You will then see the **Add a Virtual Network** box as shown in Figure 5-16.

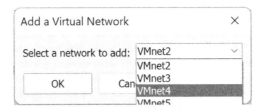

Figure 5-16. *Add a new Virtual Network*

From the drop-down menu under **Select a new network to add**, click to select one of the unused switches.

You will then see that new network has been added to the list of networks. In this example, we have added **VMnet4** which, by default, is added as a host-only network in this case as shown in the following screenshot in Figure 5-17.

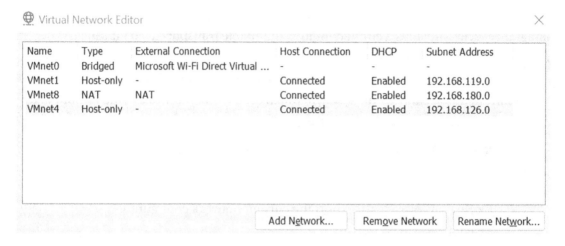

Figure 5-17. *New Virtual Network added*

The reason this has defaulted to host-only is because the host adapters are already configured in the bridged configuration.

If you tried to change this network from host-only to bridged, you will get the following warning message shown in Figure 5-18.

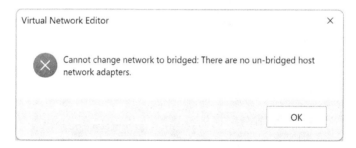

Figure 5-18. *Virtual Network Editor Warning for bridged network*

As the message says, there are no network adapters available. If you wanted to have this new network configured as a bridged network, you need to remove the adapters from the currently configured bridged network and add them to this network. Or, as we previously discussed, change the current bridged configuration from automatic to select a particular network adapter, or modify the list of those adapters that can be automatically selected.

Similarly, if you tried to change this newly added VMnet4 network to be a NAT connection, you will see the following as shown in Figure 5-19.

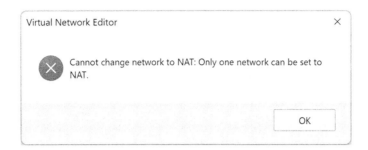

Figure 5-19. *Virtual Network Editor Warning for NAT network*

This is because only one network can be configured as NAT. If you want this new network to be the NAT network, then you will first need to remove the current NAT network configuration.

Summary

In this chapter we have discussed the components of virtual networking.

We discussed in detail the three networking modes that Workstation Pro uses, bridged, NAT, and host-only, and the difference between them along with the different use case.

Next, we discussed the Virtual Network Editor that allows you to configure network settings at a global level within Workstation Pro. This is akin to configuring your network switch infrastructure. The network adapters in the virtual machines will be discussed in Chapter 10, Configuring Virtual Machine Options.

In the next chapter we are going to discuss the different virtual hardware.

CHAPTER 6

Virtual Hardware

In this chapter we are going to discuss virtual hardware but more specifically the virtual hardware versions that VMware Workstation Pro supports.

We have already discussed virtual CPU, virtual networking, and virtual storage at a high level in previous chapters, so in this chapter we will discuss those as well as other virtual device types but focus this time on how they work and are configured for virtual machines running on Workstation Pro.

But first we are going to take a closer look at virtual machine hardware versions and hardware compatibility.

Virtual Machine Hardware Versions

The virtual machine hardware version, also known as the hardware compatibility, defines the virtual hardware functions that are supported by a virtual machine. Hardware such as the number of virtual CPUs a virtual machine can support or the maximum amount of memory a virtual machine can support.

Hardware versions can also add enhancements to virtual machines that are running an older operating system version.

When you create a new virtual machine, you can either go with the default hardware version or you can select a previous version. However, you need to be aware that if you select an older hardware version, then it may have reduced functionality as it may not support the hardware required.

Equally, if you select a higher hardware version that is not supported by the version of Workstation Pro, then the result will be that the virtual machine will not power on. This is because the hardware requirements cannot be met.

© Peter von Oven 2023
P. von Oven, *Learning VMware Workstation for Windows*, https://doi.org/10.1007/978-1-4842-9969-2_6

For example, if you create a virtual machine using the latest version of Workstation Pro, which at the time of writing this book is version 17, and the latest hardware version released with Workstation Pro 17, which is virtual hardware version 20 and you then tried to run that virtual machine on Workstation Pro 16 that only supports up to virtual hardware version 19, then the virtual machine will fail to power on.

The table in Figure 6-1 lists the virtual hardware versions and the corresponding supported versions of Workstation and Workstation Player.

Virtual Hardware Version	Workstation Pro Version
20	Workstation Pro 17.x Workstation Player 17.x
19	Workstation Pro 16.2.x Workstation Player 16.2.x
18	Workstation Pro 16.x Workstation Player 16.x
17	ESXi 7.0
16	Workstation Pro 15.x Workstation Player 15.x
15	ESXi 6.7 U2
14	Workstation Pro 14.x Workstation Player 14.x
13	ESXi 6.5
12	Workstation Pro 12.x Workstation Player 12.x
11	Workstation 11.x Player 7.x
10	Workstation 10.x Player 6.x
9	Workstation 9.x Player 5.x
8	Workstation 8.x Player 4.x
7	Workstation 7.x Workstation 6.5.x Player 3.x
6	Workstation 6.0.x
4	Player 2.x Player 1.x
3 & 4	Workstation 5.x Workstation 4.x

Figure 6-1. *Workstation Pro virtual hardware versions*

VMware does not recommend that you upgrade a virtual machine's virtual hardware version unless you need the new features that have been added to the new virtual hardware version.

The process of upgrading a virtual machine to the latest virtual hardware version is essentially the same process as that of swapping a hard drive from one machine and reinstalling it into a new and different one.

Whether or not the virtual machine boots or works correctly is purely down to the guest operating system the virtual machine is running and its plug-and-play abilities. This is its ability to update drivers to reflect what essentially is a completely different machine with a completely different set of hardware.

To give you an example, imagine what would happen if you did this in the physical world with a physical machine and you took the hard drive out of one machine and installed it in a completely different machine. The new machine may have a completely different chipset and hardware types, and potentially one of these will be a hard disk controller which would prevent the machine from booting up in the first place. In a Windows guest operating system, even if the machine did boot, you would potentially see multiple errors in the Device Manager and hardware not working.

So, we have just talked about upgrading the hardware version, but equally you can also downgrade.

You can power on a virtual machine with a virtual hardware version that is a lower version than the version it can support. For example, it may support up to version 20, but you could configure the virtual machine with virtual hardware version 18.

The only caveat here is that some of the functionality may not be available due to the difference in hardware. Lost functionality results in menu items related to virtual machine operations being grayed out and unavailable.

Having now discussed the hardware versions and compatibility, in the next section, we are going to look at the actual hardware devices and types that are configured when you create a virtual machine.

Virtual Hardware Settings

When you create a virtual machine using the **Typical** configuration, which we will cover in Chapter 9, a default set of virtual hardware is configured based on the requirements of the guest operating system.

We are going to discuss virtual hardware now, before you create a virtual machine so that you can fully understand the various configuration options for virtual hardware, what to configure, and the settings available.

You can also create a virtual machine using the **Custom** option whereby you can select the hardware, CPU, and memory resources you require. Again, this option for creating virtual machines will be discussed in Chapter 9.

The objective of this section is to discuss the default hardware types that get configured when you create a new virtual machine. This includes the specific settings for each virtual hardware component and how you can reconfigure them if you need to in order to reflect the use case for the virtual machine. This will help when we get to creating a virtual machine so that you already understand the virtual hardware that is created by default.

It also gives you an understanding of whether to go with the typical configuration or whether you need to create a custom-built virtual machine to meet your specific hardware requirements.

Memory

The first virtual machine hardware setting is for memory.

The Memory configuration screen is shown in Figure 6-2.

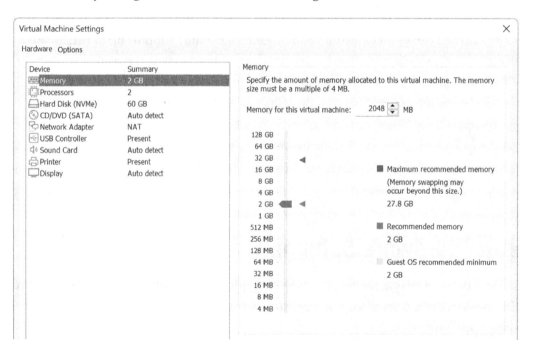

Figure 6-2. *Virtual Machine Settings - Memory*

With the typical configuration process, the amount of memory will have been automatically selected based on the standard requirements of the operating system.

However, you may need to change this to add additional memory to cater for any application requirements that are going to run on that virtual machine's guest operating system.

To change the amount of memory allocated to the virtual machine, you can either type the memory size into the Memory for this virtual machine box or use the up and down arrows to the side of it.

Note that the memory size is in megabytes (MB), and you can only increase or decrease the memory size in 4MB chunks.

You can also use the slider and drag it up and down, so it corresponds to the memory size you want. The slider also has a couple of additional colored arrows on it. The blue arrow denotes the maximum recommended memory size while the green arrow denotes the recommended amount of memory. This will be the amount selected when using the typical configuration.

Finally, you will see a yellow box by the side that states the minimum amount of memory the guest operating system requires.

Next is the option to configure the virtual processors.

Processors

The processor configuration allows you to change the number of virtual processors, the number of cores each processor has, and the configuration of the hardware-based virtualization features that the host machine can pass through the virtual machine.

This is divided into two sections, Processors and Virtualization engine, and is shown in Figure 6-3.

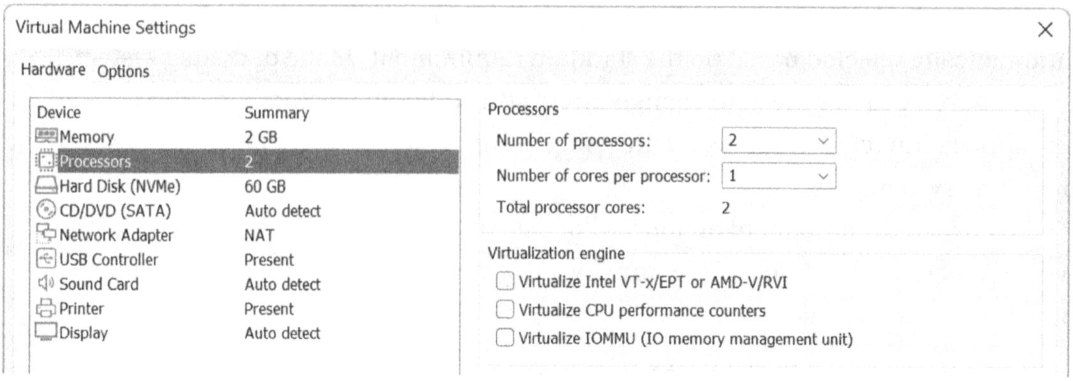

Figure 6-3. *Virtual Machine Settings - Processors*

The Processors section allows you to configure the Number of processors and the Number of cores per processor that the virtual machine has.

To configure this simply click the arrow for the drop-down and select the number from the list. Workstation Pro will also provide guidance on the values for these settings based on the processor capabilities (cores and number of processors) in the host machine and the supported values of the guest operating system running as a virtual machine.

For example, in Figure 6-4 you can see that we have tried to configure more processor cores than the supported maximum that is supported.

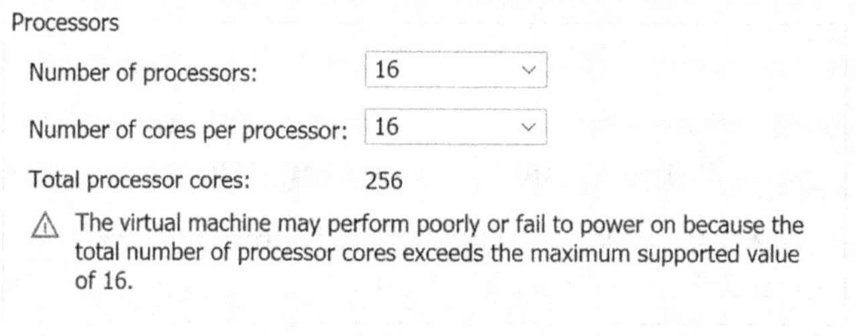

Figure 6-4. *Warning for exceeding the number of supported processor cores*

This is also the case if you try to configure more virtual processors than the host can support, and an example of this warning message is shown in Figure 6-5.

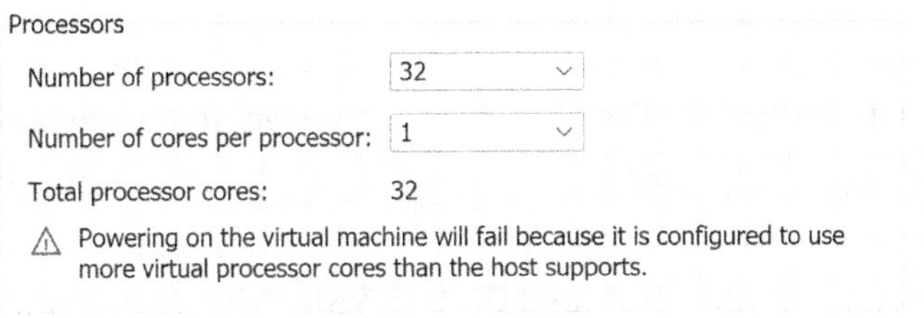

Processors

Number of processors:	32	⌄
Number of cores per processor:	1	⌄
Total processor cores:	32	

⚠ Powering on the virtual machine will fail because it is configured to use more virtual processor cores than the host supports.

Figure 6-5. *Warning for configuring more virtual cores than the host supports*

The question that springs to mind most often when configuring processors is the difference between configuring the number of processors versus the number of cores. For example, a single processor with 16 cores is the same as 16 processors. The result being you have 16 cores in total available to the virtual machine.

The key reason is software licensing. Some operating systems and applications are licensed on a per processor basis, whereas others are based on the number of cores. Therefore, you should configure the processors and cores accordingly.

For guidance on physical processor and virtual processor ratios, this was discussed back in Chapter 3.

The last section of the processors hardware configuration is for **Virtualization engine**. The settings in this section relate to the acceleration technologies we discussed in Chapter 3. The first enables virtual machines to make use of the CPU hardware acceleration technology integrated in the host machine's CPU. To use this feature, you will need to ensure that the physical CPU virtualization features are enabled in the BIOS of the host machine.

With the Virtualize CPU performance counters feature enabled, you can monitor and measure the performance of the processor using software profile tools, for example. In this case the feature allows the software and applications that are running inside the virtual machines to have access to the performance information.

Finally, there is the Virtualize IOMMU (IO memory management unit) option. This allows you to map virtual addresses to physical addresses and is typically used with Microsoft virtualization-based security or VBS that is used in Windows 10 and Windows Server operating systems.

Next, we are going to look at hard disks.

Hard Disks

As we have previously explained, the hard disk of a virtual machine is basically a file; however, there are some additional tasks that you can perform on this file as if it were an actual hard disk.

The first few sections under the **Hard Disk (NVMe)** virtual machine settings are purely informational and therefore cannot be edited or changed. These sections are for **Disk file**, **Capacity**, and **Disk information**. Just to add, the **NVMe** part in brackets is the virtual disk type configured for this disk.

In the **Disk file** box, you will see the path to where the virtual hard disk is saved to, along with the filename.

Next, you will see the **Capacity** section which gives you information about the current size of the virtual hard disk, the amount of free space, and then the size that was configured when the virtual machine was created.

In the **Disk information** box, you can see information such as how the disk space is allocated and how the disk files are stored. In this example the virtual hard disk is stored as multiple files. These are all shown in Figure 6-6.

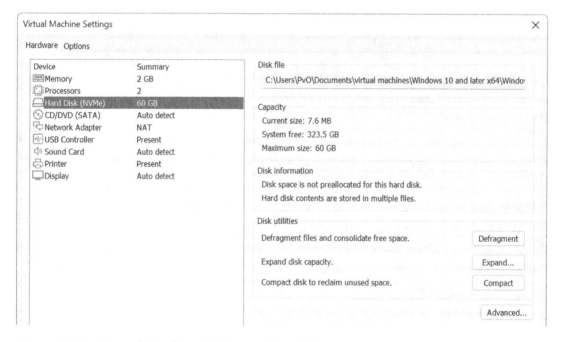

Figure 6-6. *Virtual Machine Settings - Hard Disk*

So, as we said before, these fields are the informational elements of the virtual hard disk configuration, but you will also see several buttons under the **Disk utilities** section.

The first option is for **Defragment**. Disk defragmentation is basically the process of reorganizing the contents of a hard disk so that all the pieces of the files that it stores are stored in a contiguous manner. Essentially, it is putting all the pieces of a file that may be saved in different places across the disk back in one place. This helps to reduce the time it takes to access the data as it is all in one place and therefore the virtual machine doesn't need to look all over the hard disk to find the data.

As well as speeding up file access times, it also helps to consolidate any free space on the disk.

If you click the **Defragment** button, then Workstation Pro will perform the defragmentation tasks on the virtual hard disk. Once completed you will see the message shown in Figure 6-7.

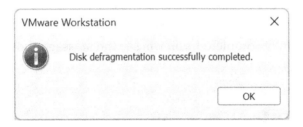

Figure 6-7. Disk defragmentation completed

The next option allows you to expand the size of the virtual hard disk. If you click the **Expand...** button, you will see the **Expand Disk Capacity** box as shown in Figure 6-8.

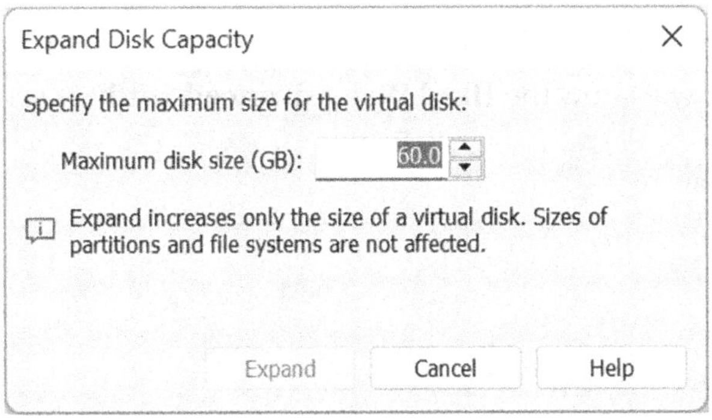

Figure 6-8. Hard disk defragmentation completed

To expand the virtual hard disk size, either type in the new size in the **Maximum disk size (GB)** box or use the arrows to the right, clicking until you get to the required size.

Once you have set the desired size in gigabytes, then click the **Expand** button to execute the expansion task. You will then see the virtual hard disk has been expanded and resized to the new size that you set.

Even though you have expanded the size of the virtual hard disk, it is worth noting that the newly expanded size will not be instantly recognized by the guest operating system. You will need to increase the size of the partition using the operating system tools or a third-party solution.

The final setting is for compacting the virtual hard disk. This process frees up unused disk space and can only be used if the virtual hard disk does not have its disk space pre-allocated, is mapped, or is a mounted disk.

To compact the virtual hard disk, click the **Compact** button. Given that modern operating systems manage disk space in a more efficient manner, then it is likely you won't see large amounts of disk space freed up once compacted. When the compacting operation has successfully completed, you will see the message shown in Figure 6-9.

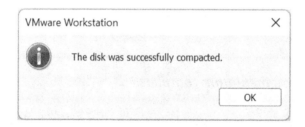

Figure 6-9. *Hard disk compacting completed*

Last but not least, on the hard disk settings, you will see the **Advanced…** button which, when clicked, will show the **Hard Disk Advanced Settings** screen shown in Figure 6-10.

Figure 6-10. *Hard Disk Advanced Settings screen*

In the drop-down for **Virtual device node**, you can select the virtual hard disk you want to configure the settings for.

Then, in the **Mode** section, you can enable **Independent mode** by checking the box and then selecting either **Persistent** or **Nonpersistent** mode by clicking the corresponding radio button. As a reminder of what these modes are used for, refer to Chapter 4 where we discussed the different types of virtual hard disks and their operational modes.

Following on from hard drives, in the next section we are going to discuss another form of storage medium, CD and DVD drives.

CD and DVD Drives

To install software or copy other data, Workstation Pro allows you to connect a CD or DVD drive to virtual machines. But it is not just a physical device that can be connected. As the process effectively mounts the drive, it also means you can directly mount an ISO image to your virtual machines as well.

In the **CD/DVD (SATA)** section of the hardware settings, you will see two sections for the status of the device and then what device is connected.

As with the hard disk, the part of the name in brackets, in this case **SATA**, is the interface type for this CD/DVD drive. You can choose IDE or SCSI which we will discuss in Chapter 10.

This settings screen is shown in Figure 6-11.

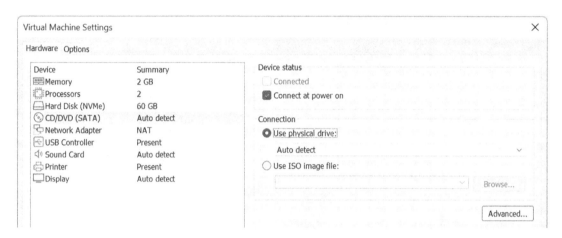

Figure 6-11. *CD/DVD Settings screen*

In the **Device status** box, you have two options. The first option is **Connected**. If you check this box, then the device will immediately be connected to the virtual machine once you click **OK** and exit the virtual machine settings screen.

The second option is **Connect at power on**. By checking this box, then the CD/DVD drive will be automatically connected to the virtual machine each time it is powered on. Next is the **Connection** settings for the type of drive.

First is the option for **Use physical drive**. If you select this option, by clicking the radio button, then, from the drop-down menu, you can select the physical drive you want to use. This is the drive in the host machine. You can either select a specific listed drive, or you can opt for the **Auto detect** option to automatically detect the drive.

You then have the **Use ISO image file** option. If you click the radio button for this option, you can then click the **Browse...** button which opens Windows Explorer allowing you to navigate to and select an ISO image from the host machine to mount to the virtual machine.

The final option for the CD/DVD settings is the advanced configuration settings that can be found by clicking the Advanced... button, which opens the advanced settings screen as shown in Figure 6-12.

Figure 6-12. *Advanced Settings for CD/DVD drives*

In the advanced settings, you can select the interface and drive node for the CD/DVD drive.

By default, this is set to **SATA**. You can change this to SCSI or IDE by clicking the corresponding radio button. From the drop-down menu for each interface type, you can change the controller and device node. In this example you can see that a SATA-based CD/DVD drive has been configured and is device 1 on controller 0.

The final option, under the **Troubleshooting** section, is for **Legacy emulation**. As this is under troubleshooting, then it is used in cases where you experience direct communication issues between a guest operating system and the DVD or CD-ROM drive.

Next, we are going to discuss network adapters.

Network Adapters

In the previous chapter, Chapter 5, we discussed in detail the setup and configuration of the actual network itself, so in this chapter we are going to focus on how to connect to the configured networks and that is using the virtual network adapter.

The Network Adapter settings screen is shown in Figure 6-13.

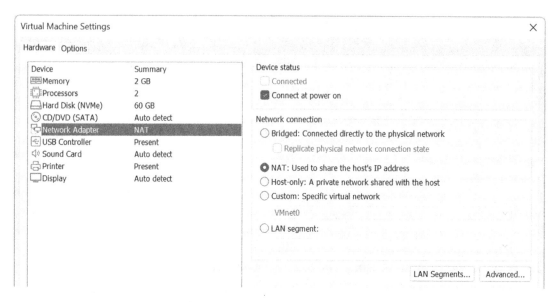

Figure 6-13. *Network Adapter Settings Screen*

In the **Device status** box, you have two options. The first option is **Connected**. If you check this box, then the network adapter will immediately be connected to the virtual machine and therefore the network. Changing this setting is only executed once you click **OK** and exit the virtual machine settings screen.

The second option is **Connect at power on**. By checking this box, then the network will be automatically connected to the virtual machine each time it is powered on.

Next is the **Network connection** settings for which network the virtual machine should connect to. These are the networks that we discussed in Chapter 5. Simply click the radio button next to the network you want to connect this virtual machine to.

There is also an additional setting on this screen for the **Custom** network configuration. When you select the **Custom** option and then select the network from the drop-down box, you will also see that there is a setting to configure a **LAN segment**.

If you click the **LAN Segments...** button, then you will see the Global LAN Segments box as shown in Figure 6-14.

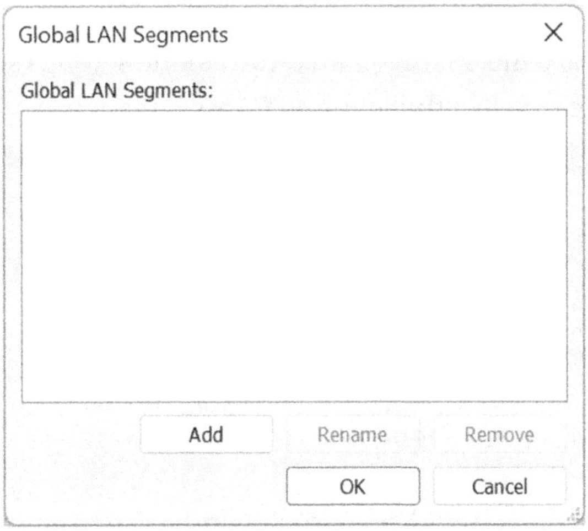

Figure 6-14. *Global LAN Segments settings*

A LAN Segment is a private network shared by other virtual machines where you need to create isolation between virtual machines.

By default, there are no LAN segments configured.

If you want to add a new Global LAN Segment, then click the **Add** button.

This will add a new entry, called **LAN Segment 1** by default, which will be highlighted in blue ready for you to add your own name as shown in Figure 6-15.

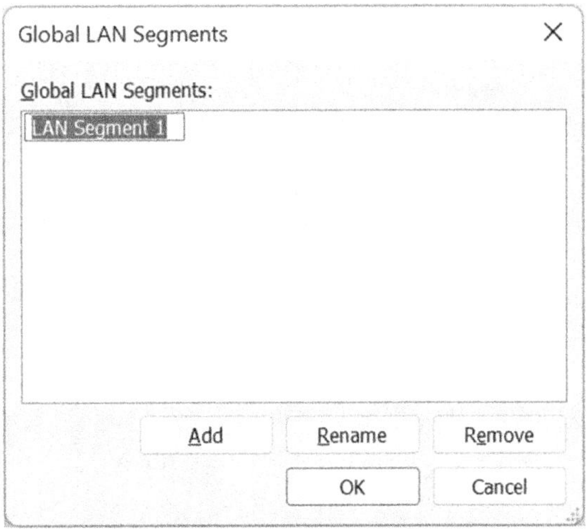

Figure 6-15. *Adding a New Global LAN Segment*

As you can see, there are also buttons for renaming and removing existing LAN segments. Click OK to save the changes and return to the settings screen.

You will now be able to select the required LAN segment from the drop-down list. In the example shown in Figure 6-16, you can see that we created three LAN segments.

○ LAN segment:

LAN Segment 1
LAN Segment 2
LAN Segment 3

Figure 6-16. Selecting a LAN Segment

The final settings for the network adapter fall under the heading of advanced and are accessed by clicking the **Advanced...** button.

If you click the **Advanced...** button, then you will see the **Network Adapter Advanced Setting** box which is divided into three sections, **Incoming Transfer**, **Outgoing Transfer**, and **MAC Address,** as shown in Figure 6-17.

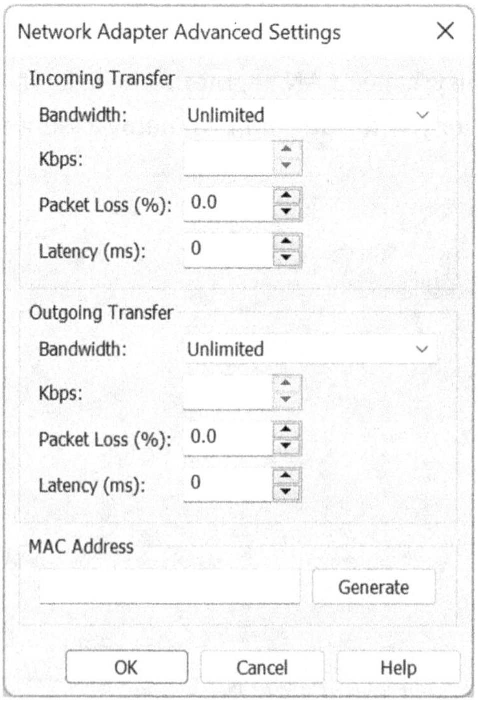

Figure 6-17. Network Adapter Advanced Settings

The advanced settings use case is to provide network simulation capabilities. By that we mean that you can configure the bandwidth for both the incoming and outgoing networks which allows you to create a simulation for networks that have limited bandwidth capabilities as shown in Figure 6-18.

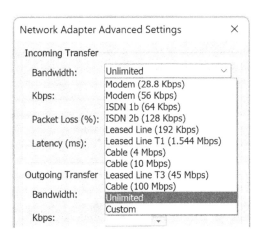

Figure 6-18. *Network Adapter Advanced Settings - Bandwidth settings*

As you can see from the options in the **Bandwidth** drop-down box, you can select different networks with different bandwidth settings from a 28k modem to a 100Mbps LAN connection.

You can also set the **Kbps** speed of the network, the amount of **Packet Loss**, and the **Latency** you want the network to simulate. For example, you might be testing a VDI solution where the best connection is with a network latency of less than 250ms. Here you could test what would happen to the end-user experience should the latency exceed that number.

You can also configure exactly the same settings on the outgoing network too as shown in Figure 6-19.

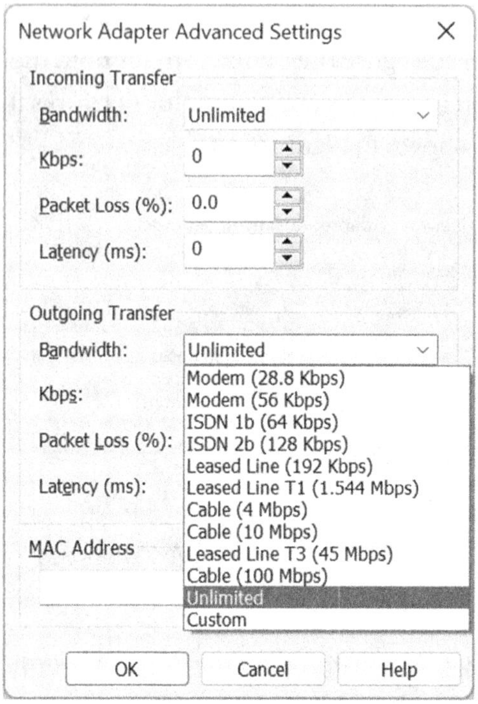

Figure 6-19. *Network Adapter Advanced Settings - Outgoing settings*

The final advanced configuration option is the **MAC Address** section.

When you power on a virtual machine, Workstation Pro will assign MAC address to each virtual network adapter in the virtual machine. The MAC address is a unique address assigned to each virtual network adapter on the network to identify it.

Virtual machines will keep the same MAC address each time they are powered on unless you move the virtual machine to a new host machine, edit specific files in its configuration file, or even move it to a new location on the same host machine.

If you are running applications that are tied to a MAC address, for licensing purposes, for example, then you need to be aware of this.

In the **MAC Address** field, you can either enter your own address, or you can click the Generate button to allow Workstation Pro to automatically create one for you. This is shown in Figure 6-20.

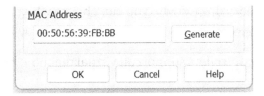

Figure 6-20. *Generating MAC addresses*

The VMware Organizationally Unique Identifier (OUI) allocation assigns MAC addresses based on the default VMware OUI 00:50:56.

Next, we are going to look at USB controllers.

USB Controllers

Virtual machines are able to make use of USB devices that are plugged into the host machine.

These devices, once plugged into the host machine, can be passed through to the virtual machines where they will be available to use.

In the virtual machine settings for USB controllers, you have the option to configure **USB compatibility**, **Show all USB input devices** and to **Share Bluetooth devices with the virtual machine** as shown in Figure 6-21.

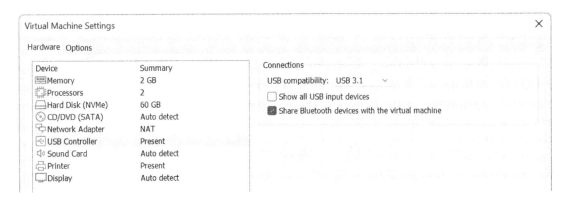

Figure 6-21. *USB controller settings*

In the **USB compatibility** drop-down, you can choose which version of USB you want the controller to support:

- **USB 1.1** UHCI controllers support all virtual machine hardware versions.

- **USB 2.0** EHCI controllers support virtual machine hardware from Workstation 6 and later.

- **USB 3.0** xHCI supports Windows 8 guest operating systems where virtual machine hardware must be compatible with Workstation 8 or later.

These options are shown in Figure 6-22.

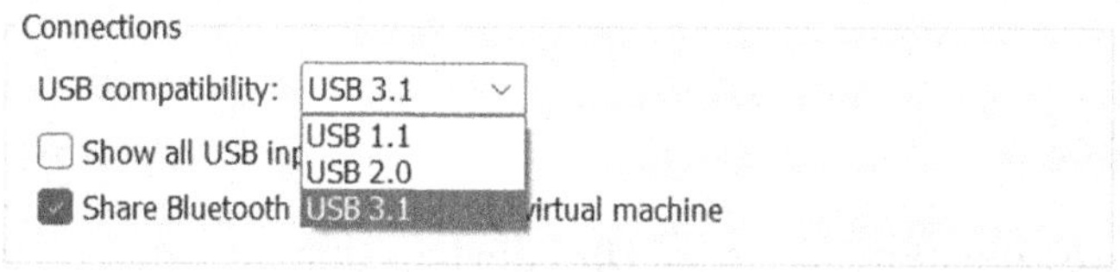

Figure 6-22. *USB compatibility settings*

The next option for USB is the **Show all USB input devices** check box. If you enable this option, then you can use USB human interface devices (HIDs), such as keyboards and mice within the virtual machine.

If you don't enable this option then this type of device, even though it may be physically plugged into the host, will not be available to the virtual machine.

The host operating system must support USB; however, you do not need to install USB device drivers in the host operating system to use those devices only in the virtual machine. You install drivers in the guest operating system.

The final option is for **Share Bluetooth devices with the virtual machine**. Enabling this option means that the Bluetooth radio device in the host, if it has one, is shared with the virtual machine.

However, the Bluetooth feature has limited functionality. See the following KB article: https://kb.vmware.com/s/article/2005315.

Once the controller has been configured then you will be able to see the devices. For example, click on **VM** from the menu, and then hover the mouse over **Removable Devices** and then hover on the device you want to connect. You can then select **Connect** which disconnects the device from the host and connects it to the virtual machine as shown in Figure 6-23.

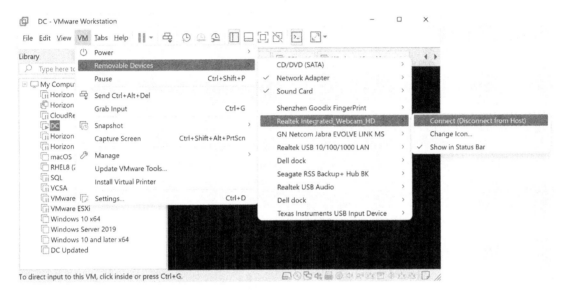

Figure 6-23. *Removable devices*

The next option is for configuring sound card settings.

Sound Cards

With this setting the virtual machine is able to use the host sound card.

In the **Device status** box, you have two options. The first option is **Connected**. If you check this box, then the sound card will immediately be connected to the virtual machine. Changing this setting is only executed once you click **OK** and exit the virtual machine settings screen.

The second option is **Connect at power on**. By checking this box, then the sound card will be automatically connected to the virtual machine each time it is powered on. This is shown in Figure 6-24.

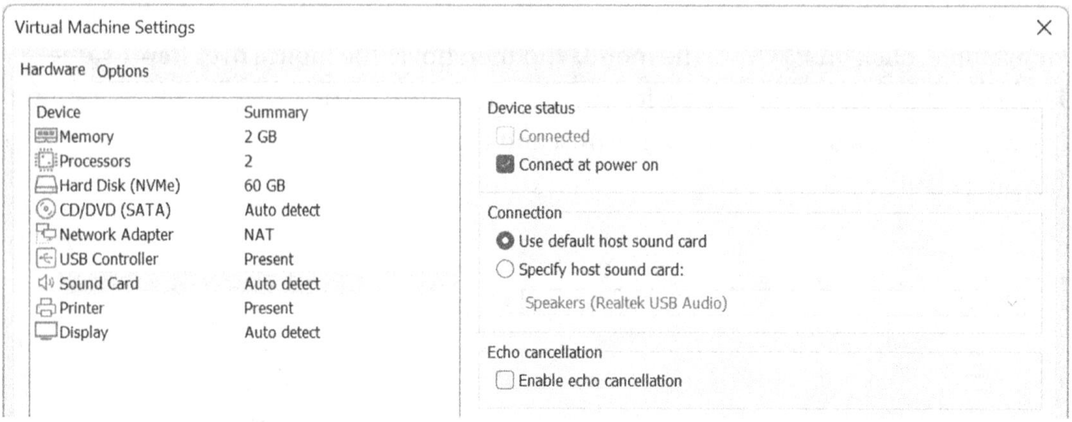

Figure 6-24. *Sound card settings*

In the next section, **Connection**, you can specify the sound card to use as shown in Figure 6-25.

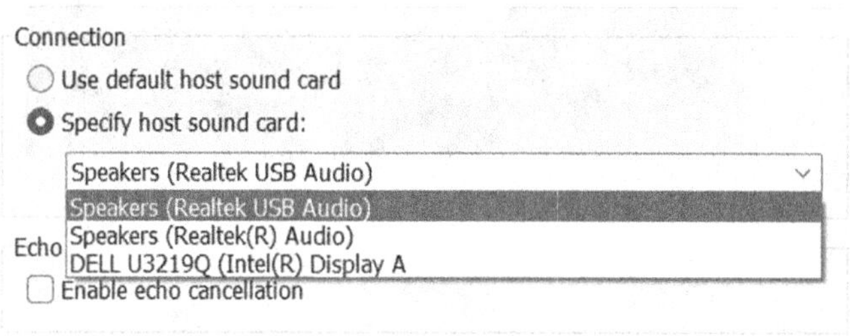

Figure 6-25. *Configuring the sound card*

You can click the radio button for **Use default host sound card** to use the default card set in the host machine, or if you click the radio button for **Specify host sound card,** you can select the sound card you want to use. This, of course, if your host has more than one sound card.

The final option is for **Enable echo cancellation**. Echo cancellation works by first analyzing incoming voice streams and at the same time analyzing the return voice stream. If any echo is detected between the two, then the echo cancellation removes it from the audio signal. To enable this feature, then you need to check the box.

The next settings are for configuring printers.

Printer

The printer setting is also part of the Workstation Pro virtual printer configuration which we will discuss in the next chapter.

This feature allows a virtual machine that is running VMware Tools to be able to print to any of the printers that are configured and connected to the host machine. There are just two options for printing.

The first option is **Connected**. If you check this box, then the printer will immediately be connected to the virtual machine. Changing this setting is only executed once you click **OK** and exit the virtual machine settings screen.

The second option is **Connect at power on**. By checking this box, then the printer will be automatically connected to the virtual machine each time it is powered on. This is shown in Figure 6-26.

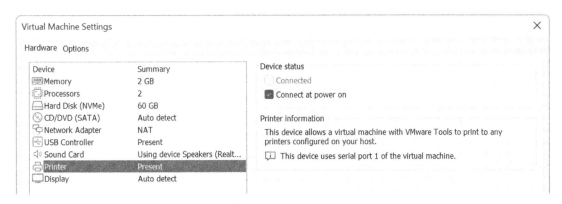

Figure 6-26. *Printer Settings Screen*

Once connected, you will have the ability to install the virtual printer driver which we will discuss in the next chapter.

In the final section, we are going to discuss the display settings.

Display

There are several different settings options when it comes to display configuration as shown in Figure 6-27.

Figure 6-27. *Display settings*

The first section is the **3D graphics** section. This just has a check box to enable or disable the **Accelerate 3D graphics** feature. Enabling this feature will allow virtual machines, running Windows XP or newer, to support DirectX 9 or DirectX 10 accelerated graphics. For this feature to work, you also need to ensure you are running the latest version of VMware Tools.

Next is the **Monitors** settings. The first option, selected by clicking the radio button, is for **Use host setting for monitors**. With the host monitor setting, the SVGA driver uses two monitors, with a maximum bounding box width of 3840 pixels and a maximum bounding box height of 1920 pixels.

The virtual machine is then configured with a minimum of two monitors with a resolution of 1920 x 1200 pixels. This configuration uses a side-by-side topology, either in normal or rotated orientations.

If the host system has more than two monitors attached, then the virtual machine will use the same number of monitors that the host machine is configured with. If the host machine's bounding box is wider or taller than the default settings, then the virtual machine will use the larger size.

You then have the option, again by clicking the radio button, to **Specify monitor settings**. If you enable this setting, then you can configure the number of monitors supported by clicking the drop-down menu for **Number of monitors** and selecting the appropriate number.

The number of monitors configured for a virtual machine is independent of the number of monitors physically attached to the host machine. This makes this feature useful for developing a multi-monitor application using a virtual machine and a host machine that has only one physical monitor attached.

When you power on a virtual machine configured with multi-monitors, then the guest operating system will be configured with the number of monitors configured in this setting.

Once you have configured the number of monitors for the virtual machine, you can then, from the maximum resolution of any one monitor drop-down menu, select the resolution you want to use. The options range from the minimum resolution of 640 x 480 up to the maximum supported of 3840 x 2160.

This is shown in Figure 6-28.

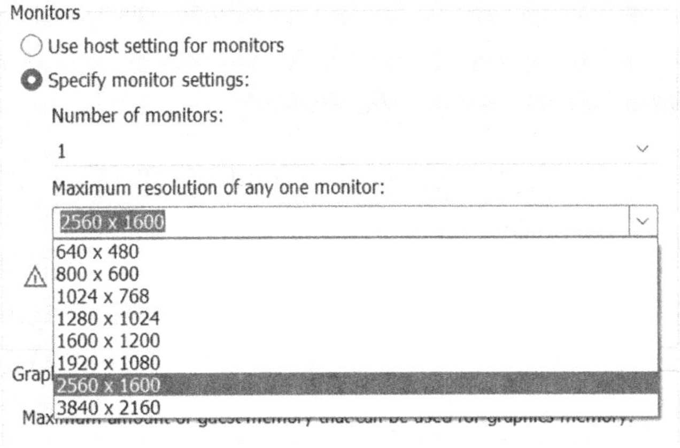

Figure 6-28. *Monitor settings*

The next settings section is to set the amount of video memory the virtual machine is configured to use. This is shown in Figure 6-29.

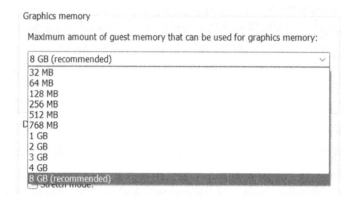

Figure 6-29. *Configuring graphics memory*

Click the drop-down and select the amount of memory you want the virtual machine to be configured with.

One thing to be aware of is that depending on what you configure for graphics memory might require you to increase the amount of RAM the virtual machine is configured with.

For example, here we have a Windows 10 virtual machine configured with 4GB of RAM. When we increase the amount of graphics memory to 4GB, you will see the warning message shown in Figure 6-30.

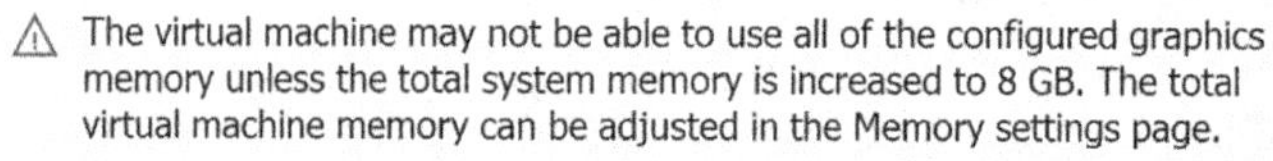

⚠ The virtual machine may not be able to use all of the configured graphics
memory unless the total system memory is increased to 8 GB. The total
virtual machine memory can be adjusted in the Memory settings page.

Figure 6-30. *Graphics memory warning message*

The final section in the **Display** settings is to configure Display scaling.

The first option, select by clicking the check box, is for **Automatically adjust user interface size in the virtual machine**. This option also needs the latest version of VMware Tools to be installed on the virtual machine. When enabled when you resize the windows in which the virtual machine is displayed, the scaling will automatically adjust to fit.

The second option is **Stretch mode**. With this option enabled, you can choose from the option for **Keep aspect ratio stretch** or **Free stretch**. You select the required option by clicking the corresponding radio button.

With the keep aspect ratio option, when you resize and stretch the virtual machine display, it will maintain the same aspect ratio of the windows in which the virtual machine is running. The free stretch option on the other hand will stretch the virtual machine display to fill the window the virtual machine is running in, but the aspect ratio will not be maintained.

Summary

In this chapter we started by discussing the hardware versions and compatibility of virtual hardware running on VMware Workstation.

We then went on to discuss each of the different types of virtual hardware device and the settings that can be configured. Although we are yet to build a virtual machine, by discussing this now will help with building a virtual machine as you can identify the different configurable virtual hardware components in preparation for virtual machine creation.

You may also have noticed in this chapter that some virtual hardware device types have not been discussed. This is because they are typically classed as being non-standard devices and therefore need to be added as additional devices depending on the use case. In this chapter we have focused on those virtual hardware components that are created as part of a standard virtual machine build.

We will discuss adding devices, both standard and non-standard, in Chapter 10 when we discuss how to configure virtual machines once they are built and running.

CHAPTER 7

Installing and Configuring VMware Workstation Pro

This chapter is the first chapter where we will start to get hands-on with VMware Workstation Pro by installing the software on the host machine.

We will work through the installation process step-by-step, explaining the different configuration option screens and using actual screenshots as we go along.

Before we start the software install process, we will first download the software from the VMware website. To do this, you will either need to have an existing VMware Customer Connect account and login details to access the download and license key (you will need to have purchased Workstation Pro first) or you can download an evaluation version.

Once we have the software downloaded, we will discuss the minimum requirements for the host machine in terms of CPU, memory, and supported operating system versions.

Now we have a host machine that meets the minimum requirement to run Workstation Pro; we will follow the steps to install Workstation Pro on the host machine, explaining the different options and what they are used for.

With VMware Workstation Pro now successfully installed, the final part of this chapter will discuss the configuration options, or preferences as to how Workstation Pro will operate. This will cover things such as controlling and managing external devices, screen resolutions, and overall end-user experience focused options.

Downloading the Software

You have several options to access and download VMware Workstation Pro. You can either download an evaluation license, buy online via the VMware Store, or access an existing license from your Customer Connect portal.

© Peter von Oven 2023
P. von Oven, *Learning VMware Workstation for Windows*, https://doi.org/10.1007/978-1-4842-9969-2_7

Downloading an Evaluation Version

To download an evaluation license for VMware Workstation Pro, you can go to the VMware page using the following link:

www.vmware.com/products/workstation-pro/workstation-pro-evaluation.html

By clicking the link, you will see the following page (Figure 7-1).

Figure 7-1. *Workstation Pro download page*

If you click **DOWNLOAD NOW** > in the Workstation 17 Pro for Windows box, you will see that the download will automatically start, and once the download has completed, the installer will be available in the Downloads folder.

As this is an evaluation version of Workstation Pro, you won't need a license key. However, you can add one before the end of the trial period to activate and keep using Workstation Pro.

Download from VMware Customer Connect

Another option for download is if you have a VMware Customer Connect account. If so, then click the following link:

`https://customerconnect.vmware.com/en/downloads/info/slug/desktop_end_user_computing/vmware_workstation_pro/17_0`

This will take you to the following page (Figure 7-2).

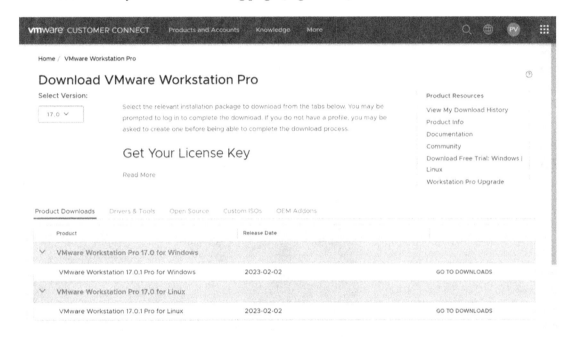

Figure 7-2. *Workstation Pro download page on Customer Connect*

If you click **GO TO DOWNLOADS** for the **VMware Workstation Pro 17.0 for Windows** option, you will see the following page (Figure 7-3).

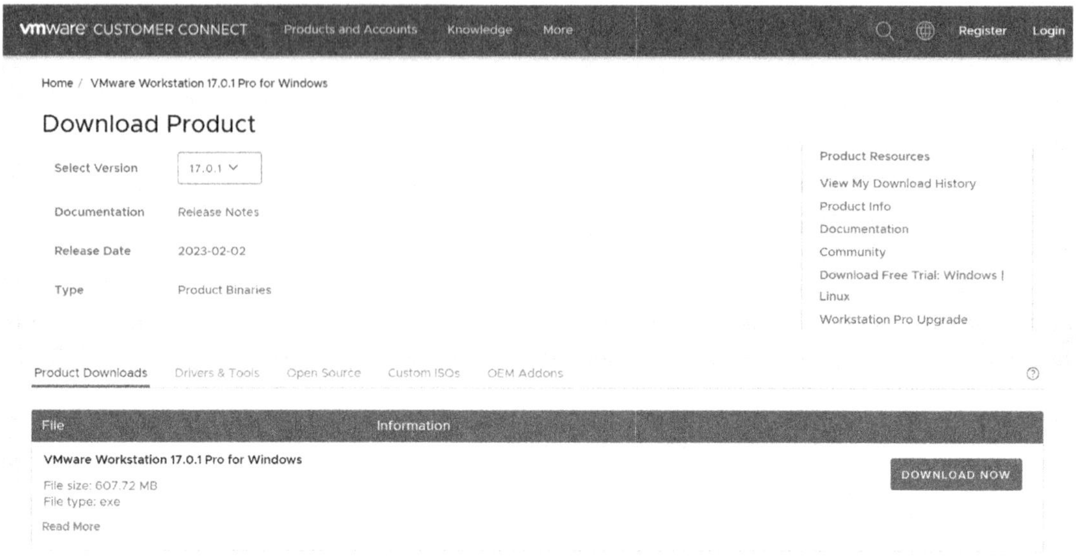

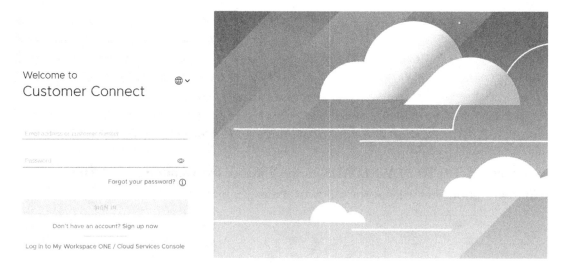

Figure 7-3. *Workstation Pro download product page on Customer Connect*

Click the **DOWNLOAD NOW** button. You will see the following page (Figure 7-4).

Figure 7-4. *Customer Connect login page*

Once you have successfully logged in, the download will start, and then once the download has completed, the installer will be available in the Downloads folder.

Purchasing Workstation Pro

You will also note on the web page, shown in Figure 7-1, that there is a blue box at the top of the screen for **BUY ONLINE**.

When you purchase the full version of Workstation Pro, you have a few different options when it comes to support. You can choose from

- **Standard Subscription** – Includes 30 days of email support

- **Basic Subscription** – Includes 1 year of major updates and office hours technical support

- **Production Subscription** – Includes 1 year of major version upgrades and 24x7 technical support

Host Requirements

One final thing to discuss before we move on to the actual installation itself is the host machine that you are going to install Workstation Pro on to, and what are the minimum requirements that host machine needs to meet to be able to run the Workstation Pro application.

It is worth noting that these are the minimum specs required just to run the Workstation Pro application on the host machine and therefore does not take into account your virtual machine resource requirements. You need the host machine to have enough resource (CPU, RAM, and disk) to run the virtual machines you intend to host on it.

In terms of architecture, Workstation Pro will run on a standard x86-based host device with either 64-bit Intel or AMD processors, running a 64-bit Windows operating system. As we have previously mentioned, there is also a Linux version of the Workstation Pro application; however, the focus of this book is the Windows version.

The host machine will need to meet the following minimum requirements:

- 64-bit Intel x86 or AMD64 CPU from 2011 or newer

- 1.3GHz or faster CPU core clock speed

- 2GB RAM (4GB RAM or more is recommended)

It is worth noting that the following CPUs are **NOT** supported:

- Intel Atom Bonnell architecture-based CPUs

- Intel Atom Saltwell architecture-based CPUs

- AMD Llano and Bobcat architecture-based CPUs

Host Operating System Requirements

Workstation Pro will run on most 64-bit Windows operating systems, including

- Windows 10

- Windows Server 2019

- Windows Server 2016

- Windows Server 2012

- Windows 8

Note   Windows 7 is no longer supported as a host operating system.

For a full list of the currently supported host operating systems, follow the link below:
https://kb.vmware.com/s/article/80807

Supported Guest Operating Systems

As we have just discussed the supported host operating systems, then in this section we are going to touch on the supported guest operating systems; the operating system that the virtual machine hosted on Workstation Pro is running.

This list is long, so the easiest way to share this information is by using the VMware online compatibility guide which you will find by clicking the following link:
www.vmware.com/resources/compatibility/search.php

Once on the compatibility page, ensure you click the drop-down for **What are you looking for** and select **Guest OS** from the list. Then select **Workstation** from the **Product Name** box and then the version in the **Product Release Version** box.

This is shown in the following screenshot (Figure 7-5).

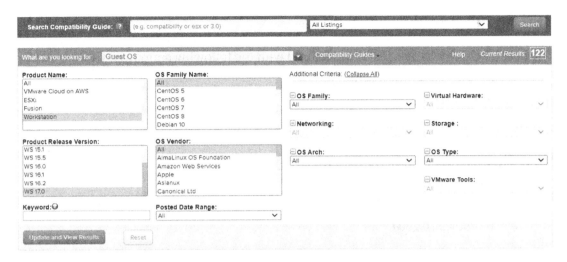

Figure 7-5. *Searching the compatibility guide*

Click **Update and View Results,** and you will see the list of support guest operating systems as shown in the following screenshot (Figure 7-6).

OS Vendor	OS Release	OS Arch	Supported Releases	
Canonical Ltd	Ubuntu 21.04	x86(64-bit)	Workstation	17.0 Legacy
Canonical Ltd	Ubuntu 20.04 LTS	x86(64-bit)	Workstation	17.0
Canonical Ltd	Ubuntu 18.04 LTS	x86(64-bit)	Workstation	17.0
Canonical Ltd	Ubuntu 16.04 LTS	x86(32-bit)	Workstation	17.0
Canonical Ltd	Ubuntu 16.04 LTS	x86(64-bit)	Workstation	17.0
Canonical Ltd	Ubuntu 14.10	x86(32-bit)	Workstation	17.0
Canonical Ltd	Ubuntu 14.10	x86(64-bit)	Workstation	17.0
Canonical Ltd	Ubuntu 14.04 LTS	x86(32-bit)	Workstation	17.0 Legacy
Canonical Ltd	Ubuntu 14.04 LTS	x86(64-bit)	Workstation	17.0 Legacy
CentOS	CentOS 8.x	x86(64-bit)	Workstation	17.0

Search Results: Your search for" Guest OS " returned **122 results.**   Back to Top   Turn Off Auto Scroll   Display: 10

Previous   1   2   3   4   5   6   7   8   9   10   11   12   13   Next

Figure 7-6. *Search results*

Hyper-V Enabled Host Requirements

If your host machine has Hyper-V enabled, then the host will need to meet the following requirements:

CPU Requirements

The host machine will need to be configured with the following supported CPUs:

- Intel Sandy Bridge CPU or later

- AMD Bulldozer CPU or later

Host Operating System Requirements

The host machine will need to be running the following supported OS as a minimum:

- Windows 10 2004

3D Hardware Accelerated Graphics Requirements

If you are planning on running virtual machines that need hardware accelerated graphics capabilities, then the following hardware and software requirements will need to be met:

Hardware Requirements

- GPU that supports DirectX 11 is required.

Software Requirements

- **Host operating system** - 64-bit Windows 8 or higher

- **Guest operating system** - Windows 7 or higher

We are now ready to move to the practical process of installing Workstation Pro on the host machine.

Installation Process

Now that we have downloaded the software and ensured we have a host machine that meets the requirements for running both the Workstation Pro application and the virtual machines it is going to be hosting, it is time to work through the installation and the required configuration steps.

The first step of the installation process is to extract the Workstation Pro installer.

You will have noticed that the file you downloaded has the GZ file extension with the type listed as a GZ file. A GZ file is an archive file that is compressed by the standard GNU zip (gzip) compression algorithm which is typically a Unix-based file compression format; however, this is the Windows version of Workstation Pro.

This file is shown in the following screenshot (Figure 7-7).

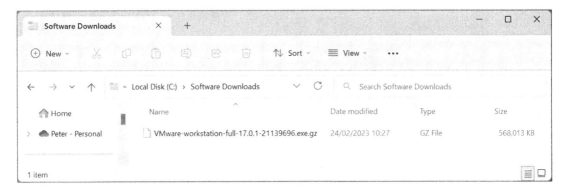

Figure 7-7. *Workstation Pro compressed .gz file shown in Explorer*

Use your choice of compression software such as 7Zip to extract the installer.

In this example we have also extracted it and saved it to a new folder called **Software Downloads** as shown in the following screenshot (Figure 7-8).

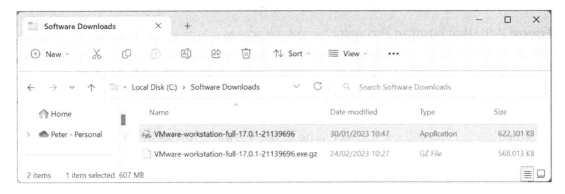

Figure 7-8. *Workstation Pro installer extracted*

With the installer now extracted, double click the **VMware-workstation-full-17.0.1-21139696** file to launch the installer.

As you can see from the filename, this is version 17.0.1 and has a build number of 21139696 and is the latest version at the time of writing this book. It is worth noting that you may have a different version or build number.

The installer will now launch, and you will see the Workstation Pro 17 splash screen and a pop-up message stating **"Preparing VMware Workstation" for installation...** as shown in the following screenshot (Figure 7-9).

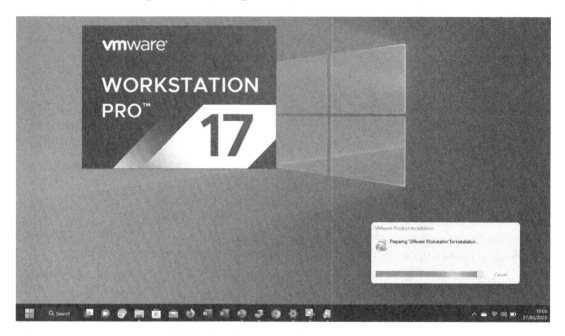

Figure 7-9. *Workstation Pro Installer splash screen*

For reference purposes, the host being used in this book is a Dell XPS15 laptop configured with an Intel Core i9-10885H CPU and 32GB RAM. It is running Windows 11 Version 21H2 (OS Build 22000.318).

Once loaded you will see the **Welcome to the VMware Workstation Pro Setup Wizard** as shown in the following screenshot (Figure 7-10).

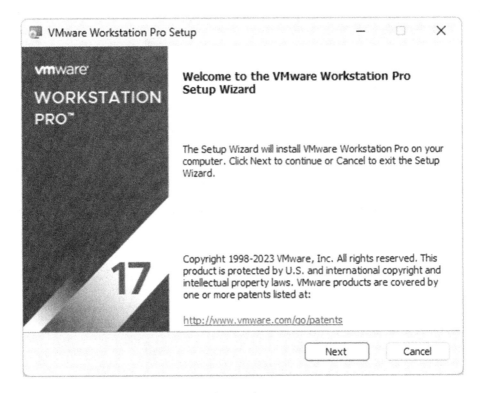

Figure 7-10. *Workstation Pro Installer welcome screen*

Click **Next** to continue. You will see the **End-User License Agreement** screen as shown in the following screenshot (Figure 7-11).

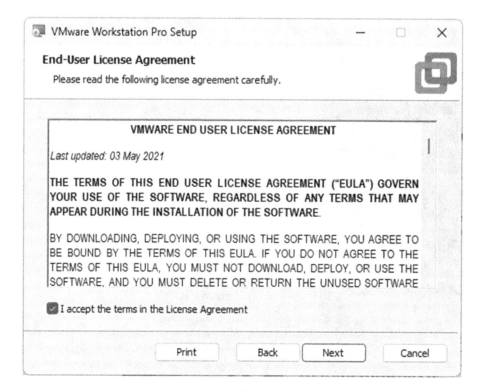

Figure 7-11. *End-User License Agreement screen*

Check the **I accept the terms in the License Agreement** box and then click the **Next** button.

You will now see the **Custom Setup** screen as shown in Figure 7-12.

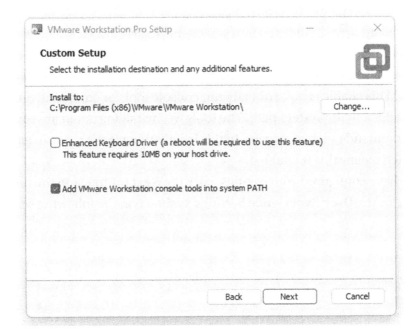

Figure 7-12. *Custom Setup screen*

The first option on this screen is to configure the destination folder for where the installation files will be copied to.

By default, it is C:\Program Files (x86)\VMware\VMware Workstation, but if you want to change the default location, click the **Change…** button. This will open another dialog box (not shown) for **Change destination folder**.

In this box you can browse to the folder location you want to use (existing folder) or create a new folder. Click **OK** when you have selected the new folder. For this example, we are going to stick with the default folder location which is the recommended option unless there is a good reason why you need to change the location.

The second option is a check box for the **Enhanced Keyboard Driver**. This is not selected by default, and to install the enhanced keyboard driver, simply check the box.

As per the notes, it says that a reboot will be required and that an additional 10MB of disk space will be used to install the files for this feature. What it doesn't tell is what the enhanced keyboard driver does and whether you need it.

The enhanced keyboard driver serves two purposes. The first is to support additional language keyboards. The second purpose is to support keyboards that have additional capabilities such as additional keys for multi-media functions or shortcut keys that launch things like calculator. Typically, these keyboards tend to work fine without the enhanced keyboard driver, but if you find you are having issues, you can always enable this feature at a later time. For now, we are going to leave this options unchecked.

Finally, you have the option to **Add VMware Workstation console tools into system PATH**. This enables you to directly run console tools or command line tools as they are now added to the system path. The tools we are talking about are some of the automation commands such as **vmrun**. In this installation we are going to leave this set as default which means this is enabled.

Once you have configured your options, click the **Next** button, and the next screen you will see is for the **User Experience Settings** as shown in the following screenshot (Figure 7-13).

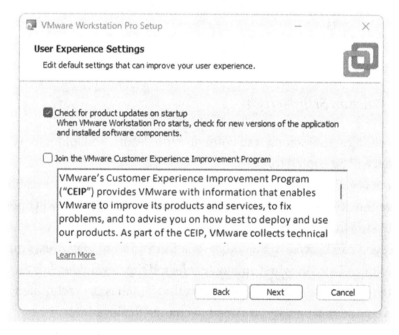

Figure 7-13. *User Experience Settings screen*

The first option on this screen, enabled by default, is for **Check for product updates on startup.** This feature checks the version you are currently running against the latest version available from VMware. You have the option to get more info which directs you to the VMware Workstation Pro web page, to skip the newer version, or to be reminded at a later stage, that is, the next time you launch Workstation Pro.

An example of the Software Updates screen, shown on startup, is shown in the following screenshot (Figure 7-14).

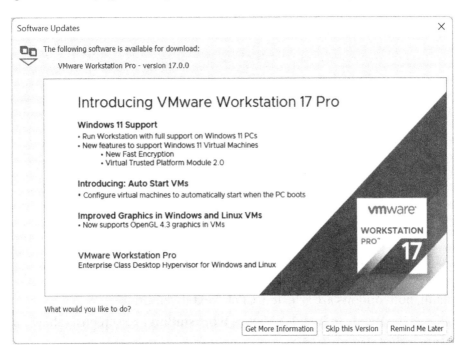

Figure 7-14. *Checking for product updates on startup*

If you don't want to check for updates each time you start Workstation Pro, then uncheck the box.

The second option is to **Join the VMware Customer Experience Improvement Program**, or CEIP. This allows VMware to collect technical information about the VMware solutions that you are using. It is not a licensing check!

In this example we are going to disable this by unchecking the box.

Click **Next** to continue.

The next configuration screen is to configure **Shortcuts**. This allows you to place shortcuts for Workstation Pro on either the Desktop of the host machine or to create a shortcut in the Programs Folder on the Start Menu of the host machine. This is shown in the following screenshot (Figure 7-15).

Figure 7-15. *Shortcuts configuration screen*

By default, both options are selected. Click **Next** to continue.

You will see the **Ready to install VMware Workstation Pro** screen as shown in the following screenshot (Figure 7-16).

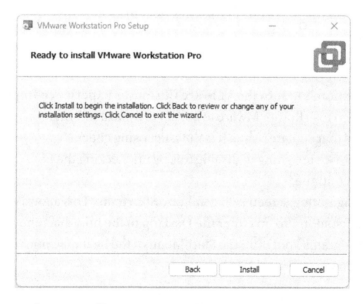

Figure 7-16. *Ready to install VMware Workstation Pro screen*

If you are happy that you have selected all the required configuration options for installation, then click the **Install** button. If you need to go back and change any of the configured options, simply click the **Back** button to review the previous screen.

The installation will now start, and you will see the following screenshots as registry keys are set, files copied, and network drivers installed (Figure 7-17).

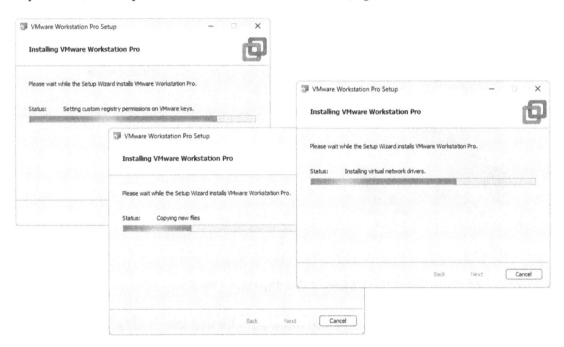

Figure 7-17. *VMware Workstation Pro installation process status*

Depending on the performance of the host machine, installation typically will take between 5 and 10 minutes to complete.

Once the installation has completed, then you will see the **Completed the VMware Workstation Pro Setup Wizard** as shown in the following screenshot (Figure 7-18).

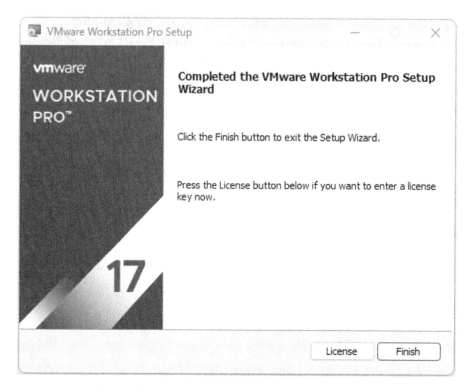

Figure 7-18. *Completed the VMware Workstation Pro Setup Wizard screen*

Before you complete the installation, you will notice that there is a **License** button shown as well as the **Finish** button. This gives you the option to enter a valid license key, if you have one, during the installation process (Figure 7-19).

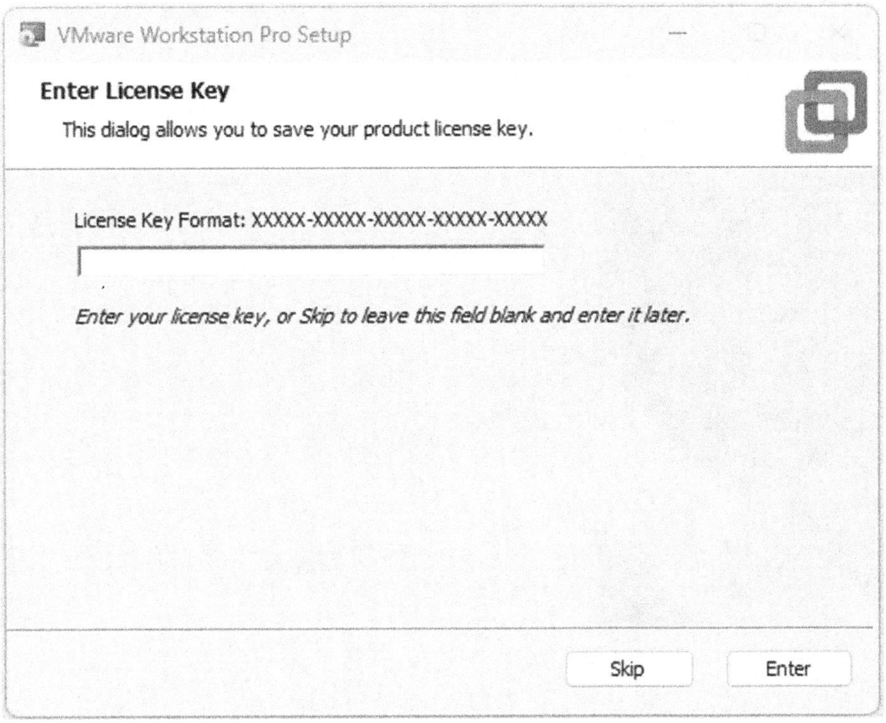

Figure 7-19. *Completed the VMware Workstation Pro Setup Wizard screen*

Enter your license key in the field, and then click the **Enter** button.

You will now see the **Completed the VMware Workstation Pro Setup Wizard** screen again, this time without the License button and just the Finish button as shown in the following screenshot (Figure 7-20).

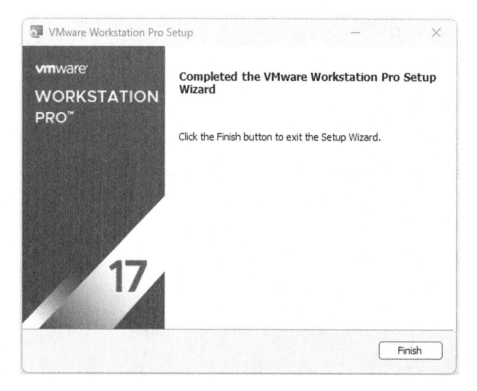

Figure 7-20. *Completed the VMware Workstation Pro Setup Wizard screen*

Click the **Finish** button to close the installer.

If you now press the Windows key and type **vm**, you will see that Workstation Pro has been added, as configured, to the Start Menu as shown in Figure 7-21.

Figure 7-21. *VMware Workstation Pro Added to the Start Menu*

You will also see that again, as configured, the icon for Workstation Pro has also been placed on the desktop of the host machine as shown in Figure 7-22.

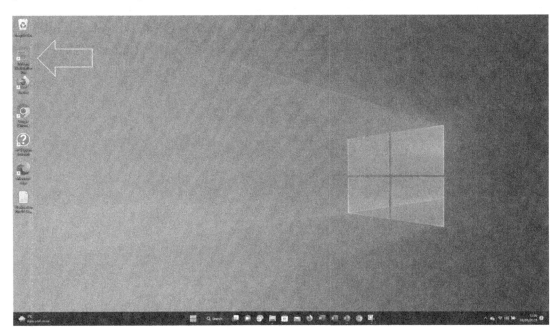

Figure 7-22. *VMware Workstation Pro desktop icon*

You have now successfully completed the installation of VMware Workstation Pro.

In the next section, we are going to launch Workstation Pro for the first time and discuss the additional preferences that you can configure.

Configuring Preferences

Once the installation of Workstation Pro has been completed, there are several configurations or preferences you can configure with the application that define how virtual machines are controlled and managed as well as some end-user experience focused options.

This includes how external peripherals are managed along with end-user experience changes that can be made on how virtual machines are displayed and how the end user interacts with them.

In this section we are going to discuss each of the different options and what they are used for.

Accessing the Preferences Menu

To access the preference settings, first ensure that Workstation Pro is running.

You can then either click the **Edit** menu and select **Preferences…,** or you can use the shortcut by pressing **CTRL + P** as shown in the following screenshot (Figure 7-23).

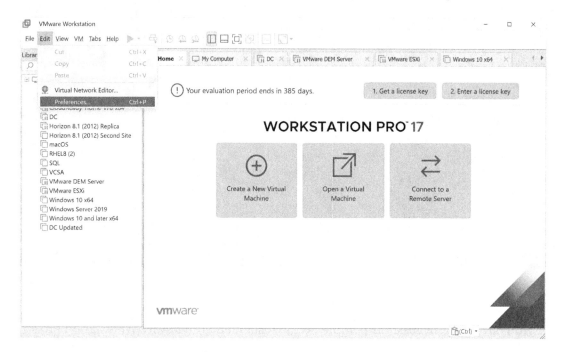

Figure 7-23. *Accessing the Preferences menu*

You will now see the **Preferences** screen with a list of the different elements that you can configure. Each one of those is also divided into different subsections. We are going to work through each one starting with the configuration options for Workspace.

Workspace Configuration Preferences

The first option is to configure the general workspace settings. There are three subsections within the workspace preference configuration.

Default Location for Virtual Machines

The first option is to configure the default location for where your virtual machines are going to be saved and stored. By default, virtual machines are saved to the **My Documents** folder on the host machine.

For example, **C:\Users\<username>\Documents\virtual machines**, where **<username>** is the name of the logged in user. In this case, in the example lab, this is **PvO** as shown in the following screenshot (Figure 7-24).

Figure 7-24. *Preferences Menu - Workspace*

One thing to note and to be aware of is if this folder is going to automatically synchronize with a cloud-based storage solution which often is the case with OneDrive as it is typically configured for the **My Documents** folder by default.

This is a great feature to ensure you have a backup of your virtual machines, but as the size of a virtual machine can be quite large and you may well have more than one virtual machine, and quite often these are GBs in size, then this might slow down the sync process depending on your connection speed, or you may not have enough space on your cloud storage.

If you want to change the default location, then you can click the **Browse...** button. You will then see the **Browse for Folder** screen as shown in Figure 7-25.

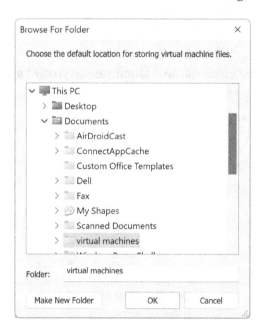

Figure 7-25. *Browse for Folder*

Scroll through the folders and select the new folder location, or you can click the **Make New Folder** button to create a new folder. Click **OK** when you have configured your default location for storing your virtual machines.

Next you have the virtual machines configuration options.

Virtual Machines

There are several different options under the virtual machine configuration.

The first option is for **Remember opened tabs between sessions** which is enabled by default with the box already checked. This feature, when enabled, means that the tabs you have open for each virtual machine will persist between Workstation Pro sessions.

So, that means that if you exit and launch Workstation Pro again, the tabs will remain in place as shown in the following screenshot (Figure 7-26).

Figure 7-26. *Virtual machine tabs*

The next option is for **Keep VMs running when Workstation Pro is closed**, which is disabled by default. This option, when enabled, simply means that if you exit Workstation Pro, any running virtual machines will continue to run in the background. If you need to manage them, then you will need to launch Workstation Pro again.

Next is the **Enable all shared folders** feature which is disabled by default. When enabled, this feature switches on the Workstation Pro shared folder feature which allows folders to be shared between the host and the virtual machine. We will cover this feature in more detail in Chapter 10.

The **Show Aero Peak thumbnails for open tabs** feature, which is enabled by default, shows thumbnails of each of the open tabs. If you hover the mouse over the Workstation Pro icon in the taskbar, then you will see each of the VMs shown where you can perform power actions or switch directly to a VM by clicking on it. An example is shown in the following screenshot (Figure 7-27).

Figure 7-27. *Aero Peak Thumbnails (Windows 11 host)*

Next is the **Show tray icon** which by default is set to **Always**. From the drop-down menu, you have the options to set this to **Never** or **When a virtual machine is powered on**. An example is shown in the following screenshot (Figure 7-28).

Figure 7-28. *Workstation Pro tray icon (Windows 11 host)*

From the **Default hardware compatibility** options, which defaults to the latest version of Workstation Pro that is currently running, from the drop-down box, you can select the hardware compatibility for each new virtual machine that gets created. So in this example, every virtual machine created is using Workstation 17.x as its hardware compatibility level. You can change this later and on a per virtual machine basis if you need to. This is shown in the following screenshot (Figure 7-29).

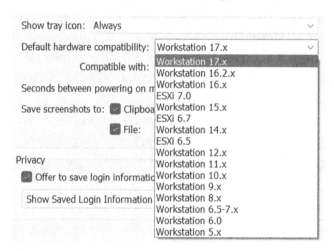

Figure 7-29. *Default hardware compatibility*

In conjunction with this option, you also have the **Compatible with ESX Server** box. This is automatically enabled and is grayed out, so it cannot be changed, meaning that the hardware compatibility you select is already compatible with ESX. However, if you select Workstation 5.x, then the option becomes available, and with this it is unchecked by default.

The next option, **Seconds between powering on multiple VMs**, allows you to configure the time delay between powering on virtual machines. By default this is set to 10 seconds, meaning that if you have multiple virtual machines, then Workstation Pro will wait 10 seconds before powering on the next virtual machine, when you power multiple virtual machines in one action.

This is useful in conjunction with the Auto Start feature where virtual machines can be configured to auto start when the host operating system boots. If you power on a few virtual machines at once, it could affect the boot time of the host machine, and so spacing out the timing of the power on action could be helpful.

The final option in this section is for saving screenshots of the virtual machines and the location of where that screenshot is saved to. You can **Save screenshots to clipboard** by checking the box to enable this which is enabled by default. This means that the screenshot you take of the virtual machine will be saved to the clipboard of the host machine.

The other option is to **Save screenshots to file** again by checking the box to enable this feature. It too is enabled by default. You then have a drop-down to select where the file is saved to on the host machine. You can select from the following options:

- **Save to desktop** - Places the screenshot on the desktop (and in the desktop folder) on the host.

- **Always ask for location** - Opens a **Save As** screen on the host machine where you can browse to the location to save the file or create a new folder.

- **Browse for custom location** - Opens a **Browse For Folder** screen where you can go and select a new default folder in which to save screenshots. You also have the option to make a new folder. All screenshots will now be saved in this new folder.

The following is an example of the default settings of save to the Desktop of the host machine and save to the clipboard of the host machine.

To take the screenshot, ensure you have the virtual machine you want to capture, in focus. From the menu click **VM** and then **Capture Screen** as shown in Figure 7-30.

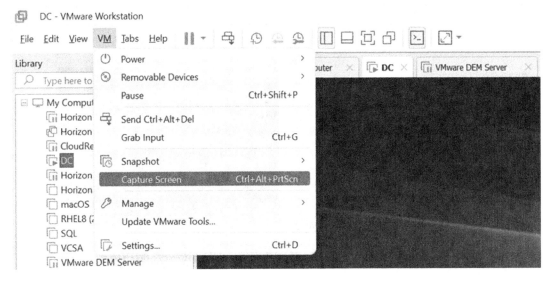

Figure 7-30. *Taking a screenshot of a virtual machine*

You will now see the **Capture Screen - VMware Workstation** dialog box which tells you where the screenshot is going to be saved to (Figure 7-31).

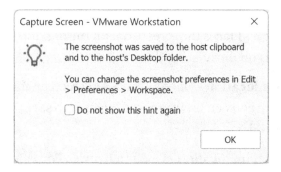

Figure 7-31. *Capture Screen*

Click **OK**. You can also check the box so that you don't see this message again the next time you take a screenshot.

As we have configured the screen capture to also save to the desktop of the host machine, if you open the desktop folder on the host machine, you will see the following (Figure 7-32).

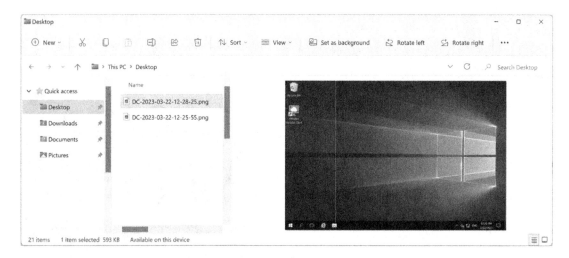

Figure 7-32. *Desktop Folder of the host machine after screen capture*

The final section in the Workstation settings is for **Privacy** which we will discuss in the next section.

Privacy

The **Privacy** setting gives you the option to save the login details for when you connect to a remote host using the **Connect to Server...** option which can be found under the **File** menu.

It's worth noting that the remote systems in question are either ESX host servers or vCenter servers and not the standard virtual machines running in Workstation Pro. Unless of course those virtual machines are ESX hosts or vCenter servers. The objective of the remote connection is so that you could move virtual machines between Workstation Pro and the other host servers.

To enable this feature, ensure that the **Offer to save login information for remote hosts** box has been checked.

You will also see a button for **Show Saved Login Information** (Figure 7-33). If you click this button, you will see details of the server name and the user name details that have been saved under the **Saved Passwords** tab. You can remove them from this screen if you need to. There is also a second tab for **Exceptions**.

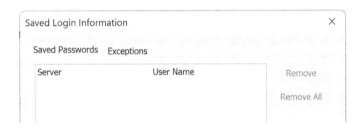

Figure 7-33. *Saved Login Information*

Next, we are going to look at configuring the Input preferences.

Input Configuration Preferences

The input preferences allow you to configure how the end user interacts with the virtual machine by configuring two elements, the keyboard and mouse, and then the cursor settings.

The Input preferences are shown in the following screenshot (Figure 7-34).

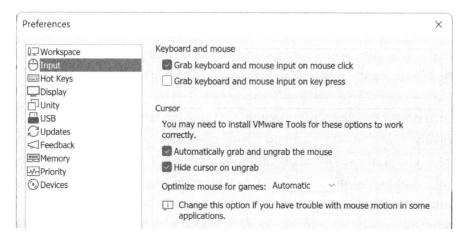

Figure 7-34. *Input configuration preferences*

The first section enables you to configure the preferences for the keyboard and mouse.

Keyboard and Mouse

Under the keyboard and mouse section, there are two options that both allow you to configure how to get focus on the running virtual machine. By focus we mean interacting with the virtual machine.

First is the option for **Grab keyboard and mouse input on mouse click** which is enabled by default. This means that focus will switch to the virtual machine when you click the mouse over the virtual machine running in Workstation Pro.

Secondly, there is the **Grab keyboard and mouse input on key press** which is disabled by default. This means that pressing a key on the keyboard will switch the focus back to the virtual machine.

Cursor

For these cursor options to work correctly you should ensure that you have VMware Tools installed and updated to the latest version.

The first option is for **Automatically grab and ungrab the mouse**, which is enabled by default. This means that whenever you move the mouse cursor over the virtual machine running in Workstation Pro, then the cursor automatically becomes active within that guest operating system. It means you don't have to click to get focus on the virtual machine.

Next, there is the **Hide cursor on ungrab** setting which is also enabled by default. This basically means that when you move the mouse and cursor outside of the virtual machine, then the cursor within that virtual machine guest operating system is no longer visible.

The final setting is the **Optimize mouse for games** feature which is set to Automatic by default. Other options are available from the drop-down menu and allow you to select **Never** or **Always**. This feature helps with the performance and speed of the cursor within games applications. It controls whether the cursor image is accelerated by the host machine, or whether it is drawn by VMware in the graphics stream as well as switching from the host machines cursor tracking speed to the guest operating systems tracking speed.

In the next section, we are going to look at configuring the preferences for hot keys.

Hot Keys

The hot keys feature allows you to configure shortcuts to commonly used operations on the virtual machines. The default settings are shown in the following screenshot (Figure 7-35).

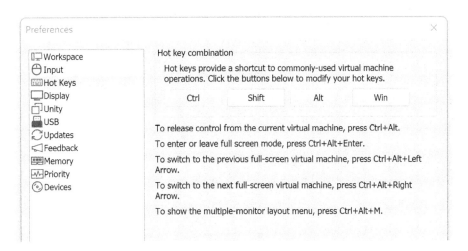

Figure 7-35. *Hot keys*

- **CTRL + ALT** - Release control from the current VM.

- **CTRL + ALT + ENTER** - Toggle between full screen mode.

- **CTRL + ALT + ←** - Switch to previous full screen VM.

- **CTRL + ALT + →** - Switch to next full screen VM.

- **CTRL + ALT + M** - Show multiple monitor layout menu.

If you want to modify the hot key sequences, simply click on the button for **Ctrl**, **Shift**, **Alt**, or **Win**. You will see with the default settings that both Ctrl and Alt are gray as they have been selected as the hot key sequence.

As an example, if you now clicked **Shift**, it would add Shift to the sequence, meaning you now need to press **Ctrl + Shift + Alt** plus the key for the function. So, **Ctrl + Shift + Alt + M** for multi-monitor layout.

Display

The Display preferences allow you to configure how virtual machines are displayed on the host and how the window is sized. The preferences are shown in the following screenshot (Figure 7-36).

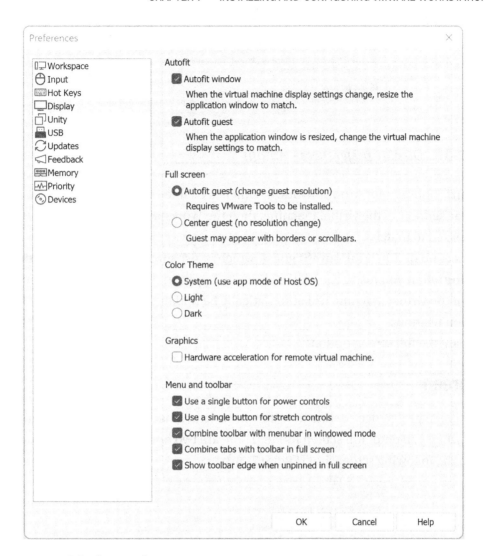

Figure 7-36. *Display preferences*

There are five different categories when it comes to configuring the display preferences. We will cover these in the next sections.

Autofit

With autofit you can define how the virtual machine will dynamically resize its window depending on whether you resize the Workstation Pro application or the virtual machine display settings. You have two options as shown in the following screenshot (Figure 7-37).

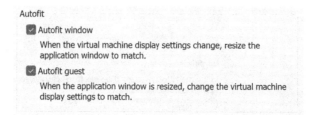

Figure 7-37. *Display preferences - Autofit*

The first option is for **Autofit window**, which is enabled by default. When you change the display settings of the virtual machine, then the Workstation Pro application window will be resized to match.

The second option is for **Autofit guest**, which is also **enabled by default. With this setting when you** resize the Workstation Pro application window, the display settings of the virtual machine will automatically be updated to match the size of the application window.

Next are the full screen options.

Full Screen

The full screen preferences define how the guest virtual machines display resolution changes when you enter full screen mode. There are two options you can configure as shown in the following screenshot (Figure 7-38).

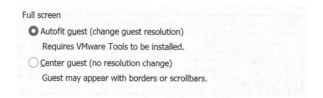

Figure 7-38. *Display preferences - Full screen*

You can select just one of these options by clicking the corresponding radio button.

First is the **Autofit guest** option which is selected by default. When you enter full screen mode, then the display resolution of the virtual machine guest operating system automatically changes to match the resolution of the host machine. For this to work, you will need VMware Tools to be installed on the virtual machines guest operating system.

An example of autofit full screen mode is shown in the following screenshot (Figure 7-39).

Figure 7-39. *Display preferences - example of autofit full screen*

The second option is for **Center guest**. As the name suggests, the virtual machine will be displayed in the center of the host machines display and will keep its current resolution and display settings.

Therefore, depending on the resolution of the virtual machine, you could see a border around the display if the resolution of the virtual machine is lower than that of the guest machine. On the other hand, if it is bigger than the host machine, you will see scroll bars to allow you to navigate the entire display size.

An example of Center guest is shown in the following screenshot (Figure 7-40).

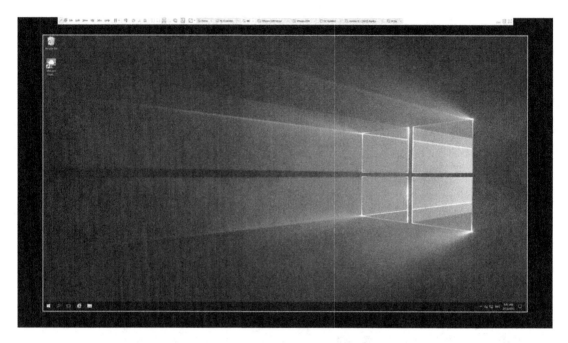

Figure 7-40. *Display preferences - example of center guest*

In this example we have drawn a white border around the virtual machines display to easier highlight the border around it.

The next set of preferences are for configuring the color theme.

Color Theme

With the Color Theme settings, you can configure the color of the theme used by the Workstation Pro application. Note, this setting does not apply to the virtual machine guest OS and applies just to Workstation Pro.

There are three settings to select from as shown in the following screenshot (Figure 7-41).

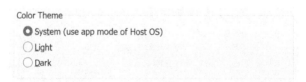

Figure 7-41. *Display preferences - color themes*

The **System (use app mode of Host OS)** option, the default setting, uses the current settings of the host machine. Typically, your host OS is set to light by default, but if you then change the color theme on the host machines operating system, then this will be reflected on the Workstation Pro app too.

If you select the option for **Light,** then the Workstation Pro application will use light mode regardless of what you set the host machines operating system to use. So if your host OS uses a dark mode, Workstation Pro will continue to use light mode regardless.

Finally, there is the **Dark** theme. This will use a dark mode using a black background with white text. Again, as with the previous options, selecting **Dark** means that the Workstation Pro application will use dark mode regardless of what you set the host machines operating system to use. So, if your host OS uses a light mode, Workstation Pro will continue to use dark mode regardless. An example of the dark theme is shown in the following screenshot (Figure 7-42).

Figure 7-42. *Display preferences - color themes*

The next preference setting is for graphics.

Graphics

The **Hardware acceleration for remote virtual machine** option was only introduced with version Workstation Pro 16.2.x and allows you to enable hardware acceleration for remote virtual machines. Remote virtual machines are those that are running on another platform such as ESXi.

Menu and Toolbar

With the menu and toolbar preference settings, you can define the behavior of the menus and the toolbars in Workstation Pro. There are five different options you can configure, all enabled by default, as shown in the following screenshot (Figure 7-43).

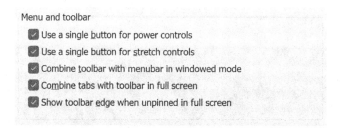

Figure 7-43. *Display preferences - Menu and toolbar*

The **Use a single button for power controls** shows a single button on the menu for controlling the power actions on a virtual machine. The other power actions are then shown by clicking the drop-down arrow as shown in the following screenshot (Figure 7-44).

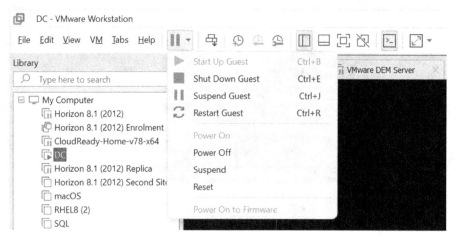

Figure 7-44. *Use a single button for power controls.*

If you disable this feature, by unchecking the box, then the power actions will all be displayed next to each other on the menu as shown in Figure 7-45.

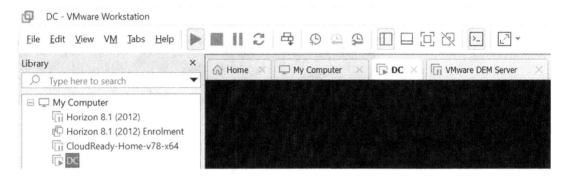

Figure 7-45. *Disable single button for power controls*

Next is the option for **Use a single button for stretch controls**. As with the power action buttons, by default there is a single button for the stretch controls as shown in the following screenshot (Figure 7-46).

Figure 7-46. *Use a single button for stretch controls.*

If you disable this feature, by unchecking the box, then the stretch controls will all be displayed next to each other on the menu as shown in the following screenshot and highlighted by the red box (Figure 7-47).

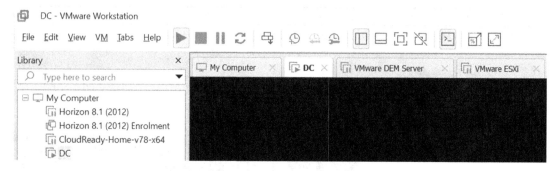

Figure 7-47. *Disable single button for stretch controls.*

The next preference setting is **Combine toolbar with menu bar in window mode**. This option combines the icons for the various actions you can perform on virtual machines (toolbar) along with the standard menu options (menu bar). This is shown in the following screenshot (Figure 7-48).

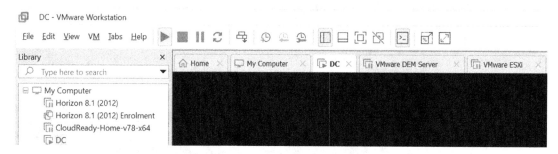

Figure 7-48. *Combined Toolbar and Menu Bar*

If you disable this feature, by unchecking the box, then the toolbar is separated from the menu bar, and they appear on two separate lines as shown in the following screenshot (Figure 7-49).

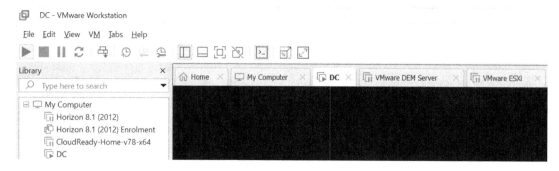

Figure 7-49. *Separate Toolbar and Menu Bar*

Next is the **Combine tabs with toolbar edge in full screen mode**. This works in a similar way as the Combine toolbar with menu bar as shown in Figure 7-50.

Figure 7-50. *Combined Toolbar, Menu Bar, and Tabs in Full Screen*

As you can see, the virtual machine is in full screen mode and the menu bar, toolbar, and virtual machine tabs are shown in a single one-line menu.

If you disable this feature, by unchecking the box, then the menu bar and toolbar are on one line, and the virtual machine tabs are on a separate line as shown in the following screenshot (Figure 7-51).

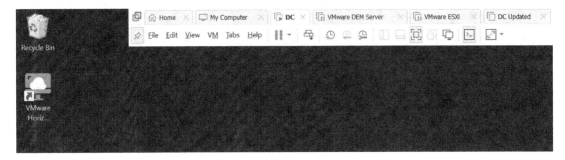

Figure 7-51. *Separate Toolbar, Menu Bar, and Tabs in Full Screen*

Finally, there is the **Show toolbar edge when unpinned in full screen mode**. When you have the toolbar unpinned, that is, hidden when you are in full screen mode, then a line will be displayed across the top of the screen where the menu bar would normally be visible. This line represents the bottom edge of the toolbar.

This is shown in the following screenshot (Figure 7-52).

Figure 7-52. *Show toolbar edge when unpinned in full screen*

If you disable this feature, by unchecking the box, then the line at the top of the screen, the edge of the toolbar, will no longer be visible.

This is shown in the following screenshot (Figure 7-53).

Figure 7-53. *Show toolbar edge when unpinned in full screen*

The next preference settings we are going to discuss is for unity mode.

Unity

Unity mode is a feature that allows applications running on VMs to be displayed on the host's desktop as if they were running on the host, effectively hiding the virtual machines console but still allowing access to the Start menu and applications menu of that virtual machine (Figure 7-54). We will cover this in more detail in the next chapter, Chapter 8.

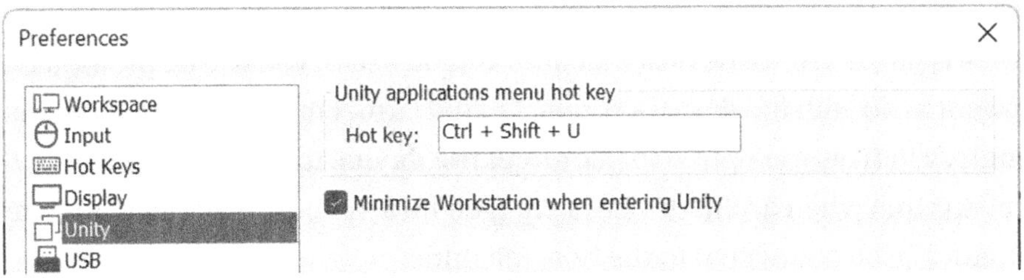

Figure 7-54. *Unity mode preferences*

There are just two options you can configure in the **Unity** preferences. The first is to change the Hot key sequence used to invoke Unity mode. To change the Hot key sequence, simply click in the **Hot key** box and press the key you want to use. This also includes using arrow keys.

If you press the delete key, then this sets the Hot key to **None**.

The other option is to Minimize Workstation when entering Unity. This is enabled by default and means that when you invoke Unity mode then the Workstation Pro application is minimized.

Next is the USB preference settings.

USB

This preference setting controls how a USB device, when plugged into the host machine and detected by Workstation Pro, should connect to a guest virtual machine running in Workstation Pro.

The following screenshot shows the **Connections** configuration options (Figure 7-55).

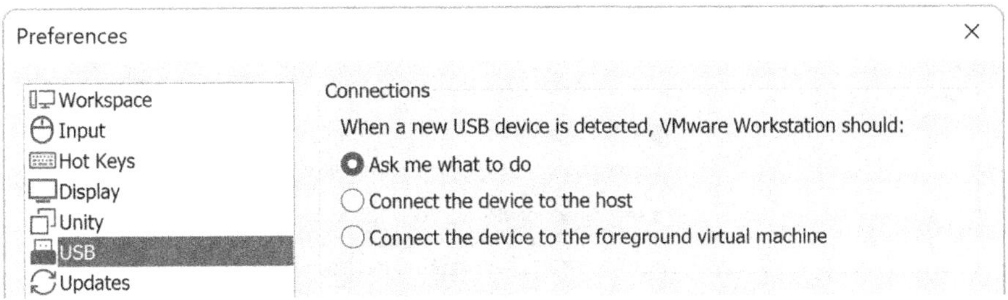

Figure 7-55. *USB Connections*

The first option is **Ask what to do**, which is enabled by default. This means that when a USB device is plugged into the host machine and detected, you will be prompted as to what you want to do with the device - connect to the virtual machine or the host machine.

Secondly, you have the option for **Connect the device to the host**. Selecting this options means that when a USB device is plugged into the host machine and detected, it will automatically be connected to the host machine.

Finally, you have the **Connect the device to the foreground virtual machine**. When a USB device is plugged into the host machine and detected, it is automatically connected to the virtual machine that is in the foreground, that is, the virtual machine currently in focus.

In the next section, we are going to discuss the software updated for Workstation Pro.

Updates

The updates section is used to manage and configure software updates. There are two different updates covered in this section. The first is to update the Workstation Pro application itself, and then the second preference settings manage how to upgrade the current version of VMware Tools that is installed on the virtual machine.

The preference settings are shown in the following screenshot (Figure 7-56).

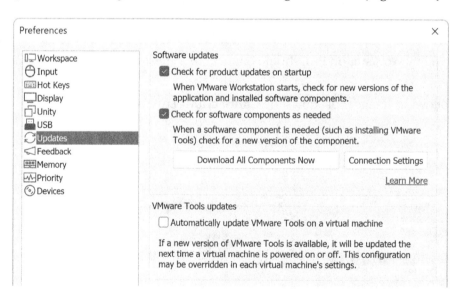

Figure 7-56. *Updates*

We will start by discussing the Software updates.

Software Updates

The first option in the Software updates section is for **Check for product updates on startup**, which is enabled by default. This means that when Workstation Pro launches, it will check the VMware software update website to see if there is an update or newer version available. This is covered in more detail in Chapter 21.

Next is the **Check for software components as needed** option, which is also enabled by default. This feature checks whether there is an update to a specific component as and when it is required.

You will see that there is also a button for **Download All Components Now**. Clicking this button will check for newer versions of all components, and if there are newer versions available, then they will be downloaded immediately.

The last option in the Software Updates section is a second button for Connection Settings. This takes you to another configuration screen where you can check the details of the update server as well as configuring a proxy server if you need to. You can either select, by clicking the corresponding radio button, No proxy, Windows proxy settings, and Manual proxy settings with the two latter options allowing you to enter the username and password for the proxy settings.

These options are shown in the following screenshot (Figure 7-57).

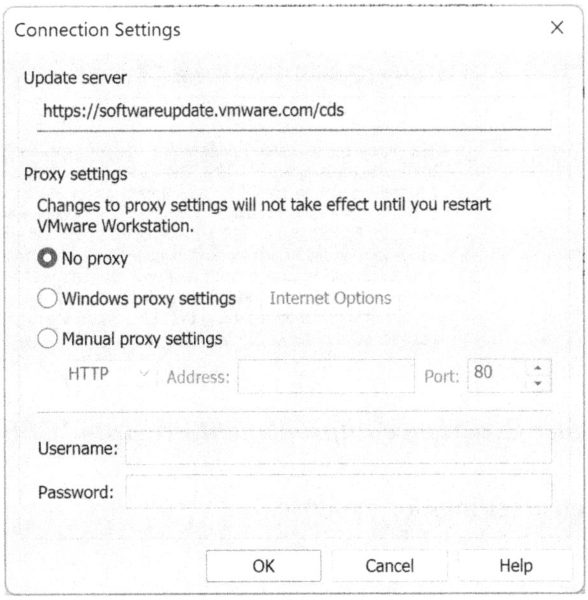

Figure 7-57. *Connection Settings*

The next updates relate to the updating of VMware Tools.

VMware Tools Updates

The final setting is for **Automatically update VMware Tools on a virtual machine**, which is disabled by default. If you enable this setting, then when a new version of VMware Tools is available, then it will automatically update the virtual machines the next time they are powered on or off.

This setting, although enabled here at a global level, can also be overridden in the configuration at an individual virtual machine level.

The next set of preferences relate to customer feedback.

Feedback

The **Feedback** option configures whether you want to join the Customer Experience Improvement Program or CEIP. It was also one of the questions asked during the installation, and so if you enabled this during install, then you now can disable it, by unchecking the box and vice versa.

This is shown in the following screenshot (Figure 7-58).

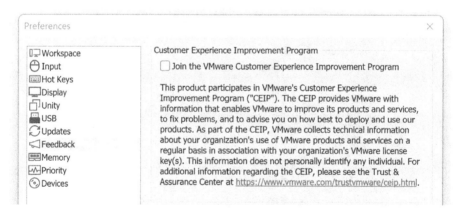

Figure 7-58. *Customer Experience Improvement Program (CEIP)*

Next is the preference settings for memory.

Memory

There are two memory preferences that you can set, reserved memory and additional memory, as shown in the following screenshot (Figure 7-59).

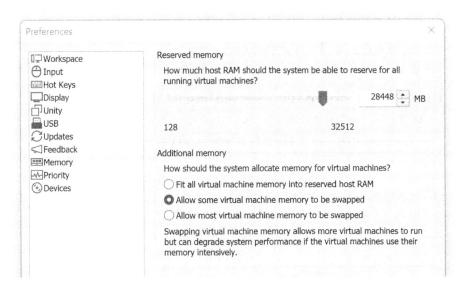

Figure 7-59. *Memory*

Reserved Memory

With the **Reserve memory** setting, you will see slider that allows you to set the amount of memory that the host machine can reserve for running virtual machines.

This allows you to set an amount of memory that is reserved for use by the host only as well as configuring the amount of memory that is usable by the virtual machines. The minimum amount of memory you can reserve is 128 MB, and the maximum amount of memory you can reserve will equal the total amount of memory the host is configured with. In this case, you can see that the host machine has 32GB of memory.

It is worth noting that the total amount of memory that can be assigned to all virtual machines hosted on a single instance of Workstation Pro is only limited by the amount of memory you can fit in the host machine. Also don't forget the maximum memory you can allocate to a virtual machine is 64GB.

The recommendation is not to reserve all memory and leave a minimum of 4 GB available to the host. If you go above the recommended amount of memory reserves, then a warning will be displayed.

Additional Memory

The other memory setting allows you to configure how memory should be allocated to the virtual machines. It enables you to configure the memory manager of the host machine so that it can efficiently swap the physical memory available between them. This allows for more virtual machines to run and possibly with greater memory requirements as memory can be swapped out to disk.

There are three options from which you can select:

- **Fit all VM memory into the reserved host RAM** - This option provides the best performance as virtual machines are running 100% in memory with no swapping. However, you need to ensure you have enough memory for this to work.

- **Allow some VMs RAM to be swapped** - This is enabled by default. It allows for some of the virtual machine memory to be swapped to disk enabling you to potentially run more virtual machines or virtual machines configured with more memory. Remember there might be a performance penalty as memory is now being swapped to disk.

- **Allow most VM RAM to be swapped** - This option means that Workstation Pro can swap as much memory as it needs to, to disk. It allows even more virtual machines to be hosted, or virtual machines configured with more memory; however, there will again be a performance penalty for swapping to disk.

The next preference setting is for priority.

Priority

There are two different priority settings that you can configure. The first is for the priority between the host machine and the virtual machines, and the second is for taking snapshots.

These options are shown in the following screenshot (Figure 7-60).

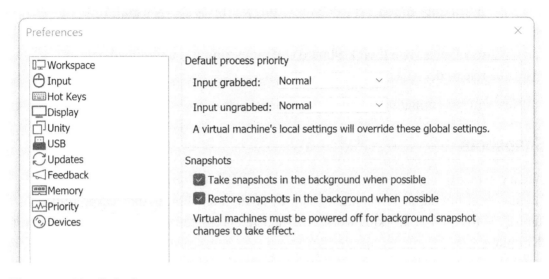

Figure 7-60. *Priority*

Let's look at the default process priority.

Default Process Priority

The default process priority preferences allow you to configure the priority that the Windows process scheduler gives to the virtual machines.

It's also worth noting that these settings could potentially affect the performance of the host system as well as the virtual machines.

There are two options to configure:

- **Input grabbed** - The default setting is **Normal**. This means that the processes running on virtual machines contend equally for resources with all the other processes that are currently running on the host machine. You have the option to change this to **High**. This setting is used for virtual machines when their keyboard and mouse input is grabbed.

- **Input ungrabbed** - The default setting for this is also **Normal**. You have the option to change this to **Low**. This setting is used for virtual machines when their keyboard and mouse input is ungrabbed or released.

Next you can configure the priority for snapshots.

Snapshots

When you take a snapshot of a virtual machine in Workstation Pro, that snapshot creation does not happen instantaneously. By taking snapshots in the background, it allows you to continue working work. The snapshot is created in the background without disruption.

There are two settings you can configure, with both being enabled by default:

- **Take snapshots in the background** - Snapshots are taken in the background with this option enabled meaning you can continue to work.

- **Restore snapshots in the background** - If you need to restore a snapshot, then this is also processed in the background allowing you to continue working.

If you change any of these snapshot background settings, then for them to take effect, then the virtual machines will need to be powered off and then powered back on again. A restart will not work.

The final preference settings relate to devices.

Devices

In the devices preferences setting, you can configure the behavior of removable media devices and printers as shown in the following screenshot (Figure 7-61).

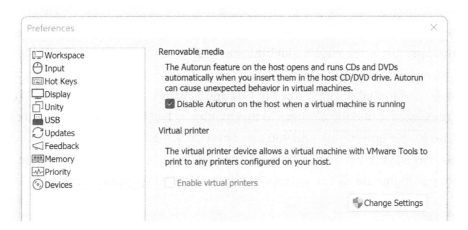

Figure 7-61. *Devices*

The first setting is for removable media devices.

Removable Media

The Autorun feature allows CDs and DVDs to run automatically when they are inserted into the drive in the host machine. While this is a great feature for the host machine and the host operating system, it doesn't work so well for virtual machines.

For this feature to work, any programs configured with Autorun programs, means that the operating systems poll the media drive every second or so. It does this to check whether you have inserted a disk. This action of continually polling the drive can cause Workstation Pro to connect to the host machines media drive making the drive spin up. When this happens, the virtual machine appears to hang while it waits for the drive to spin up and check whether a disk has been inserted. Therefore, this feature is disabled by default as it doesn't give the best end-user experience, and it also is generating unnecessary processes and load in checking the media drive.

You can switch this feature back on should you so wish, but it is recommended to leave it disabled.

Virtual Printer

The virtual printer setting enables a virtual machine that is running VMware Tools to be able to print to any of the printers that are configured on the host machine. By default, this option is disabled.

It is worth noting that this is a global setting that enables the **Install Virtual Printer** option to be available from the menu. For virtual printing to work, you will still need to add a virtual printer to the virtual machine you wish to print from as well as installing the VMware Virtual Printer Application. We will cover this in more detail in Chapter 10.

To enable the global setting, click the **Change Settings** button, accept the UAC warning message for making changes to this machine. The **Enable virtual printers** button is no longer grayed out, and you can now check the box.

Once enabled you will see the **Install Virtual Printer** option is now available from the **VM** menu (highlighted in red) as shown in the following (Figure 7-62).

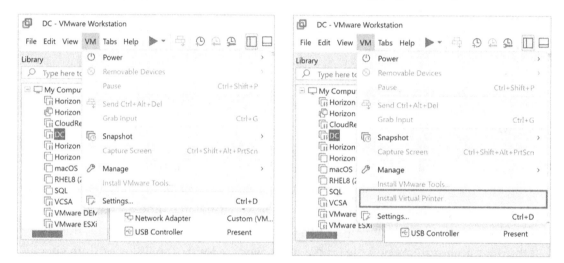

Figure 7-62. *Enabling virtual printers*

Summary

In this chapter we have discussed how to download and install VMware Workstation Pro. After discussing the prerequisites, we went on to install Workstation Pro, detailing each step of the process, explaining the different options, and showing the steps using actual screenshots.

Once workstation was successfully installed, we walked through configuring the preferences to control and manage the behavior of the virtual machines.

CHAPTER 8

A Guided Tour of the UI

Now that we have installed and configured Workstation Pro on a host machine, the main objective of this chapter is to give you an overview of the user interface and where you find the different features and settings. This will allow you to "drive" Workstation Pro.

Screen Layout

When you launch Workstation Pro for the first time, you will see the following as shown in Figure 8-1.

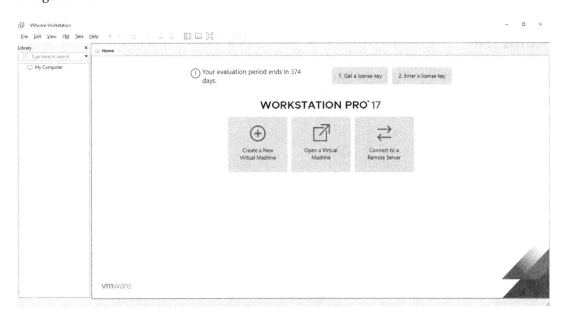

Figure 8-1. *Workstation Pro screen - first launch*

© Peter von Oven 2023
P. von Oven, *Learning VMware Workstation for Windows*, https://doi.org/10.1007/978-1-4842-9969-2_8

As part of the overview of the UI, we will look at the layout of the Workstation Pro screen, which is made up of three sections, the menu options, and also the icons. Where icons or menu options relate to a specific feature, we will show how that feature works and how it appears to the end user.

Just as a side note, the version running in these examples and throughout the book is using a vExpert license and therefore shows as an evaluation copy.

The Workstation Pro application window is divided into four core views:

- Menu bar

- Toolbar

- Library

- Virtual machines

When VMs are running, then the virtual machine pane view will change depending on whether the virtual machine is running, suspended, or powered off.

In the following sections, we are going to look at each view, starting with the menu bar.

Menu Bar

The first thing we are going to look at is the menu options as highlighted in red in Figure 8-2.

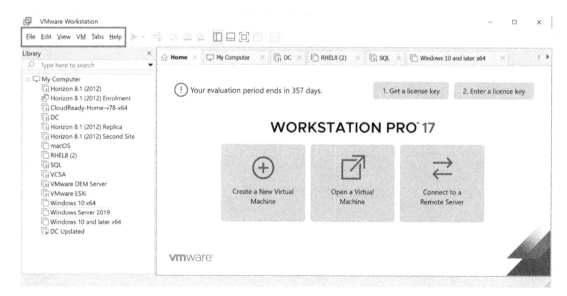

Figure 8-2. *Workstation Pro screen - menu bar*

The first menu option is for **File**, and the menu options are shown in Figure 8-3.

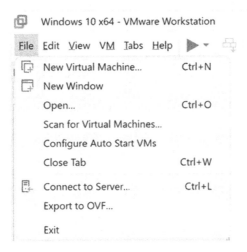

Figure 8-3. *Workstation Pro screen - File menu*

The options available on this menu are as follows:

- **New Virtual Machine** - Starts the new virtual machine wizard to guide you through the process of creating and configuring a new virtual machine. You can also select the New Virtual Machine option by right clicking in the **Library** pane under **My Computer**.

- **New Window** - Opens another Workstation Pro window. This could be used to view two virtual machines at the same time.

- **Open** - Allows you to open an existing virtual machine. When selected, a Windows Explorer box will open to allow you to browse to an existing VM configuration file or an OVF template.

- **Scan for Virtual Machines** - Scans the folder location you enter for virtual machines that are not currently listed in the library.

- **Configure Auto Start VMs** - Allows you to configure which virtual machines should be automatically started when Workstation Pro is launched. We will cover this in more detail in Chapter 11.

- **Close Tab** - Closes the currently selected tab and removes that view into that specific virtual machine.

- **Connect to Server** - Allows you to connect to an ESXi host server or a vCenter server. VMs hosted on that platform will then be listed in the library view within Workstation Pro.

- **Export to OVF** - Exports the selected virtual machine to an OVF or OVA template. The virtual machine needs to be powered off to do this.

- **Exit** - Exits and closes the Workstation Pro application.

The next option on the menu bar is for the **Edit** options as shown in Figure 8-4.

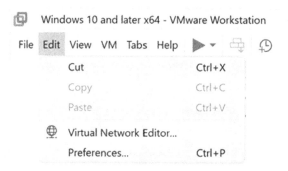

Figure 8-4. *Workstation Pro screen - Edit menu*

The options available on this menu are as follows:

- **Cut**, **Copy**, and **Paste** - Enabled by default, enables you to paste text between virtual machines and between applications running in virtual machines. You can also cut, copy, and paste images, plain text, formatted text, and email attachments as long as the size does not exceed 4MB.

  You can also cut and paste the virtual machines listed in the Library pane to reorder the listings; however, you can also just drag and drop these in the order in which you want to see them listed.

- **Virtual Network Editor** - Launches the virtual network editor enabling you to reconfigure and create networks for virtual machines running in Workstation Pro. This was covered in detail in Chapter 5.

- **Preferences** - Launches the preferences configuration screen. This was covered in more detail in Chapter 7.

Next, we are going to look at the **View** options from the menu bar. With the view options, you can choose how the virtual machine is displayed within the VM window as well as customize which panes are visible within the Workstation Pro application window.

The menu options are shown in Figure 8-5.

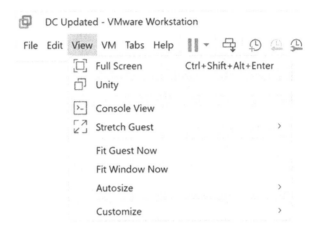

Figure 8-5. *Workstation Pro screen - View menu*

The following options are available on the **View** menu:

- **Full Screen** - This option switches the currently selected virtual machine, when running, to full screen mode, meaning the virtual machine will use the entire screen real estate of the host machine.

    If you select full screen for a virtual machine that is not running, then the Workstation Pro application will switch to full screen which hides the menu and toolbars of the application along with the Windows Taskbar.

- **Unity Mode** - In Unity mode, the application running on virtual machines will appear on the desktop of the host machine. This means that you can launch these application from the host machine. When launched the virtual machine console view is hidden.

    Applications from the virtual machine will appear on the host machine's taskbar the same way as and other host applications.

Once running in unity mode, you can use keyboard shortcuts to copy, cut, and paste images, plain text, formatted text, and email attachments between applications. You are also able to drag and drop as well as copy and paste files between the host machine and the virtual machine.

When you save a file or open a file when running an application in Unity mode, the file system displayed for opening and saving that file is the virtual machine's file system. It is not the host machine's file system, and therefore, you will not be able to open a file from the host machine or save a file to the host machine.

Figure 8-6 shows an example of the virtual machine named DC being switched to Unity mode.

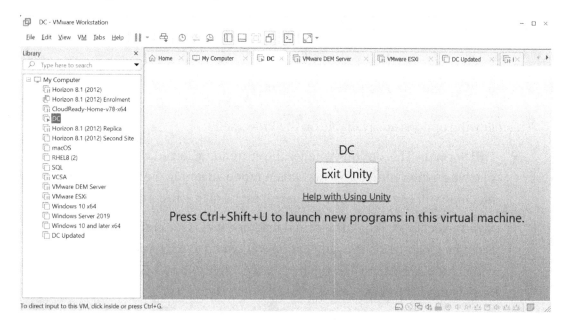

Figure 8-6. *Workstation Pro screen - Unity mode*

In Figure 8-7 you will see the host machine view of Unity mode running.

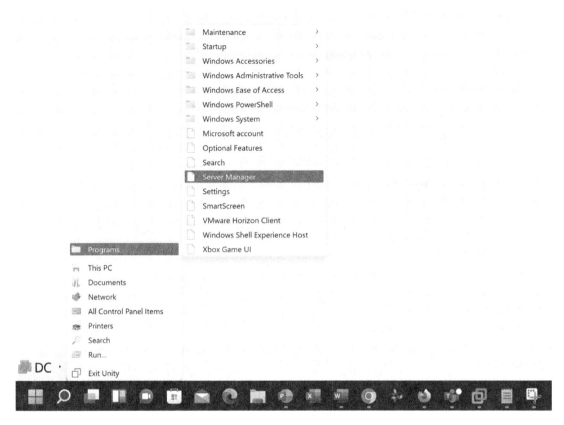

Figure 8-7. *Workstation Pro screen - Unity mode host machine view*

As you can see in the example in Figure 8-7, the DC virtual machine appears on the desktop of the host machine where you are able to launch the applications running on the virtual machine with them opening and appearing on the desktop of the host machine.

- **Console view** - Switches between the VM pane showing just the console of the virtual machine or the view that also has the devices, description, and details of the virtual machine displayed.

- **Stretch guest** - Provides the following two options for how the virtual machine screen is displayed:

  - **Keep aspect ratio stretch** - When you resize and stretch the virtual machine display, it will maintain the same aspect ratio of the window in which the virtual machine is running.

- **Free stretch** - The free stretch option will stretch the virtual machine display to fill the window the virtual machine is running in, but the aspect ratio will not be maintained.

- **Fit guest now** - The virtual machine display size will now change to match that of the current Workstation Pro window.

- **Fit window now** - The Workstation Pro window will now change to match the current display size of the virtual machine.

- **Autosize** - Enables you to size the display of the virtual machine to match the display size of the Workstation Pro VM window in which the virtual machine is running. There are three different options for the autosize feature:

  - **Autofit guest** - The virtual machine resizes the guest display resolution to match the size of the Workstation Pro console window in which the running virtual machine is displayed.

  - **Center guest** - The virtual machine resolution remains the same and is displayed in the center of the windows that is displaying the running virtual machine. The virtual machine, depending on the resolutions setting, may display surrounded by a border.

  - **Autofit window** - The windows in which the virtual machine is displayed keeps the size of the virtual machine display resolution regardless of whether the resolution of the virtual machine changes. Workstation Pro will resize accordingly in order to match any changes to the resolution.

  - **Customize** - The customize option allows you to select which element you want to be displayed. These are as follows:

  - **Library** - Toggles whether or not the library pane is displayed. The library pane is shown in Figure 8-8.

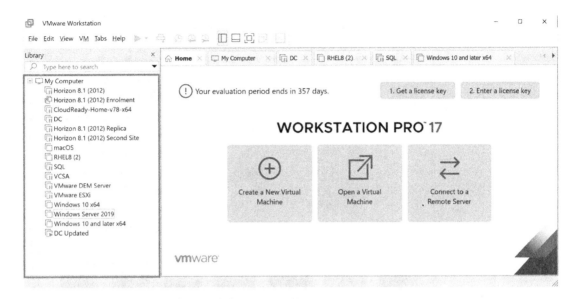

Figure 8-8. *Workstation Pro screen - Library*

- **Thumbnail bar** - Toggles whether or not the thumbnail bar is displayed. The thumbnail bar can be found at the bottom of the virtual machine pane and can display two different views selectable by clicking the drop-down menu shown highlighted in Figure 8-9.

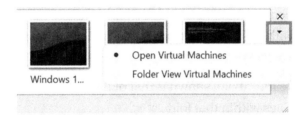

Figure 8-9. *Selecting a thumbnail view*

The first view you can select is the **Open Virtual Machines** view that shows the virtual machines that are configured in Workstation Pro, effectively a thumbnail view of the library view.

They are displayed as a thumbnail view of the virtual machine's screen as shown in Figure 8-10.

165

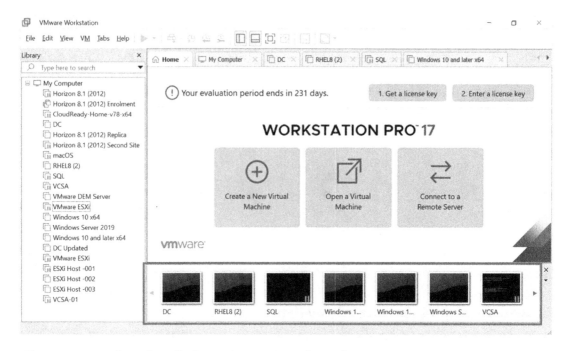

Figure 8-10. *Thumbnail view - Open virtual machines*

The other view is the **Folder View Virtual Machines** view.

If you select this option, then the thumbnails of the virtual machines shown are those in the folder that you select. In the example screenshot in Figure 8-11, we have a folder called Test Folder, and within that folder there is a virtual machine called Windows Server 2019.

Therefore, the thumbnail shown is that of the virtual machine or virtual machines within that folder:

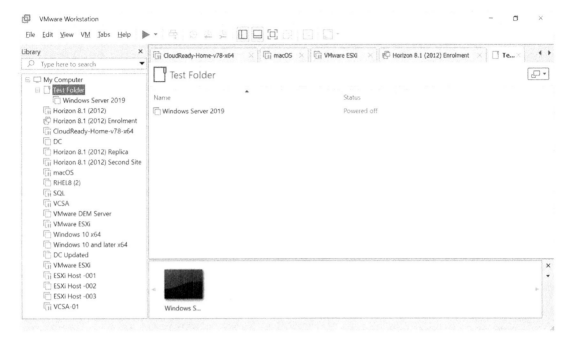

Figure 8-11. *Thumbnail view - Folder view virtual machines*

- **Toolbar** - Toggles whether or not the toolbar is displayed. The
  toolbar is shown in Figure 8-12.

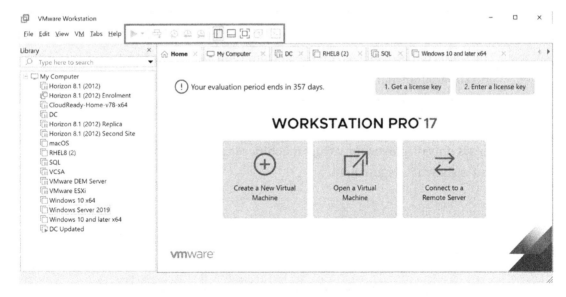

Figure 8-12. *Toolbar*

- The icons on the toolbar will be discussed in more detail later on in this chapter.

  - **Tabs** - Toggles whether or not the virtual machine tabs appear in the VM window as highlighted in Figure 8-13.

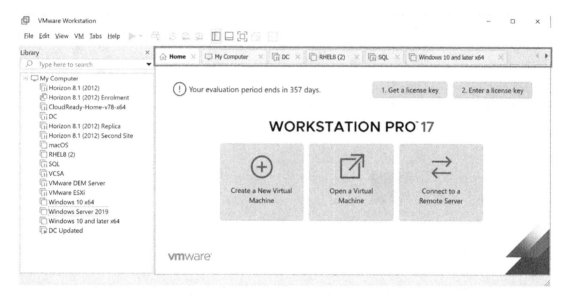

Figure 8-13. *Tabs view*

- **Status bar** - Toggles whether or not the status bar is displayed.

  The status bar is displayed on the bottom right side of the screen and shows information about the currently selected virtual machine such as hard disk activity, network activity, and devices connected.

  This is only displayed for virtual machines that are powered on and is shown in Figure 8-14.

Figure 8-14. *Status bar*

Next, we are going to look at the **VM** options from the menu bar which relates to options and features of the virtual machines and is shown in Figure 8-15.

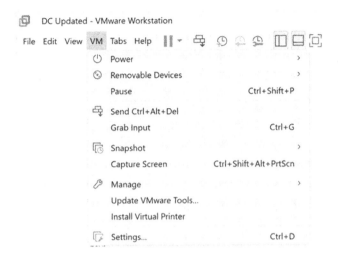

Figure 8-15. *Workstation Pro screen - VM menu*

The following options are available on the **VM** menu:

- **Power** - Under the power option, there are a number of power-
  related functions that can be actioned on a virtual machine.
  The power functions listed will reflect the current power state of
  the selected VM. For example, if a virtual machine is currently
  suspended, then you won't see the option for power on as technically
  it is already powered on. Instead, you will see the option to resume
  the virtual machine back to the state where it was originally
  suspended:

  - **Start Up Guest** - Classified as a soft power option, this option
    starts the virtual machine, and then VMware Tools will run a
    script on the virtual machine. If DHCP is being used, then this
    script will renew the virtual machine's IP address.

  - **Shutdown Guest** - This initiates a graceful shutdown of a virtual
    machine by sending a power off command to the operating
    system running in the virtual machine. The virtual machine will
    then power off using the correct procedure depending on the
    operating system it is running. It is worth noting that not all guest
    operating systems will support a graceful shut down.

- **Suspend Guest** - The suspend feature saves the current state of a virtual machine. When the virtual machine is resumed, it continues from the exact point where it was suspended, including any applications that were running at the time the virtual machine was suspended. When you initiate a suspend action, then a virtual machine suspended state or vmss or .vmem file is created in the same folder as the virtual machine is stored. The virtual machine is also disconnected from the network, and if the IP address was acquired using DHCP, then the IP address will be released. Once resumed the virtual machine will continue to work from where it left off, and you cannot return to the same state as when the virtual machine was first suspended. That is where snapshots come in to play.

- **Restart Guest** - Another soft option which first gracefully shuts down the virtual machine and then performs a startup guest action. To do this VMware Tools runs scripts both before the virtual machine shuts down and then again when the virtual machine starts up.

- **Resume Guest** - Resuming the guest brings a suspended virtual machine back online ready to use from the same point in time as when it was suspended.

- **Power On** - Classified as a hard option, this essentially turns on a virtual machine.

- **Power Off** - Another hard option then turns the virtual machine off as if you removed the power. There is no graceful shutdown with this option.

- **Suspend** - The virtual machine is suspended but is left connected to the network.

- **Reset** - This is a hard option that immediately resets the virtual machine without warning and is like turning it off and back on again.

- **Power on to Firmware** - Switches the virtual machine on and automatically launches the BIOS configuration page as shown in Figure 8-16.

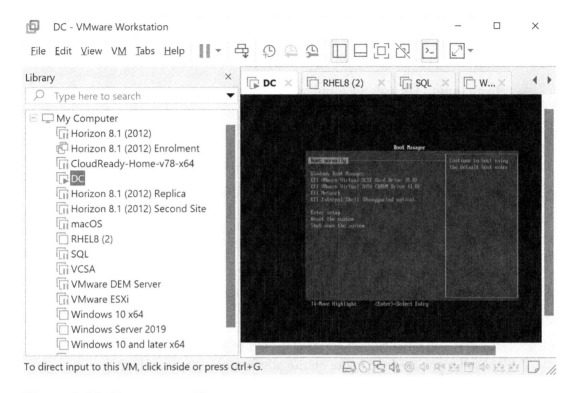

Figure 8-16. *Power on to Firmware screen*

- **Removable Devices** - When clicked you will see a list of hardware devices that can be connected to the virtual machine currently selected.

- **Pause** - A virtual machine can be paused to temporarily stop it using resources.

  This would be used if a particular virtual machine was using too much CPU resource, for example, which was preventing you from running something on another virtual machine or the host machine. This is not the same as suspending as no files are written or created to save the virtual machine state. When paused the virtual machine will display a green play button, which you click to resume, and the display itself will be dimmed.

- **Send Ctrl+Alt+Del** - Sends the Ctrl+Alt+Del command to the virtual machine selected to either logon or access the Lock, Switch User, Sign Out, Change Password, or launch the Task Manager.

- **Grab Input** - Focuses the input to the virtual machine selected. This means that the keyboard and mouse become active on the virtual machine.

- **Snapshot** - There are three functions under the snapshot menu:

  - **Take Snapshot** - Takes a snapshot of the selected virtual machine.

  - **Revert to Snapshot** - Reverts to a previously taken snapshot.

  - **Snapshot Manager** - Launches the snapshot manager. We will discuss snapshots and how to manage them in Chapter 11.

- **Capture Screen** - Takes a screenshot of the selected virtual machines display. The screenshot is saved to the clipboard of the host machine as well as the Desktop folder on the host machine as stated in the pop-up message shown in Figure 8-17.

Figure 8-17. *Capture Screen dialog box*

- **Manage** - The manage option comprises a number of management functions as described in the following points:

  - **Change Hardware Compatibility** - Launches the Change Hardware Compatibility Wizard that allows you to change the hardware version of the selected virtual machine.

172

- **Clone** - Creates a clone or exact copy of the selected virtual machine.

- **Upload** - Launches the Upload Virtual Machine Wizard which allows you to upload the selected virtual machine to another host by copying the virtual machine files to the selected vSphere host and selected datastore.

- **Download** - Allows you to download a virtual machine from a vSphere platform to Workstation Pro.

- **Clean Up Disk** - Returns disk space that was previously used by files that have been deleted from the virtual machine. This space is the space used in the virtual disk file and has no bearing on the host machine's disk space. We will cover in Chapter 10.

- **Delete from Disk** - Deletes all files, configuration, and virtual disk files, for the virtual machine selected.

- **Permissions** - Allows for the control of which users can access remote hosts and shared virtual machines consisting of a number of predefined privileges.

- **VNC Connections** - A virtual machine can act as a Virtual Network Computing (VNC) server that enables users on other machines to use VNC client software to connect to that virtual machine.

This does not require any VNC software to be installed on the virtual machine itself. You simply enable VNC connections on the virtual machine settings page which we will cover in Chapter 10.

The VMC Connections dialog box showing the current connections is shown in Figure 8-18.

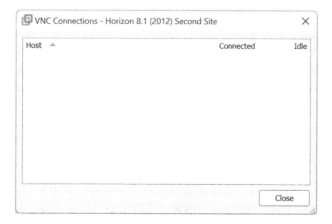

Figure 8-18. *VNC Connections screen dialog box*

- **Message Log** - Messages stored in the message log include warning information about the virtual machine such as devices being connected and other tasks such as disk cleanup.

  The Message Log dialog box showing the current connections is shown in Figure 8-19.

Figure 8-19. *Message Log dialog box*

- **Install/Reinstall VMware Tools** - Depending on the status of VMware Tools, this option will allow you to install VMware Tools on a virtual machine that currently does not have it installed, or if it is already running, then you have the option to reinstall.

- **Install Virtual Printer** - Installs the virtual printer feature on the virtual machine.

- **Settings** - Launches the settings screen for the virtual machine's hardware settings configuration. This was discussed in Chapter 6.

Toolbar

When selected, the toolbar is displayed at the top of the screen next to the menu options, and each feature is represented by an icon as shown in Figure 8-20.

Figure 8-20. *Toolbar*

The first icon is for virtual machine power functions and can also be found in the VM → Power menu.

This icon will also change as it displays the current power option available for the virtual machine that is selected. For example, if a virtual machine is powered on, then the suspend or pause button is shown.

If the virtual machine is already paused or suspended, then the resume or play button will be shown. The power options are shown in Figure 8-21.

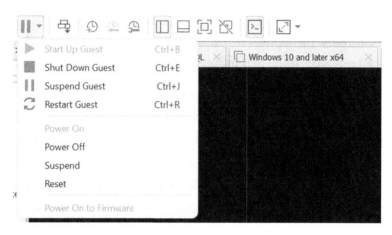

Figure 8-21. *Toolbar power options*

The other icons on the toolbar, which are also defined in the various menu options, are described in the following table in Figure 8-22.

Figure 8-22. *Toolbar icons*

Now that we have discussed the menu bars and toolbars; in the next couple of sections, we will complete the discussion on the other areas on the Workstation Pro application screen starting with the library pane.

Library

The library pane is used to show the virtual machines that have been configured within Workstation Pro.

Each virtual machine is shown, listed by the name you configured when you created the virtual machine, along with an icon showing its current power state. If you have created any folders, these will also be shown in the library pane along with any virtual machines within that folder structure.

If you have connected to any remote ESXi servers or vCenter Servers, then these will also be listed in the library.

At the top of the library pane, you will see that there is a search bar from where you can search for virtual machines.

The library pane is shown in Figure 8-23.

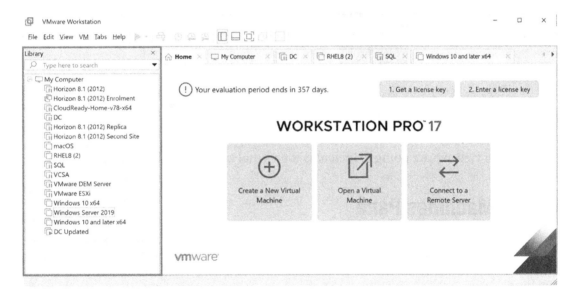

Figure 8-23. *Library pane*

The final functionality you will find in the library pane is a contextual menu.

When you right click on a virtual machine in the library, you will see a contextual menu. The menu options shown are dependent on the power state of the virtual machine, and therefore some options might not be available.

For example, you can't remove a virtual machine when it is powered on or you can't add a device or capture screen on a virtual machine that is suspended or powered off.

These contextual menu examples are shown in Figure 8-24.

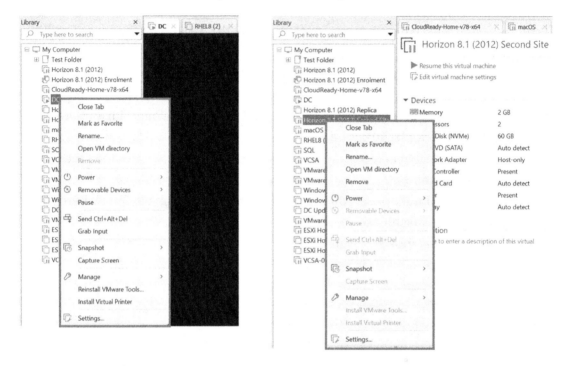

Figure 8-24. *Library pane contextual menus*

The final view we are going to look at is the virtual machines pane.

Virtual Machines Pane

The virtual machines pane is where you see the configuration and settings details of virtual machines as well as providing a console view of the desktop of the virtual machine.

Each virtual machine can be selected from the library or the tabs. The first tab is the **Home** tab and is shown in Figure 8-25.

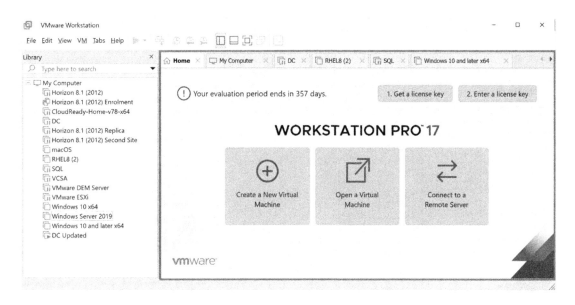

Figure 8-25. *Home tab*

The next tab is the My Computer tab and mirrors the My Computer section in the library. This view shows the virtual machines and their current status as shown in Figure 8-26.

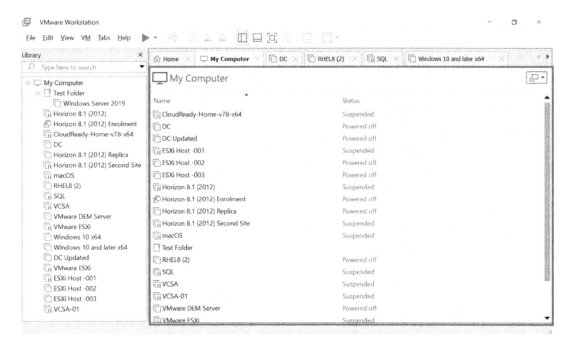

Figure 8-26. *My Computer tab*

If you click on a virtual machine, then you will see the following screenshot (Figure 8-27).

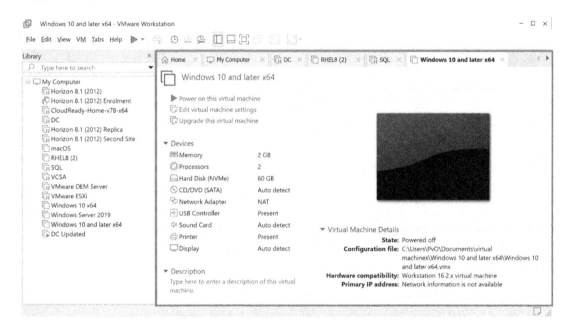

Figure 8-27. *Virtual machine view - powered off virtual machine*

The virtual machine selected in this example is powered off. From this screen you can power on the virtual machine and view the devices, configuration, and the details such as snapshot, config file, and hardware compatibility.

You will also see a black square where the console would normally be displayed as this virtual machine is powered off.

If the virtual machine had been suspended or paused, you would see something like the example shown in Figure 8-28.

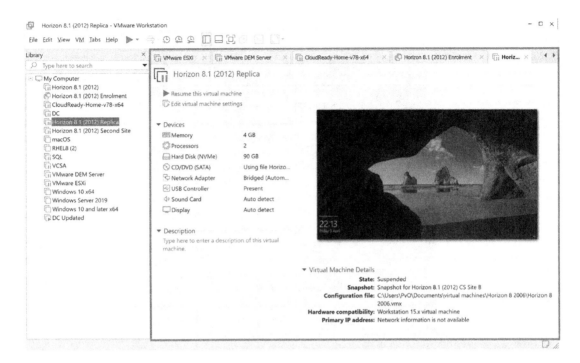

Figure 8-28. *Virtual machine view - suspended virtual machine*

In this example you will see the same details as shown in the previous screenshot; however, the console screen will now show a grayed-out version of the virtual machines screen at the point it was suspended.

If the virtual machine is powered on and running, then you would see something like the example screenshot in Figure 8-29.

Figure 8-29. *Virtual machine view - running virtual machine*

As this virtual machine is running, you will also see the status bar in the bottom right-hand side of the screen.

Summary

In this chapter we have given you an overview of the different screen views within VMware Workstation Pro so that you are familiar with how to work with the solution more effectively.

As well as describing the different features and functions available in Workstation Pro, this chapter gives you the information that allows you to "drive" the application interface to build, configure, and manage virtual machines and the available options and what each one means and how to use it.

CHAPTER 9

Creating a Windows VMs

Now that we have discussed the virtual hardware, installed VMware Workstation Pro on our device, and given an overview of the user interface, it is now time to build the first virtual machines.

In this chapter we are going to focus on building Windows-based virtual machines and will build, configure, and install three Windows operating systems:

- Windows 10

- Windows 11

- Windows Server 2022

With the two desktop-based operating systems, we are going to use two different build methods. First, we will build Windows 10 using the **Typical** mode whereby Workstation Pro selects the appropriate configuration, and then we will build a second virtual machine but this time using a more manual method with the **Custom** option to build a Window 11 virtual machine.

Finally, we will build a Windows Server virtual machine.

Building a Windows 10 Virtual Machine

In this first section, we are going to build a virtual machine running the Windows 10 operating system, and to build and configure it, we are going to use the **Typical** method which is also highlighted as the recommended way to build a virtual machine.

It is also the quickest and easiest way to build and configure a virtual machine as Workstation Pro will make the decision on the virtual hardware configuration based on the requirements of the operating system chosen.

© Peter von Oven 2023
P. von Oven, *Learning VMware Workstation for Windows*, https://doi.org/10.1007/978-1-4842-9969-2_9

To build and configure a new virtual machine, follow the steps described:

1. Click the **File** option from the menu and then select the option for
   New Virtual Machine as shown in Figure 9-1. For this example,
   we also have a folder called **Chapter 9 VMs** in which we are going
   to create these virtual machines.

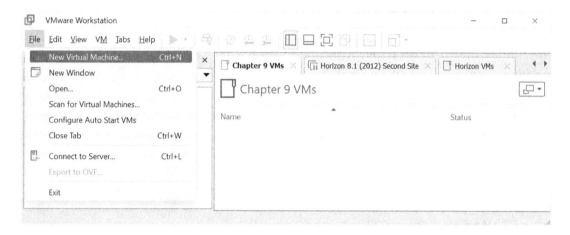

Figure 9-1. *Creating a New Virtual Machine*

2. You will now see the **Welcome to the New Virtual Machine
   Wizard** screen as shown in Figure 9-2.

Figure 9-2. *Welcome to the New Virtual Machine Wizard screen*

3. Click the radio button for **Typical (recommended)**.

4. Now click the **Next >** button. You will see the **Guest Operating System Installation** screen as shown in Figure 9-3.

Figure 9-3. *Guest Operating System Installation screen*

5. On this screen you have the option of selecting the source of the
    installation. You have the following choices:

    •   The first option is for installing the operating system from an
        installation disk with that installation disk inserted into a CD
        ROM drive, for example. You would then select the drive letter
        from the drop-down menu.

    •   The second option is to install from an ISO image to which you
        can browse to.

    •   The final option is to choose not to install the operating system at
        this point in time. Instead, you would just create a blank virtual
        hard drive and then install the chosen operating system at a
        later date.

6. In this example, click the radio button for **Installer disc image file (iso)**, and then click **Browse….** You will see a File Explorer window open to allow you to browse to the location of the ISO file required as shown in Figure 9-4.

Figure 9-4. *Browse for ISO Image screen*

7. Navigate to the location of the ISO file required, click to select it, in this case the Windows 10 ISO image, and then click **Open**.

8. You will return to the **Guest Operating System Installation** screen.

9. In the **Installer disc image file (iso)** box, you will now see the full path to the selected ISO image entered as shown in Figure 9-5.

Figure 9-5. *ISO Image selected*

10. Now click **Next >**. You will now see the **Easy Install Information** screen.

11. In the **Windows product key** box, type in the product/license key for the operating system being installed. You can miss this step out and enter the key once the operating system has been installed or if you have an alternative way, such as KMS, to activate and register the operating system. You will see a pop-up warning box as shown in Figure 9-6.

Figure 9-6. *Product Key warning box*

12. In the Version of Windows to install, click the drop-down box, and select the version of the operating system you want to install.

13. Next you have the option to personalize Windows by adding your **Full name**, **Password**, and **Confirm** password. These are optional and if selected will then allow you to check the box for **Log on automatically**. The **Easy Install Information** screen is shown in Figure 9-7.

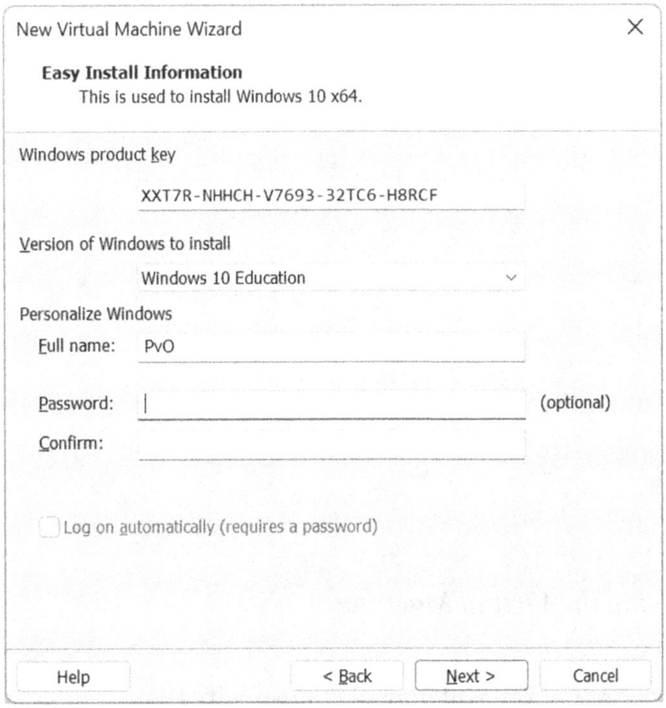

Figure 9-7. *Easy Install Information*

14. Now click **Next >**. You will now see the **Name the Virtual Machine** screen.

15. In the **Virtual machine name** box, type in a unique name for the virtual machine. Don't forget that the virtual machine name doesn't just appear in the library; it is also used as the filenames for the virtual machine configuration file and virtual hard disk files. In this example we have called it **Chapter 9 - Windows 10**.

16. In the Location box you will see that the default folder location is used to store the virtual machine files. If you want to change this, then click the Browse... button, and select a new folder location. the **Name the Virtual Machine** screen is shown in Figure 9-8.

Figure 9-8. *Naming the Virtual Machine*

17. Now click **Next >**. You will now see the **Specify Disk Capacity** screen.

18. The first option is for **Maximum disk size (GB)** which allows you to specify the size of the virtual hard disk that will be created for the operating system of this virtual machine. In this case the recommended size of 60GB has already been entered. You can change this if required by typing in a new size value or by using the up and down arrows.

19. The next two options define how the virtual hard disk is created
     and stored, with the following two options available:

- **Store virtual disk as a single file** - This basically does as the
  name suggests and creates one large virtual hard disk of the size
  specified.

- **Split virtual disk into multiple files** - Again, as the name
  suggests, instead of one big file, Workstation Pro will create
  multiple smaller files which are easier to manage if you need
  to migrate or copy the virtual machine. Each individual file will
  grow sequentially as the virtual hard disk fills. We will show this
  once the virtual machine has been created when we look at
  the different files Workstation Pro creates when creating a new
  virtual machine. The **Specify Disk Capacity** screen is shown in
  Figure 9-9.

Figure 9-9. *Specify Disk Capacity screen*

20. In this example, click the radio button for **Split virtual disk into multiple files** and then click **Next >**.

21. You will now see the **Ready to Create Virtual Machine** screen. This screen displays the selected configuration of how the virtual machine will be created. You also have the option to customize the hardware by adding additional hardware to the virtual machine. We will cover this in more detail in Chapter 10.

22. The final option is the check box for Power on this virtual machine after creation. Selecting this option means that as soon as the virtual machine has been configured, it will power on, and, in this case, as we have attached an ISO image of Windows 10, this will boot from that ISO to the Windows 10 setup and installation screens. The **Ready to Create Virtual Machine** screen is shown in Figure 9-10.

Figure 9-10. *Ready to Create Virtual Machine*

23. Now click **Finish**.

24. You will see the creation of the virtual hard disk and the following
    message as shown in Figure 9-11.

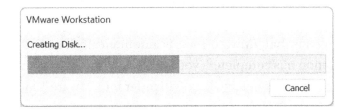

Figure 9-11. *Creating the virtual hard disk*

25. The virtual machine will boot to **Windows Setup** as shown in
    Figure 9-12.

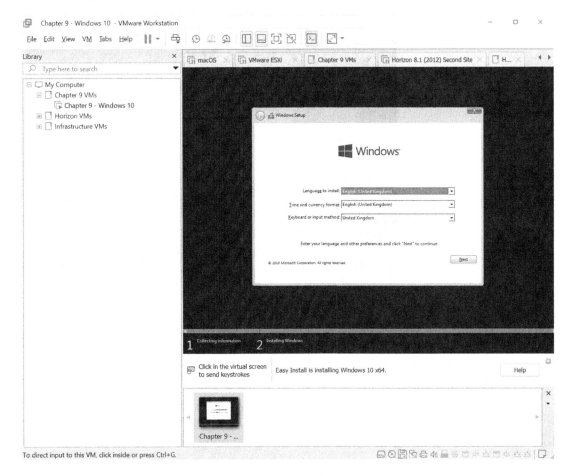

Figure 9-12. *Virtual Machine booted to Windows Setup*

The next steps are not VMware Workstation related and are the standard tasks you would complete to install Windows 10 regardless of this being a virtual machine.

As such one of the most important tasks is to install VMware Tools which in this case was completed automatically as we selected the typical installation method. Being a typical installation means that VMware Tools is automatically installed.

Once the installation has completed, you will see a VMware Tools message, as shown in Figure 9-13, stating that you need to log off in order for VMware Tools to take effect. If you click OK, then you will be logged off; however, it is recommended to restart the virtual machine instead to ensure drivers load correctly.

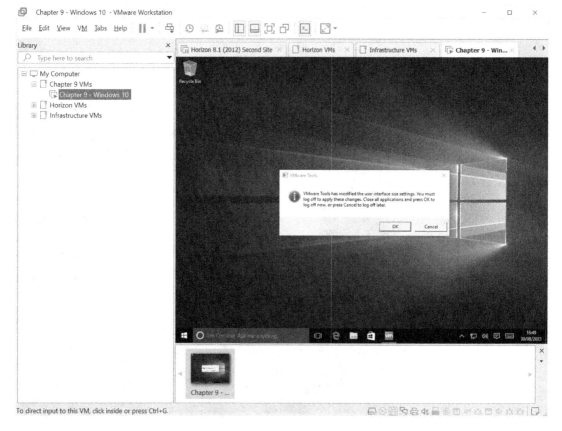

Figure 9-13. *VMware Tools*

Once the virtual machine has restarted and you have logged back in, check VMware Tools is running by clicking the up arrow on the right-hand side of the task bar and ensuring that you can see the VM logo as shown in Figure 9-14.

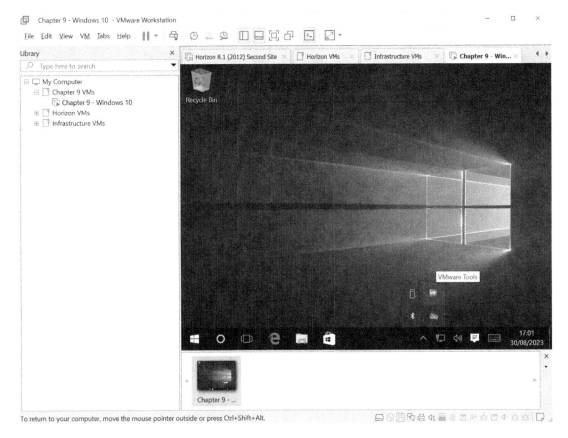

Figure 9-14. *VMware Tools running*

You have now successfully built and configured a Windows 10 virtual machine.

The next question is what exactly was created given a virtual machine is just a set of files?

What Gets Created As Part of a VM Build?

Now that the Windows 10 virtual machine has been built, configured, and is up and running, we can look at what happened behind the scenes and the files that got created.

The virtual machine was created in the default folder location in My Documents, in a sub-folder called Virtual Machines.

If you open a File Explorer window and navigate to that location then you will see that the folder shares the same name as the virtual machine. In this case Chapter 9 - Windows 10.

You will see the following as shown in Figure 9-15.

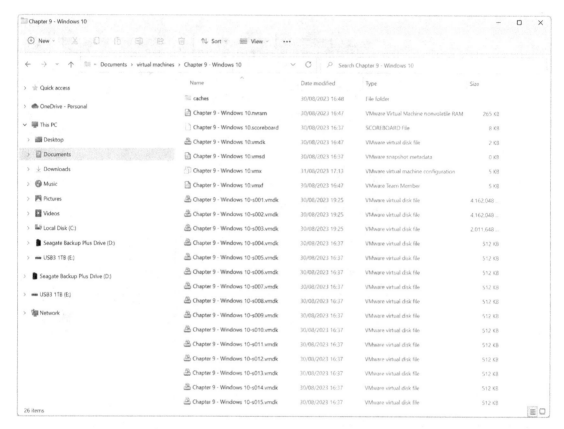

Figure 9-15. *File Explorer shown VM files*

These files are used for the following:

- **.nvram** - Stores the saved state of the BIOS of the virtual machine in a form similar to non-volatile memory.

- This file is used by Workstation Pro to store the architecture of the virtual machine.

- **.scoreboard** - Stores performance information and stats on the virtual machine. This is an optional feature and can be disabled. We will cover this in Chapter 11.

- **.vmdk** - This is the virtual hard disk file of the virtual machine.

- In this example you can see that there is multiple .vmdk files. This is because when we created the virtual machine, we selected the option to split the virtual hard disk into smaller files.

- You will see that s001 and s002 are the same size, which is the maximum size of each disk. Then s003 is half the size while s004 to s015 are all just 512k.

- What you are seeing here is the disks fill sequentially as the storage space being used increases.

- **.vmsd** - Used to store snapshot information. We will cover snapshots in Chapter 11.

- **.vmxf** - Contains configuration information that relates to creating teams in Workstation Pro that allows admins to group virtual machines together for management.

- A vmxf file might still be present even if the virtual machine in question has not been configured as part of a team.

- **.vmx** - This is a virtual machine configuration file that contains the settings and configuration of the virtual machine. You can open the .vmx file manually and make changes.

- The .vmx file, used in the example Windows 10 virtual machine is shown in Figure 9-16 and has been opened using Notepad ++. Before making any changes, it is worth taking a backup copy of the .vmx file.

Figure 9-16. *.vmx File for Windows 10 virtual machine*

In the next section, we are going to create another virtual machine, this time using the custom option and Windows 11 as the operating system.

Building a Windows 11 Virtual Machine

In this section, we are going to create a second virtual machine; however, this time we are going to select the custom build option and install Windows 11 as the operating system.

1. Click the **File** option from the menu and then select the option for **New Virtual Machine** as shown in Figure 9-17. For this example, we also have a folder called **Chapter 9 VMs** in which we are going to create these virtual machines.

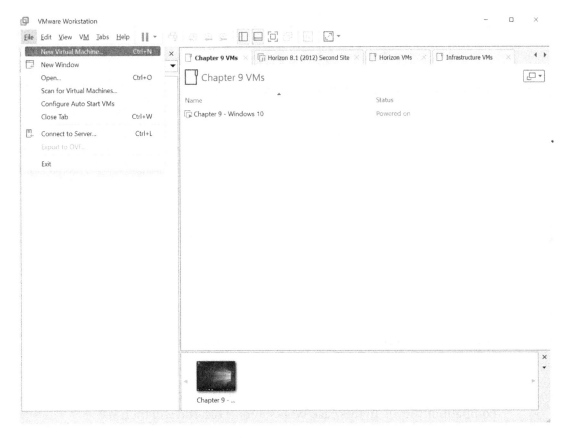

Figure 9-17. *Creating a New Virtual Machine*

2. You will now see the Welcome to the **New Virtual Machine Wizard** screen as shown in Figure 9-18.

Figure 9-18. *Welcome to the New Virtual Machine Wizard*

3. Click the radio button for **Custom (advanced)**.

4. Now click the **Next >** button.

5. You will see the **Choose the Virtual Machine Hardware Compatibility** screen.

6. From the Hardware compatibility drop-down box, select the compatibility level. In this case Workstation 17.x. You will then see the compatible products listed along with the virtual hardware configuration limits for the selected hardware compatibility.

7. The **Choose the Virtual Machine Hardware Compatibility** screen is shown in Figure 9-19.

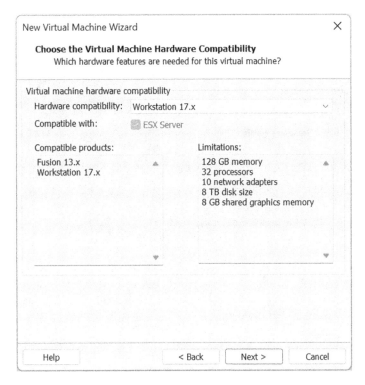

Figure 9-19. *Choose the Virtual Machine Hardware Compatibility screen*

8. Now click the **Next >** button.

9. You will see the **Guest Operating System Installation** screen where you will see the three different options as previously discussed.

10. Click the radio button for **Installer disc image file (iso)** and then click the **Browse...** button.

11. the **Guest Operating System Installation** screen is shown in Figure 9-20.

Figure 9-20. *Guest Operating System Installation screen*

12. Now click the **Next >** button.

13. You will see a File Explorer windows open where you can navigate
     to the location of the iso image that contains the operating system
     that you want to install. In this case the Windows 11 iso image.

14. Navigate to the folder location that contains the iso image, select
     it, and then click the **Open** button.

15. This is shown in Figure 9-21.

Figure 9-21. *File Explorer*

16. You will return to the **Guest Operating System Installation**
     screen where you will see the iso image has now been added.

17. You will also see that Windows 11 x64 has been detected as the
     operating system.

18. This is shown in Figure 9-22.

Figure 9-22. *ISO image selected*

19. Now click the **Next >** button.

20. You will see the **Name the Virtual Machine** screen.

21. In the **Virtual machine name** box, type in a name for this virtual machine. Remember that this name will also be used for the virtual machine files that get created as well.

22. In this example we have called the virtual machine **Chapter 9 - Windows 11**.

23. The default location has been used to store the virtual machine files as shown in Figure 9-23.

Figure 9-23. *Entering the Virtual Machine Name*

24. Now click the **Next >** button.

25. You will now see the **Encryption Information** screen as shown in Figure 9-24. If you recall this screen did not appear with the Windows 10 installation. This is because the latest operating systems such as Windows 11 require a Trusted Platform Module in order to install and run. Workstation Pro supports a virtual Trusted Platform Module (vTPM).

26. You have two configuration options for **Choose Encryption Type**:

- **All the files** - Encrypts every file that is created as part of the virtual machine. Includes the virtual hard disk file, configuration files, and all others.

- **Only the files needed to support a TPM** - Encrypts just the minimum files that are needed to support a TPM.

27. You then need to enter a password that is used for the encryption.
     Enter a password of your choice in the **Password** box and then type
     it in again in the **Confirm Password** box. You also have the option to
     automatically generate a password by clicking the Generate button.

28. Finally, check the box if you want to remember the password on
     the virtual machine in the Credential Manager.

Figure 9-24. Encryption Information screen

29. Now click the **Next >** button.

30. You will now see the **Firmware Type** screen.

31. You have the option of either **BIOS** or **UEFI** booting. The
     difference is the process that the firmware uses to find the boot
     target. Legacy boot is the boot process used by BIOS firmware, and
     UEFI boot is used by UEFI firmware. UEFI is the newer standard
     and is more secure and therefore the option to choose in this case
     as we are installing Windows 11.

32. The final option is the check box for **Secure Boot** which is an option when choosing UEFI. Secure Boot is a security standard that helps ensure that PCs boot only using software trusted by the PC manufacturer.

33. With secure booting, each component of the boot software is signed, including the bootloader, the operating system kernel, and the operating system drivers.

For this to work on a virtual machine, the virtual machine will need to be running VMware Tools 10.1 or later, and hardware compatibility version 13 or newer.

---

34. The **Firmware Type** screen is shown in Figure 9-25.

Figure 9-25. *Firmware Type screen*

35.   Now click the **Next >** button.

You will see the Processor Configuration screen.

36.   From the drop-down boxes, select the Number of Processors and
then the Number of cores per processor as shown in Figure 9-26.

Figure 9-26. *Processor Configuration screen*

37.   Now click the **Next >** button.

38.   The next screen is the **Memory for the Virtual Machine**
configuration screen.

39.   You will see that the guest OS minimum and the recommended
memory configuration is 4GB which is where the slider points
to and the amount that is shown in the **Memory for this virtual
machine** box stated 4GB also, although this is express in MB and
so reads 4096 MB.

40.   This is shown in Figure 9-27.

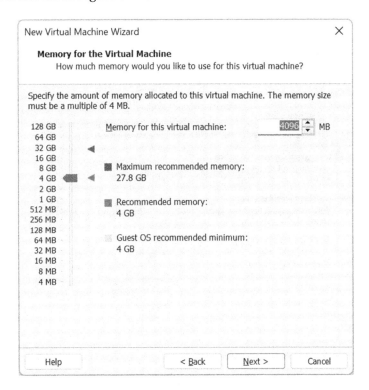

Figure 9-27.   *Memory Configuration screen*

41.   Now click the **Next >** button.

42.   The next screen is the **Network Type** screen where you can
configure the type of connection that this virtual machine will use.
You have the choice from the following options:

- Use bridged networking

- Use network address translation (NAT)

- Use host-only networking

- Do not use a network connection

43.   For this example, click the radio button for **Use network address
translation (NAT)**so that this virtual machine uses the IP address
of the host machine to connect to the network.

44.   This is shown in Figure 9-28.

Figure 9-28. *Network Type screen*

45.   Now click the **Next >** button.

46.   You will see the **Select I/O Controller Types** screen.

47.   As you will see in Figure 9-29, you can only select the option for
LSI Logic SAS (Recommended) as the other three options are not
supported by the Windows 11 operating system.

Figure 9-29. *I/O Controller Type screen*

48. Now click the **Next >** button.

49. The next screen is the **Select a Disk Type** screen where you can configure the type of virtual hard disk that this virtual machine will use. You have the choice from the following options:

- IDE

- SCSI

- SATA

- NVMe (Recommended)

50. For this example, click the radio button for **NVMe (Recommended)**

51. This is shown in Figure 9-30.

Figure 9-30. *Virtual Hard Disk Type screen*

52. Now click the **Next >** button.

53. Next you have the **Select a Disk** screen where you can choose the virtual hard disk that will be used for the virtual machine. You have the choice of the following options:

    - Create a new virtual disk

    - Use an existing virtual disk

    - Use a physical disk (for advanced users)

54. In this example, as we are creating a new virtual machine with a brand-new copy of the operating system, click the radio button for **Create a new virtual disk**. We will cover the existing virtual disk option later in this chapter.

55. These options are shown in Figure 9-31.

Figure 9-31. Select a virtual hard disk type screen

56. Now click the **Next >** button.

57. You will now see the **Specify Disk Capacity** screen where you can choose the size for the new virtual hard disk that will be created. You also have the option of choosing how the disk will be allocated and stored.

58. In the **Maximum disk size (GB)**, enter the size you want for the virtual hard disk. You will see that the recommended size for Windows 11 is 64GB which has been entered already as the default value.

59. The next option is a check box for **Allocate al disk space now**. Selecting this option means that the virtual hard disk file that is created will match the size specified. In this case 64GB. In this example we will leave the box unchecked which basically means the virtual hard disk will be thin provisioned meaning it will grow as required to the maximum size specified.

60. The next two options are for specifying how the virtual hard disk file is created. Either as one single file or split into multiple smaller files. In this example click the radio button for **Split virtual disk into multiple files** as shown in Figure 9-32.

Figure 9-32. *Configuring virtual disk size screen*

61. Now click the **Next >** button.

62. You will see the **Specify Disk File** screen.

63. In the box you will see that the disk file will be named using the name you provided for the virtual machine name, in this example **Chapter 9 - Windows 11**. This is shown in Figure 9-33.

Figure 9-33. *Naming the virtual hard disk file screen*

64. Now click the **Next >** button.

65. Finally, you will see the **Ready to Create Virtual Machine** screen.

66. Check the settings that you have selected, and if you need to make any updates, then click the **< Back** button to scroll back through the configuration options.

67. You will also see a **Customize Hardware...** button. If you click this button, then you will be taken to the hardware configuration screen where you can change or add virtual hardware device for the virtual machine. We will cover this in more detail in Chapter 10.

68. As we want to switch this virtual machine on and start the operating system installation, ensure that the **Power on this virtual machine after creation** box is checked.

69.   This is shown in Figure 9-34.

Figure 9-34. *Ready to Create the Virtual Machine screen*

70.   Click the **Finish** button.

71.   You will see that the virtual machine and the virtual disk file
      are created, and you will see the following message shown in
      Figure 9-35.

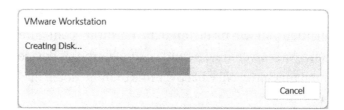

Figure 9-35. *Creating virtual machine virtual disk*

Once the virtual machine has been created, it will power on, and as the Windows 11 ISO image has been attached, then the virtual machine will start to boot Windows 11 as shown in Figure 9-36.

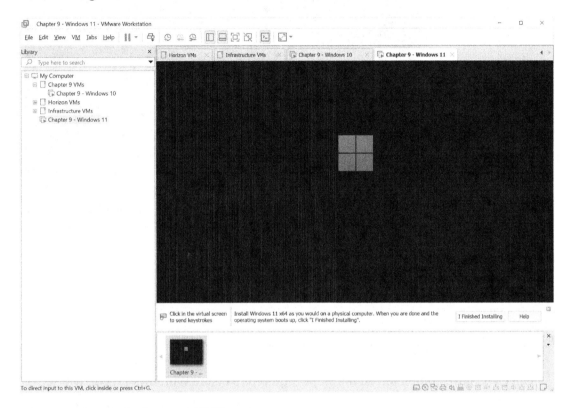

Figure 9-36. *Windows 11 VM booting*

As the virtual machine boots, then you will see a message appear stating that you should install Windows 11 as you would on any other computer, physical or virtual.

You will also see the **I Finished Installing** button. Once you have completed the Windows 11 installation, then you can click the button, but for now continue with the Windows 11 installation as shown in Figure 9-37.

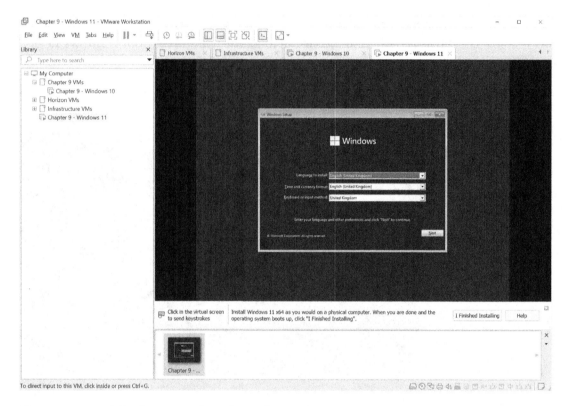

Figure 9-37. *Windows 11 virtual machine setup screen*

Once you have completed all the steps required to install Windows 11, you will see the following screen as shown in Figure 9-38. At this point you can click the **I Finished Installing** button.

Figure 9-38. *Finalizing the Windows 11 VM installation*

Now that the virtual machine has been built and configured, the final step is to install VMware Tools. This is done manually in this process as we selected the custom install option which does not automatically include the installation of VMware Tools.

To install VMware Tools, follow the steps described:

1. Click and highlight the virtual machine from the library pane. In this case the **Chapter 9 - Windows 11** virtual machine.

2. Right click and then from the contextual menu, select the option for **Install VMware Tools...** as shown in Figure 9-39.

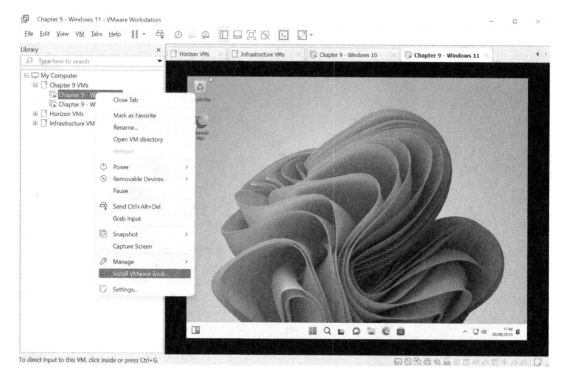

Figure 9-39. *Installing VMware Tools*

3. You will see a message in a yellow box that states if VMware Tools
    does not automatically start installing, then you will need to
    manually start the installation by clicking the **Start** button and
    selecting **Run**.

    In the Run box, type **D:\Setup**. The D:\ will contain the VMware
    Tool ISO that gets mounted as a CD-ROM drive when you start the
    installation.

4. This is shown in Figure 9-40.

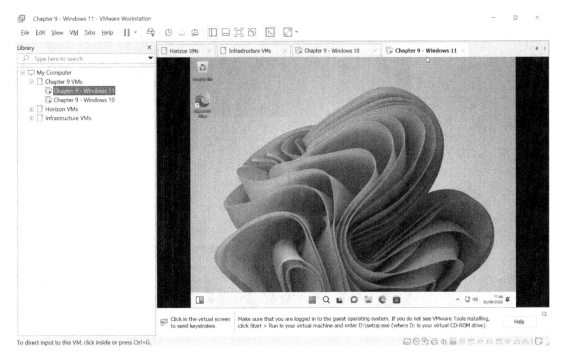

Figure 9-40. *Starting the VMware Tools installation*

5. You will now see the User Account Control (UAC) message appear asking if you want to allow the VMware Tools app to be able to make changes to your device.

6. Click **Yes** to continue as shown in Figure 9-41.

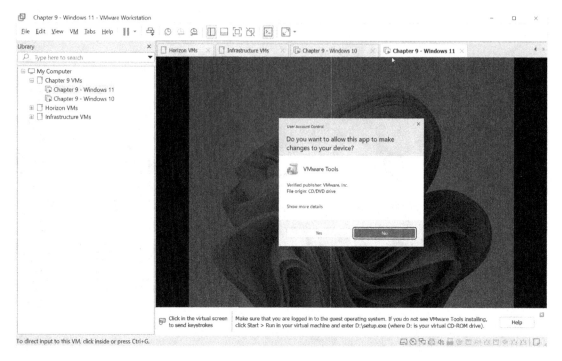

Figure 9-41. *Launcing the VMware Tools installer*

7. You will now see the status box that states **Preparing VMware Tools for installation**. You will also see a message pop up in the yellow box stating that VMware Tools is installing.

8. This is shown in Figure 9-42.

Figure 9-42. *Preparing VMware Tools installation*

9. Next you will see the **Welcome to the installation wizard for VMware Tools** screen.

10. Click the **Next >** button to continue.

11. This is shown in Figure 9-43.

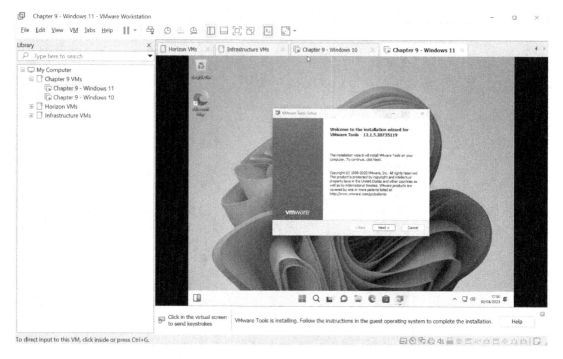

Figure 9-43. *Welcome to the VMware Tools Installation Wizard*

12. Next you will see the **Choose Setup Type** screen.

13. Click the **Typical** radio button.

14. Click the **Next >** button to continue.

15. The **Choose Setup Type** screen is shown in Figure 9-44.

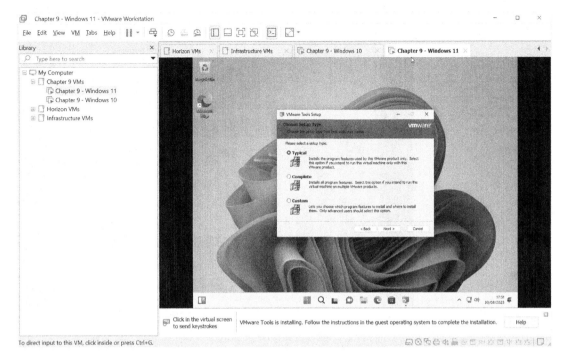

Figure 9-44. *VMware Tools Installation Wizard - Setup Type*

16. The final screen you will see is the **Ready to install VMware Tools** screen.

17. Click the **Install** button.

18. The **Ready to install VMware Tools** screen is shown in Figure 9-45.

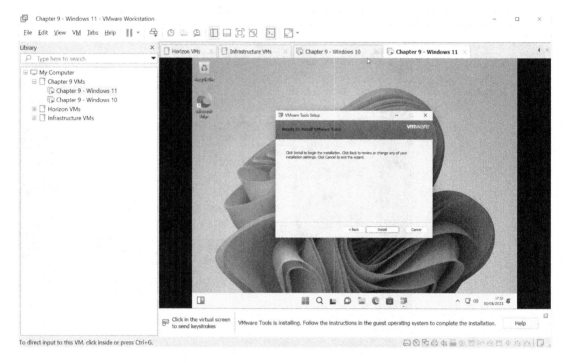

Figure 9-45. *VMware Tools Installation Wizard - Ready to Install*

19.   You will see the status bar as shown in Figure 9-46.

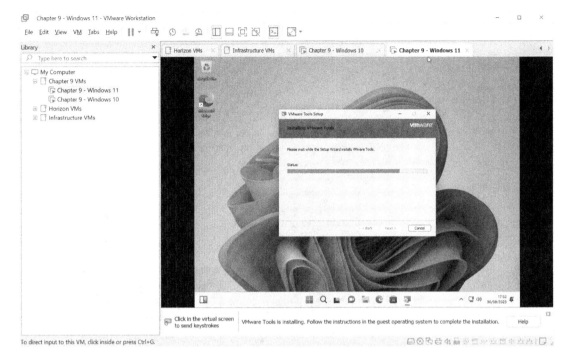

Figure 9-46. *VMware Tools Installation Wizard - Install Status*

20. Once the installation has completed, you will see the **Completed the VMware Tools Setup Wizard** as shown in Figure 9-47.

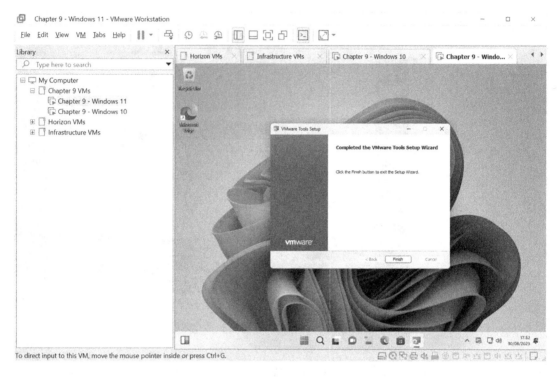

Figure 9-47. *VMware Tools Installation Wizard - Completed*

21.   Click the **Finish** button to complete the installation.

22.   You will then be prompted to restart the virtual machine to complete the installation of VMware Tools.

23.   Click **Yes** to restart the virtual machine.

24.   This is shown in Figure 9-48.

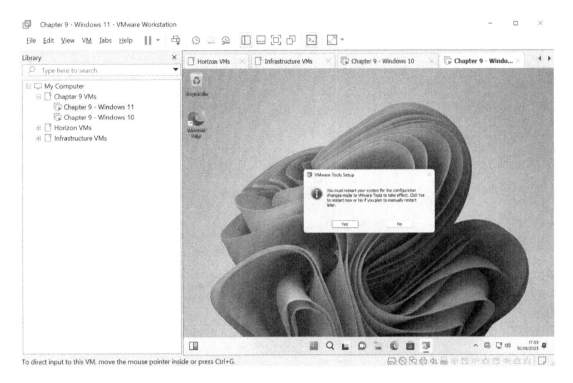

Figure 9-48. *Restarting VMware Tools Installation*

25. Once the virtual machine has restarted, log in and then click the
     up arrow on the taskbar.

26. Check that the VM icon is shown - hover the mouse over the icon,
     and you will see VMware Tools shown as shown in Figure 9-49.

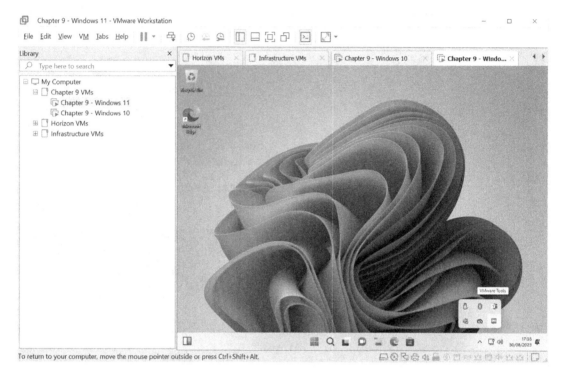

Figure 9-49. *VMware Tools running*

You have now successfully built and configured a Windows 11 virtual machine using the custom build method.

Creating a Windows Server VM

Another virtual machine that is popular to run in Workstation Pro is a Windows Server. Running this enables you to use the functionality of a server operating system for testing and development.

This not only helps with testing server applications but can also allow you to deploy some of the infrastructure side of things with components such as Active Directory or DHCP to enable you to test client server apps with the required user accounts, group policy and networking requirements.

To create a Windows Server virtual machine, follow the steps described:

1. Click the **File** option from the menu, and then select the option for **New Virtual Machine** as shown in Figure 9-50. For this example, we are again using the **Chapter 9 VMs** folder in which we are going to create these virtual machines.

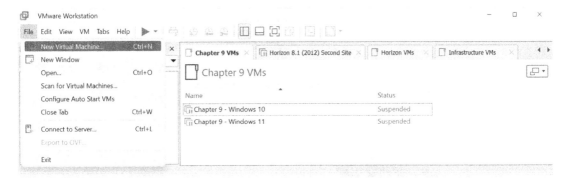

Figure 9-50. *Creating a New Virtual Machine*

2. You will now see the Welcome to the **New Virtual Machine Wizard** screen as shown in Figure 9-51.

Figure 9-51. *Welcome to the New Virtual Machine Wizard - Typical Configuration*

3. Click the radio button for **Typical (recommended)**.

4. Now click the **Next >** button.

5. You will see the **Guest Operating System Installation** screen as shown in Figure 9-52.

Figure 9-52. *Selecting an OS installer*

6. Click the radio button for **Installer disc image file (iso)** and then click **Browse....**

7. You will see a File Explorer window open to allow you to browse to the location of the ISO file required as shown in Figure 9-53.

    X

Figure 9-53. *File Explorer - Browse for ISO Image*

8. Navigate to the location of the ISO file required, click to select it, in this case the Windows 10 ISO image, and then click **Open**.

9. You will return to the **Guest Operating System Installation** screen.

10. In the **Installer disc image file (iso)** box, you will now see the full path to the selected ISO image entered as shown in Figure 9-54.

Figure 9-54. *ISO Image selected*

11. Now click **Next >**.

12. You will now see the **Easy Install Information** screen.

13. In the **Windows product key** box, type in the product/license key for the operating system being installed. You can miss this step out and enter the key later once the operating system has been installed.

14. In the **Version of Windows to install** field, click the drop-down box and select the version of the Windows Server you want to install.

15. Next, you have the option to personalize Windows by adding your **Full name**, **Password**, and **Confirm** password. These are optional and if selected will then allow you to check the box for **Log on automatically**. The **Easy Install Information** screen is shown in Figure 9-55.

Figure 9-55. *Easy Installation*

16. Now click **Next >**. You will now see the **Name the Virtual Machine** screen.

17. In the **Virtual machine name** box, type in a unique name for the virtual machine. Don't forget that the virtual machine name doesn't just appear in the library it is also used as the filenames for the virtual machine configuration file and virtual hard disk files. In this example we have called it **Chapter 9 - Windows Server 2022**.

18. In the **Location** box, leave the default folder location as shown in Figure 9-56.

Figure 9-56. *Naming the Virtual Machine*

19. The next option is to **Specify Disk Capacity**.

20. Leave the **Maximum disk size (GB)** as the default shown, the recommended size for Windows Server 2022.

21. The next two options are for specifying how the virtual hard disk file is created. In this example click the radio button for **Split virtual disk into multiple files** as shown in Figure 9-57.

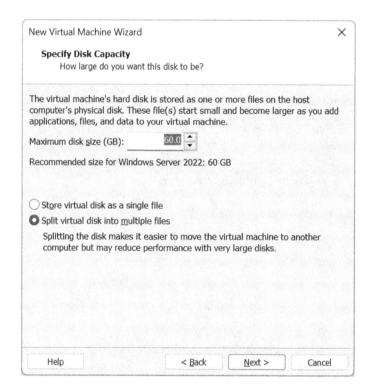

Figure 9-57. *Specifying the Virtual Hard Disk Capacity*

22. Now click **Next >**.

23. You will now see the **Ready to Create Virtual Machine** screen which details the settings that will be created.

24. Check the box for **Power on this virtual machine after creation**.

25. Click the **Finish** button as shown in Figure 9-58.

Figure 9-58. *Ready to Create Virtual Machine*

26. You will now see the Windows Server boot, and the Easy
     Installation for Windows Server 2022 will start as shown in
     Figure 9-59.

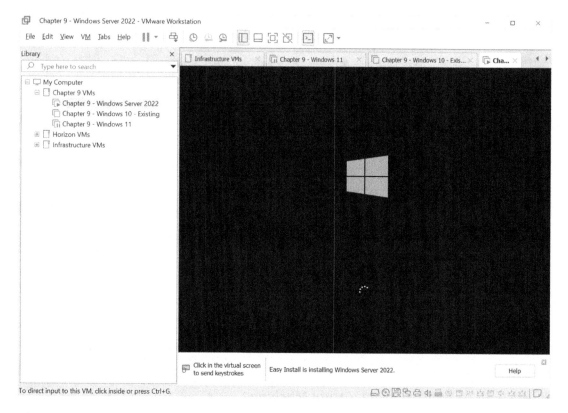

Figure 9-59. *Operating System Installation*

27. Complete the steps for installing Windows Server 2022 as you
would for any machine whether physical or virtual.

As this is a typical installation, then VMware Tools will be automatically installed as
part of the process.

You have now successfully built and configured Windows Server 2022.

In the next section, we are going to look at building another virtual machine but this
time using a virtual hard disk that already exists and has an operating system already
installed on it.

Creating a New VM Using an Existing Image

In this section we are going to create a new virtual machine; however, we are going to use
a virtual disk file that has already been created and also contains an installed operating
system. For this example, we are going to use a virtual hard disk that has Windows

10 installed on it. It is the machine created earlier on in this chapter; however, before starting this exercise, the virtual machine was deleted from the inventory, but the virtual hard disk was not deleted.

The use case for this is if you have built a gold image and want to use it for several different virtual machines. The virtual disk file can be copied and used when creating new virtual machines. It could also be if the virtual machine was deleted from the inventory and the virtual hard disk file was kept, you can simply recreate the virtual machine using the existing hard disk.

To create a virtual machine using an existing virtual hard disk, follow the steps described:

1. Click the **File** option from the menu and then select the option for **New Virtual Machine** as shown in Figure 9-60.

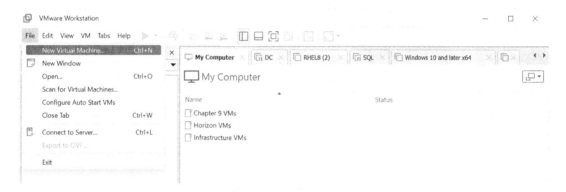

Figure 9-60. *Create a New Virtual Machine*

2. You will now see the **Welcome to the New Virtual Machine Wizard** screen.

3. Click the radio button for **Custom (advanced)**.

4. The **Welcome to the New Virtual Machine Wizard** screen is shown in Figure 9-61.

Figure 9-61. *Custom Virtual Machine Configuration*

5. Now click the **Next >** button.

6. You will see the **Select a Guest Operating System** screen.

7. In the **Guest Operating System** field, you will see listed Microsoft Windows, Linux, VMware ESX, or Other. In this example we are going to create a Windows 10 virtual machine, so click the radio button for Microsoft Windows.

8. Then, in the **Version** field, click the drop-down menu and select the version of Windows you will be running. In this example Windows 10 x64.

9. The **Select a Guest Operating System** screen is shown in Figure 9-62.

Figure 9-62. *Selecting the Guest Operating System*

10.   Now click the **Next >** button.

11.   You will see the **Name the Virtual Machine** screen.

12.   In the **Virtual machine name** box, type in a name for this virtual
       machine. In this example we have called the virtual machine
       Chapter 9 - Windows 10 - Existing.

Remember that this name will not be reflected in the virtual machine files and the
existing virtual hard disk that we will be using. The virtual hard disk will keep its
existing name. This is important when managing files on the host machine as the
virtual machine name and the virtual disk file names will not match.

---

13. The default location has been used to store the virtual machine files as shown in Figure 9-63.

Figure 9-63. *Naming the New Virtual Machine*

14. Now click the **Next >** button.

15. You will now see the **Firmware Type** screen.

16. Click the radio button for **UEFI**.

17. The **Firmware Type** screen is shown in Figure 9-64.

Figure 9-64. *Firmware Type*

18. Now click the **Next >** button.

19. You will now see the **Processor Configuration** screen.

20. From the drop-down boxes, select the **Number of Processors** and then the **Number of cores per processor** as shown in Figure 9-65.

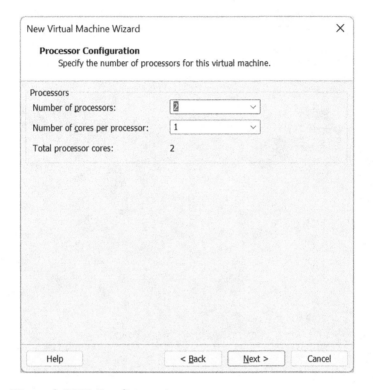

Figure 9-65. *Virtual CPU Configuration*

21. Now click the **Next >** button.

22. You will now see the **Memory for the Virtual Machine**
     configuration screen.

23. Select the amount of memory you want to configure for this virtual
     machine either by typing in the value or using the slider.

24. This is shown in Figure 9-66.

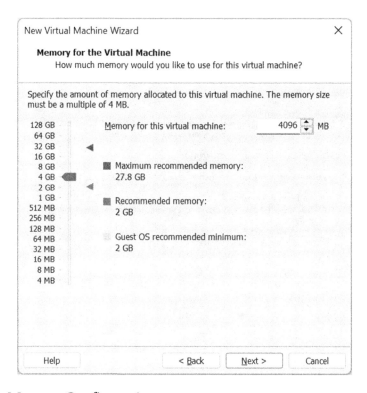

Figure 9-66. *Memory Configuration*

25. Now click the **Next >** button.

26. The next screen is the **Network Type** screen where you can configure the type of connection that this virtual machine will use.

27. For this example, click the radio button for **Use network address translation (NAT)**so that this virtual machine uses the IP address of the host machine to connect to the network.

28. This is shown in Figure 9-67.

Figure 9-67. *Configuring the Network Type*

29.   Now click the **Next >** button.

30.   You will see the **Select I/O Controller Types** screen.

31.   Select the option for **LSI Logic SAS (Recommended)**

32.   The **Select I/O Controller Types** screen is shown in Figure 9-68.

Figure 9-68. *I/O Controller Type Configuration*

33.   Now click the **Next >** button.

34.   The next screen is the **Select a Disk Type** screen.

35.   For this example, click the radio button for **NVMe (Recommended)**

36.   This is shown in Figure 9-69.

Figure 9-69. *Selecting a Virtual Hard Disk Type*

37.   Now click the **Next >** button.

38.   Next you have the **Select a Disk** screen where you can choose the
       virtual hard disk that will be used for the virtual machine.

39.   In this example, as we are going to use an existing virtual hard disk
       with Windows 10 already installed, click the radio button for **Use
       an existing virtual disk**.

40.   the **Select a Disk** screen is shown in Figure 9-70.

Figure 9-70. *Selecting an Existing Virtual Hard Disk*

41. Now click the **Next >** button.

42. You will see the **Select an Exiting Disk** screen as shown in Figure 9-71.

Figure 9-71. *Selecting the Existing Virtual Hard Disk file*

43. In the **Existing disk file** field, click the **Browse...** button.

44. You will see a File Explorer windows open to Browse for
     Existing Disk.

45. Navigate to the folder location of the existing virtual hard disk file
     you want to use. The default location will be \Documents\Virtual
     Machines.

46. In this example the file to be used is the **Chapter 9 - Windows
     10.vmdk**. Remember that this virtual disk file will not be renamed
     to reflect the new name for this virtual machine.

47. The virtual disk file is shown in Figure 9-72.

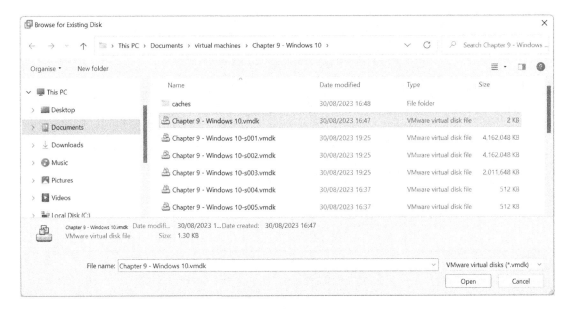

Figure 9-72. *Browse for Existing Virtual Hard Disk file*

48. Click to select the file as shown in Figure 9-72.

49. Now click the **Open** button.

50. You will return to the **Select an Existing Disk** screen which
    will now show the Existing disk file field populated with the
    selected file.

51. This is shown in Figure 9-73.

Figure 9-73. *Existing Virtual Hard Disk file selected*

52. Now click the **Next >** button.

53. Finally, you will see the **Ready to Create Virtual Machine** screen.

54. This is shown in Figure 9-74.

Figure 9-74. *Ready to Create the New Virtual Machine*

55. Click the **Finish** button.

56. Once the virtual machine has been created, you will return to the
Workstation Pro screen where you will see the virtual machine.
As there is no operating system to build and no ISO image to
boot from for setup, the virtual machine is created in a powered
off state.

57. This is shown in Figure 9-75.

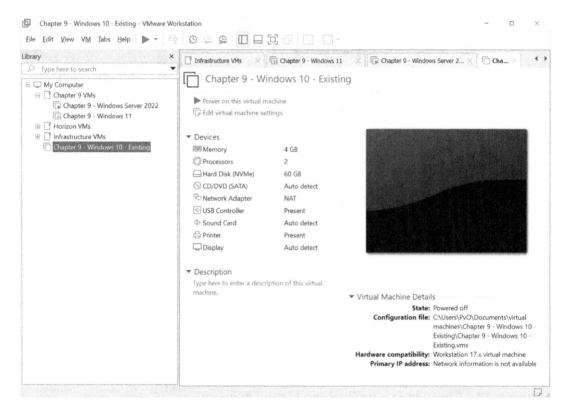

Figure 9-75. *Virtual Machine successfully created*

The virtual machine has now been successfully created using an existing virtual hard disk.

Supported Windows Operating Systems

When it comes to guest operating systems, VMware Workstation Pro supports a large number of different operating systems. The most popular are listed as follows:

- Windows 11

- Windows 10

- Windows 8

- Windows 7

- Windows XP

- Ubuntu

- RedHat

- SUSE

- Oracle Linux

- Debian

- Fedora

- openSUSE

- CentOS

- Solaris

- FreeBSD, and various other Linux Distros

To check exactly which operating systems are supported, then you can use the **VMware Compatibility Guide** which you can find online on the VMware website.

Click the following link to access the compatibility guide:

www.vmware.com/resources/compatibility/search.php?deviceCategory=softwar
e&details=1&releases=650&productNames=3&page=1&display_interval=10&sortColu
mn=Partner&sortOrder=Asc&testConfig=16

An example screenshot of the compatibility guide web page for Workstation 17.x supported guest operating systems is shown in Figure 9-76.

VMware Compatibility Guide

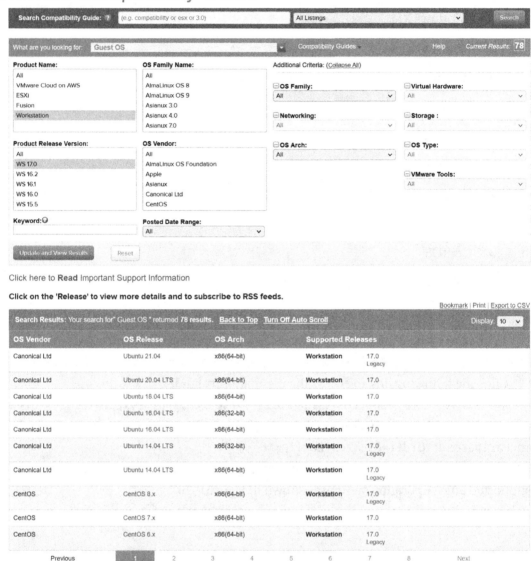

Figure 9-76. *VMware Compatibility for Workstation Pro*

Summary

In this chapter we have demonstrated, by working through the steps required, to create a number of Windows-based virtual machines, Windows 10, Windows 11, and a Windows Server 2022 virtual machine.

We looked at different ways in which to create the virtual machines using the typical configuration option and then the custom configuration option to change the virtual hardware to a configuration to suit the requirements of the virtual machine.

CHAPTER 10

Configuring Virtual Machine Options

In this chapter, now that we have built some example virtual machines to work with, we are going to look at how to configure additional options for these virtual machines. These are options that could only be configured once the virtual machine has been built and is running.

The first thing we are going to look at is the virtual machine option settings and configuration. These settings are configured on a per virtual machine basis and should not be confused with the preferences configuration which allows for configuring the general behavior of the Workstation Pro application rather than individual virtual machines, for example, configuring VM power options, shared folder access, and snapshots.

Next, we are going to look at how to configure additional virtual hardware resources to existing virtual machines. Adding additional virtual hardware components such as additional virtual hard drives or additional virtual network adapters.

You would have already seen the option to do this with the Add… button that is found at the bottom of the hardware tab in the Virtual Machine Settings configuration screen.

Configuring Virtual Machine Options

In this section we are going to look at the various options that you can configure on a **per virtual machine basis**. These can be used to override the globally set preferences. We are going to use the Windows 10 virtual machine that was created previously as an example.

To access the options configuration, perform the following steps:

1. Once the VMware Workstation Pro application is running and you have virtual machines created and configured, click and select the virtual machine for which you want to configure the options for.

© Peter von Oven 2023
P. von Oven, *Learning VMware Workstation for Windows*, https://doi.org/10.1007/978-1-4842-9969-2_10

2. From the virtual machines tab and the virtual machine pane, click
    on **Edit virtual machine settings**. Alternatively, from the **Library**
    pane, right click on the virtual machine you want to configure the
    options for, and from the contextual menu, select **Settings...**

3. You will see the **Virtual Machine Settings** screen as shown in
    Figure 10-1.

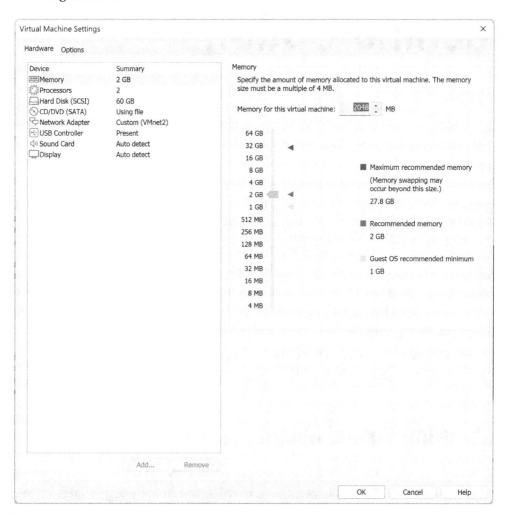

Figure 10-1. Virtual Machine Hardware Settings screen

4. Now click the **Options** tab as shown in Figure 10-2.

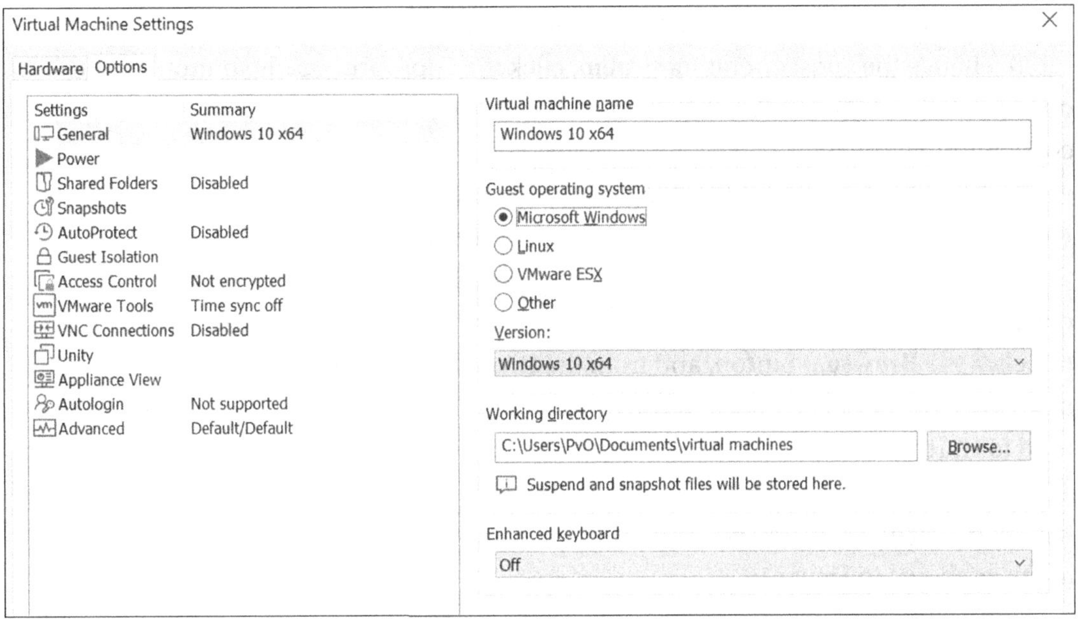

Figure 10-2. *Virtual Machine Options Settings screen*

You will now see, in Figure 10-2, all the available options that can be configured. In the next sections, we will work through these options explaining what they mean and how to configure them.

General

The **General** section contains high-level information about your virtual machines.

First is the **Virtual Machine Name** box. This contains the name of the virtual machine from when you created it and is shown in the library view and will also be shown in the tabs view.

You can edit the name and change it to something else which will update the name in the library view and the tab; however, the virtual machine files, such as the VMX configuration file and the virtual hard disk files, will not be updated with the new name when you change or edit the virtual machine name.

Next is the **Guest Operating System** section which shows the currently selected guest OS the virtual machine is running by the selected radio button. This option should only really be used if you change the version of the operating system. For example, if

263

you upgrade to a new edition or a new version of an operating system, then you would change this to reflect the new guest operating system. Also remember that the version of VMware Tools that is used is based on the guest operating system version.

To change the guest operating system, click the appropriate radio button for the operating system you want to select, and then from the drop-down menu, select the corresponding version.

The next field shows the **Working directory**. This is the location of where all the virtual machine files are stored. The location shown will be the default location you set when you installed Workstation Pro and by default is the **Documents** folder on the host machine. To change the location, either type the new location directly in the box or you can click the **Browse...** button, and from the **Browse for Folder** dialog box that appears, navigate to the folder you want to use to store this virtual machine. This folder will be used to store snapshot files and suspend files.

The final option is the **Enhanced keyboard** setting. If the enhanced keyboard driver has been installed, you will have the following options to select from the drop-down menu as shown in Figure 10-3.

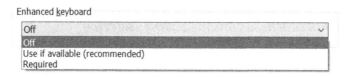

Figure 10-3. *Enhanced Keyboard Settings screen*

Next, we have the power options.

Power

With the power options, you can configure what happens when virtual machines are powered on and off as well as configuring the various power controls.

From the **Virtual Machine Settings** screen and the **Options** tab, click **Power**. The **Power options** are then shown in the right-hand pane as shown in Figure 10-4.

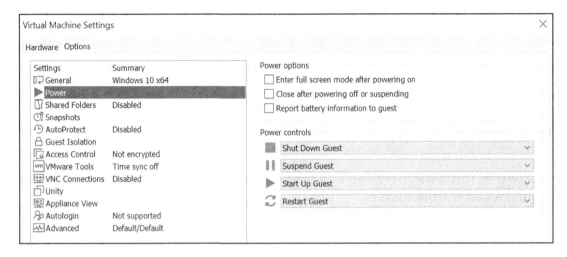

Figure 10-4. *Power Options screen*

The first section is for **Power options**. Here you have three options to choose from with three corresponding check boxes:

- **Enter full screen mode after powering on** - As the name suggests, when the virtual machine is powered on, it will automatically do so in full screen mode as it is booting.

- **Close after powering off or suspending** - The virtual machine tab in the tab view will close after the virtual machine is either powered off or suspended.

- **Report battery information to guest** - If you are running Workstation Pro on a laptop and in full screen, this option enables you to determine when the battery is running low by displaying the battery icon on the task bar of the guest operating system.

The next section is to configure the **Power controls** where you select what action each of the power button delivers. These buttons can be found on the toolbar, and the default settings are shown in Figure 10-5.

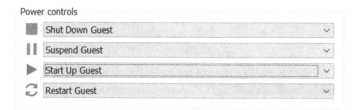

Figure 10-5. *Power Controls screen*

With each setting you can change the action. Figure 10-6 shows the alternative power controls for each of the buttons.

Figure 10-6. *Alternative Power Controls Settings screen*

Next, we will look at the shared folders configuration.

Shared Folders

VMware Workstation Pro allows you to create shared folders on your host machine and share them with your virtual machines. This is particularly useful for things such as installing software and making the installers available to the virtual machine. Or saving documents on the host machine so that they are available without having to power on the virtual machine.

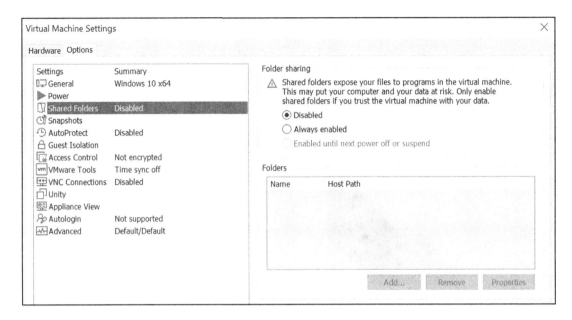

Figure 10-7. *Shared Folders Settings screen*

Figure 10-7 shows the **Shared Folder** screen. To enable the shared folder feature, follow the steps described:

1. Click the **Always enabled** button.

2. Now click the **Add...** button.

3. You will see the **Welcome to the Add Shared Folder Wizard** as shown in Figure 10-8.

Figure 10-8. *Welcome to the Add Shared Folder Wizard*

4. Click **Next >** to continue.

5. You will see the **Name the Shared Folder** screen. The first field to complete is add the path to the folder that resides on the host and that you want to share with this virtual machine.

   You can either type the path directly into the box, or you can click the **Browse...** button.

   The **Name the Shared Folder** screen is shown in Figure 10-9.

Figure 10-9. *Name the Shared Folder screen*

6. Click **Browse...**

7. You will see the **Browse For Folder** screen as shown in Figure 10-10.

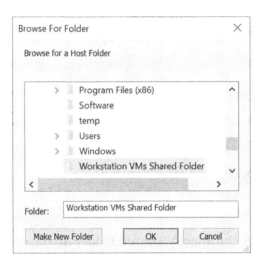

Figure 10-10. *Browse for a Host Folder to Share screen*

8. Navigate to the folder location. In this example we have created a folder on the host machine called **Workstation VMs Shared Folder**. You will also see on this screen that you have the option to create a folder if it doesn't already exist on the host. Just click the **Make New Folder** button.

9. Now click **OK**.

10. You will return to the Name the Shared Folder screen where you will see the host path has now been entered. You will also see that by default the **Name** field has been populated with the same name as the folder. If you want to change the name of the shared folder, then simply type a new name directly into the box. This is shown in Figure 10-11.

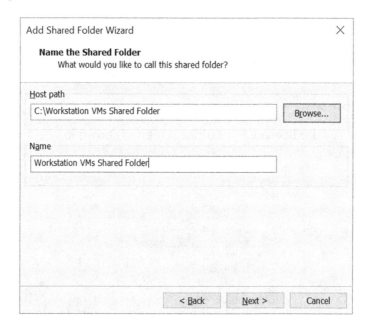

Figure 10-11. *Name the Shared Folder screen*

11. Click the **Next >** button.

12. You will now see the **Specify Shared Folder Attributes** screen as shown in Figure 10-12.

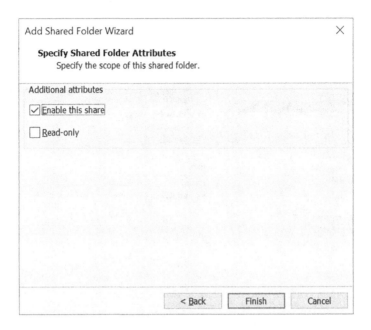

Figure 10-12. *Specify Shared Folder Attributes screen*

13. Check the **Enable this share** box to make the folder available to the virtual machine. You also have a second check box for **Read-only**. Enabling this, by checking the box, makes the folder read only. This means that the virtual machine can only read the contents of the folder and not be able to write to it.

14. Click **Finish** to complete the configuration.

15. You will return to the **Shared Folders** configuration on the **Options** screen as shown in Figure 10-13.

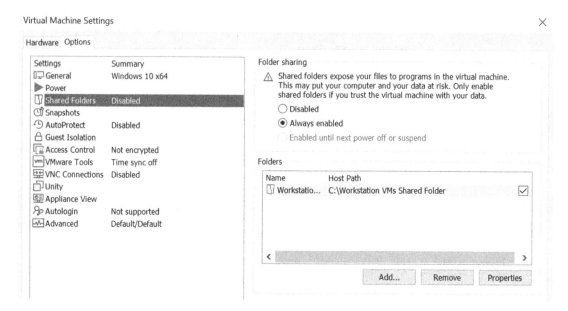

Figure 10-13. Specify Shared Folder Configured

You will also see, under the **Folders** section, that you can add another folder, remove an existing folder (this removes the sharing functionality but does not delete the folder or any files it contains from the host), or edit the properties of the existing shared folder.

If you click the **Properties** button, you will see the **Shared Folder Properties** screen as shown in Figure 10-14.

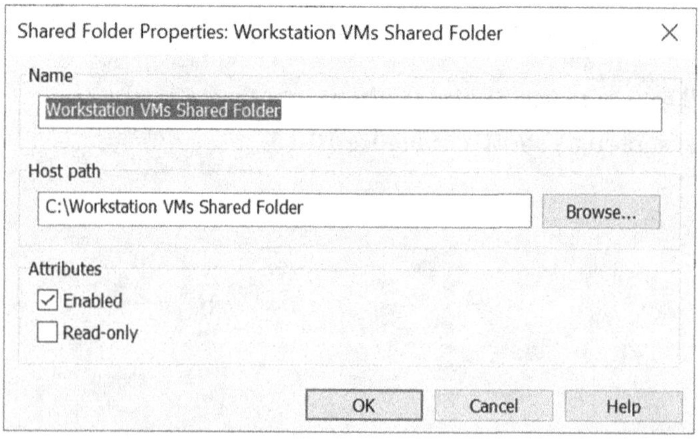

Figure 10-14. Shared Folder Properties

Snapshots

With the snapshot options configuration, rather than giving you the ability to take snapshots and manage snapshots manually, this setting allows you to configure snapshotting when powering off a virtual machine.

You can only change this configuration when the virtual machine is powered on and you have the four options as shown in Figure 10-15.

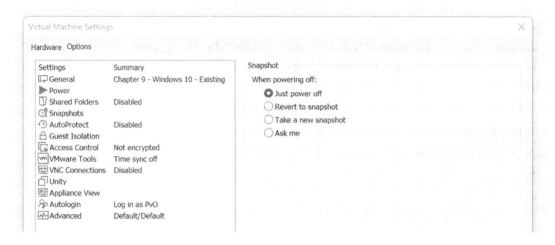

Figure 10-15. *Snapshots*

- **Just power off** - Virtual machine is powered off and no snapshot is created.

- **Revert to snapshot** - Virtual machine powers off and reverts to the previous snapshot.

- **Take a new snapshot** - A new snapshot is taken when the virtual machine is powered off.

- **Ask me** - You are prompted whether or not you want to create a snapshot.

We will cover managing snapshots in more detail and how to create and manage them manually in the next chapter, Chapter 11.

AutoProtect

The AutoProtect feature allows you to protect virtual machines by periodically taking automatic snapshots. Even with the process automated, you are still able to create snapshots manually.

To use this feature, check the **Enable AutoProtect** box.

First you can configure how often the snapshots are taken. From the **AutoProtect interval** field, click the drop-down box and select from **Daily**, **Half-Hourly**, or **Hourly**. This time interval is only measured when the virtual machine is powered on. For example, if you set the interval at half-hourly and then power off after 10 minutes, then when the virtual machine is powered back on, then the snapshot will be taken after 20 minutes.

The next option is to configure how many snapshots should be kept as a maximum. In the **Maximum AutoProtect snapshots** box, either type in the maximum number of snapshots or use the arrows. Once the maximum number of AutoProtect snapshots is reached, the oldest AutoProtect snapshot gets deleted each time a new AutoProtect snapshot is taken.

Underneath this field, when the feature is enabled, you will see displayed an estimation of the minimum amount of disk space that will be taken up by the snapshots. This minimum is affected by the memory settings for the virtual machine. The more virtual machine memory a virtual machine has, the more disk space is available for AutoProtect snapshots.

This is shown in Figure 10-16.

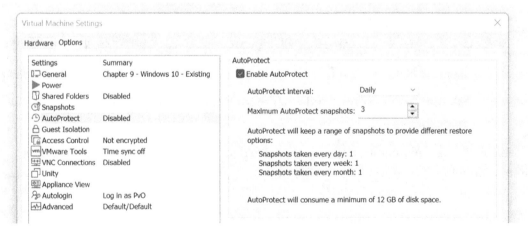

Figure 10-16. *AutoProtect configuration*

There are also a couple of points to note with this feature.

First of all, snapshots are only taken when a virtual machine is powered on, so therefore any snapshots created using the AutoProtect feature cannot be cloned. Virtual machines can only be cloned when they are powered off.

Secondly, AutoProtect does not work with remote virtual machines. Just those that are running on the local host machine.

Guest Isolation

The Guest Isolation feature is in part a security feature to prevent guest and host interaction, but also allows some of the host features to work with the guest virtual machines.

The first part is the actual **Guest Isolation** section and is configurable when the virtual machine is powered off. There are two configurable options:

- **Enable drag and drop** - Allows you to drag and drop between guest virtual machines and the host

- **Enable copy and paste** - Allows you to cut and paste between guest virtual machines and the host

This is shown in Figure 10-17.

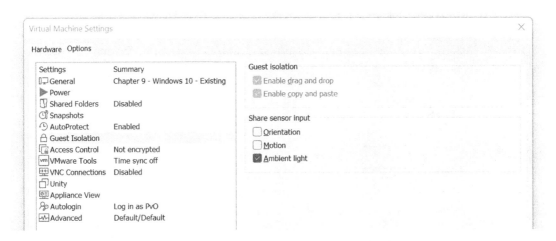

Figure 10-17. *Guest Isolation configuration*

The other field is for **Share sensor input**. This allows you to share the features of any sensors between the host machine and the guest virtual machine.

Access Control

The Access Control feature is essentially the ability to encrypt the virtual machine and protect it with a password. To enable encryption, follow the steps described:

1. Click the **Encrypt…** button as shown in Figure 10-18.

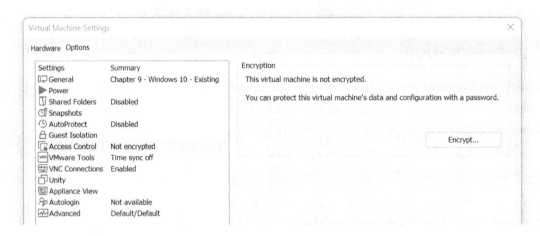

Figure 10-18. *Enabling Encryption*

2. You will see the **Encrypt Virtual Machine** screen as shown in Figure 10-19.

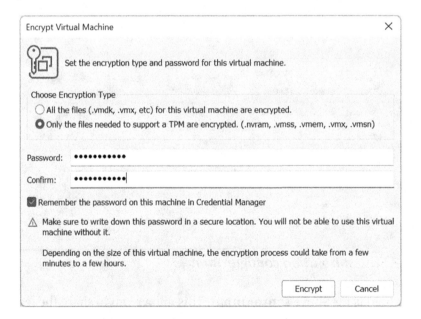

Figure 10-19. *Configuring Encryption*

3. Click the radio button to select the encryption type and whether you want to encrypt all files or just those that are needed to support a Trusted Platform Module (TPM).

4. Once selected, in the **Password** box, enter a password that will be used to protect the encryption, and then type it in again in the **Confirm** box.

5. Click the **Encrypt** button to complete the encryption. Once completed you will see that encryption has been enabled as shown in Figure 10-20.

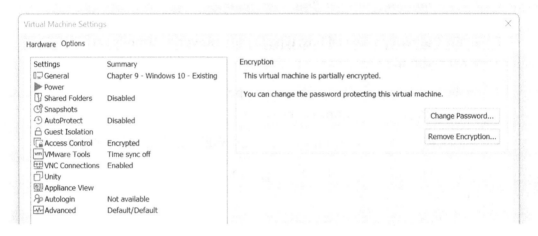

***Figure 10-20.** Encryption successfully configured*

Once encryption has been configured, you have two options; the first option is to change the password.

6. Click the **Change Password…** button. You will see the **Change Password** screen as shown in Figure 10-21.

Figure 10-21. *Changing the encryption password*

7. In the **Current password** box, type in the password currently set for encryption.

8. In the **New password** box, type in the updated password, and then type it in again in the **Confirm password** box.

9. Click **OK** to update and change the password.

   The other option is to remove encryption. To do this, follow the steps:

10. Click the **Remove Encryption** box.

11. You will see the Remove Encryption screen shown in Figure 10-22.

Figure 10-22. *Removing encryption*

12. You will be prompted to enter the encryption password in the **Password** box. Type the password in the box and then click the **Remove Encryption** box.

13. You will see the following message shown in Figure 10-23.

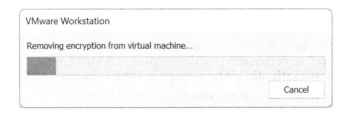

Figure 10-23. *Removing encryption from the virtual machine*

VMware Tools

The next set of configurable virtual machine options defines the behavior of VMware Tools with the specific virtual machine.

These options are shown in Figure 10-24.

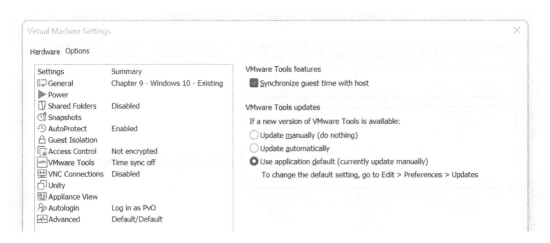

Figure 10-24. *VMware Tools options*

The first option is for the **VMware Tools features** and consists of a check box for **Synchronize guest time with the host**. Enabling this feature, by checking the box, ensures that the virtual machine and the host machine both show the same time, with the virtual machine using the time that is set on the host machine.

In the next section are the options that relate to how VMware Tools gets updated inside the virtual machine. You can select, by clicking the corresponding radio button, the following options for what to do when a new version of VMware Tools becomes available to the virtual machine:

- **Update manually** - VMware Tools doesn't get updated and relies on you doing it manually. However, you will be notified that a new version becomes available.

- **Update automatically** - When a new version becomes available, then the virtual machine will automatically be updated.

- **Use application default** - Uses the default setting that is currently configured in the preferences section.

VNC Connections

With the VNC Connections option, you can allow a virtual machine to be accessed remotely using a VNC client. These options are shown in Figure 10-25.

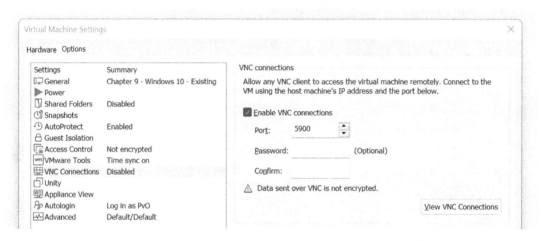

Figure 10-25. *VNC connections*

To enable remote VNC connections, check the **Enable VNC connections** box.

You then, in the **Port** box, have the option to specify the port on which to connect. By default, this is set to port 5900 which is the default port used by VNC clients. You can update this to reflect a different port if required.

Finally, if you click the **View VNC Connections** button, you will see the currently connected host machines as shown in Figure 10-26.

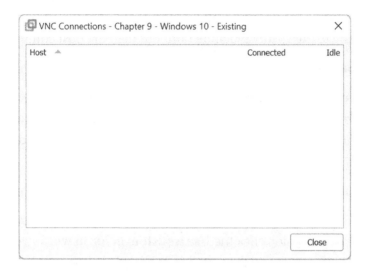

Figure 10-26. *VNC connections*

Unity

We have already discussed what the Unity feature delivers in Chapter 7, so in this chapter we are looking at the additional configurable options for running in Unity mode.

These are shown in Figure 10-27.

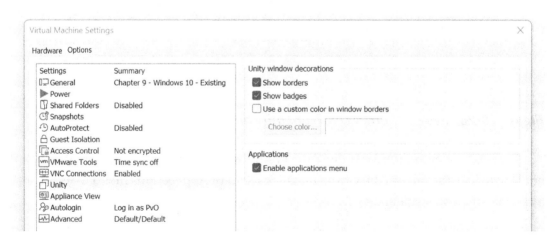

Figure 10-27. *Unity Configuration options*

The first set of options manage the windows decorations. You can choose from the following three options:

- **Show borders** - Set a window border that identifies the application as belonging to the virtual machine rather than to the host computer.

- **Show badges** - Display a logo in the title bar.

- **Use a custom color in window borders** - This feature provides a way to distinguish between the application windows that belong to virtual machines, by allowing you to use a different color for the window borders on each one.

  For example, you can set one virtual machine to have a red border and then set a green border for another virtual machine.

  To set a border color, click the **Use a custom color in windows border** button. You will then be able to click the **Choose color...** button as shown in Figure 10-28.

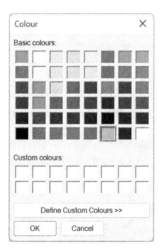

Figure 10-28. *Select a border color for Unity mode*

The final option setting for Unity is the **Enable applications** menu option. When enabled this feature allows the virtual machines Start or Applications menu to be available on the host machine.

Appliance View

The Appliance View option allows you to display a version number and author information for a virtual machine and is shown in Figure 10-29.

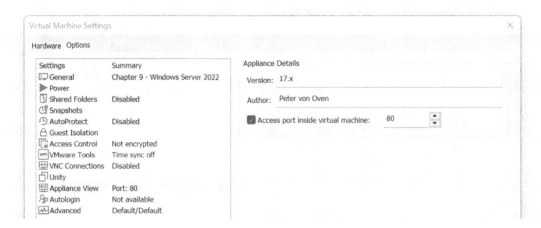

Figure 10-29. *Appliance View configuration details*

In the **Appliance Details** section in the **Version** box, type in a version number that helps you identify this virtual machine. This is useful if you have different versions of what is essentially the same virtual machine that is being used for development. This feature can aid easy identification.

Then in the **Author** box, type in the name of the author or person/team that created the virtual machine.

The following example in Figure 10-30 shows how the information is displayed on the summary screen of the virtual machine.

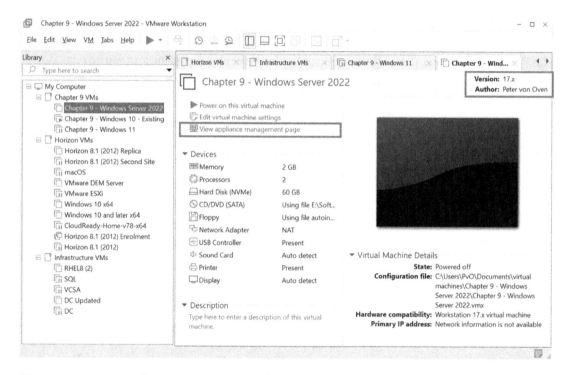

Figure 10-30. *Appliance View example*

Finally, you have the option to specify an access port inside the virtual machine by checking the box to enable the feature and then specify a particular port that you want to use to access the virtual machine.

Autologin

With the **Autologin** feature, you can configure the virtual machine to automatically login whereby you don't need to type in a username or password each time. The Autologin configuration is shown in Figure 10-31.

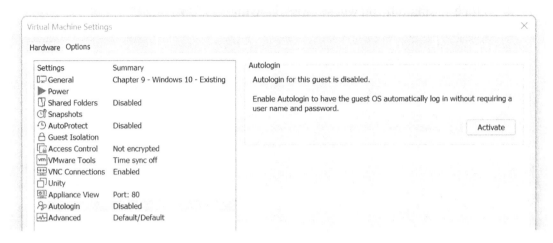

Figure 10-31. *Autologin configuration screen*

To configure Autologin, follow the steps described:

1. To enable Autologin, click the **Activate** button.

2. You will see the **Set Autologin User** screen as shown in Figure 10-32.

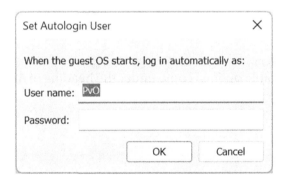

Figure 10-32. *Autologin User configuration screen*

3. In the **User name** box, type in the username. Remember that the user account will need to be present on the virtual machine.

4. Then in the **Password** box, type in the password for the username that you entered.

5. Once configured you will see the following as shown in
    Figure 10-33.

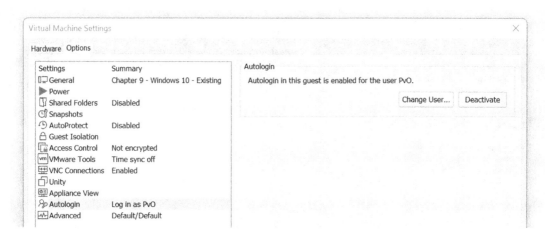

Figure 10-33. *Autologin configured*

The final part is that you now have two button. The **Change User...** button allows you
to update and change the username and password, and the **Deactivate** button disables
the Autologin feature for this virtual machine.

Advanced

The final set of configurable options come under the heading of **Advanced** and are
shown in Figure 10-34.

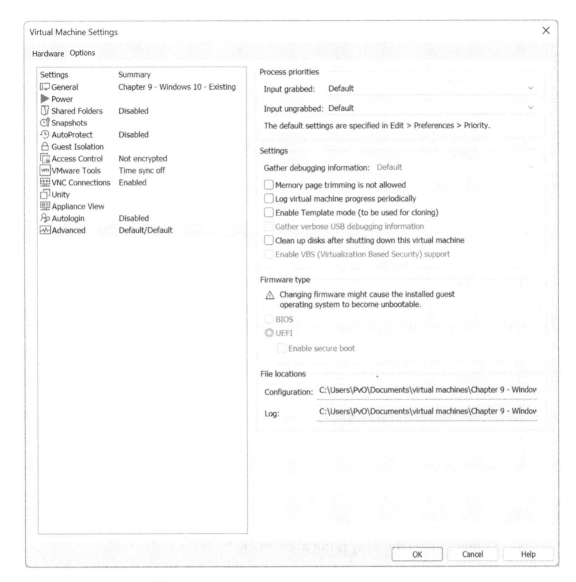

Figure 10-34. Advanced Settings screen

The first section of this configuration screen is for configuring Process priorities. There are two configurable options that in turn you can set:

- **Input grabbed** - Selects the priority level for virtual machines when their keyboard and mouse input is grabbed. From the drop-down you can select one of the following:

- Default

- Normal

- High

- **Input ungrabbed** - Selects the priority for virtual machines when their keyboard and mouse input is not grabbed. From the drop-down you can select one of the following:

    - Default

    - Normal

    - High

The default settings for process priorities can be found under the preferences configuration screen.

Next is the **Settings** section. The first setting, **Gather debugging information**, defines the level of how debug information is collected for the virtual machine. From the drop-down menu you can select from the following options:

- Default

- None

- Full

- Statistics

You then have a number of other settings that can be enabled or disabled by checking the corresponding check box:

- **Memory page trimming is not allowed** - Returns unused virtual machine memory to the host machine for other uses. While trimming usually has little effect on performance and might be needed in low-memory situations, the I/O caused by memory trimming can sometimes interfere with disk-oriented workload performance in a guest.

- **Log virtual machine progress periodically** - Adds information the virtual machine's virtual CPU state, instruction pointer, and code segment registers in the log file and is used primarily for troubleshooting or performance optimization.

- **Enable Template mode (to be used for cloning)** - With a linked clone virtual machine, the clone depends on the parent virtual machine in order to run. If the linked clone cannot access the parent virtual machine or the snapshot from which the clone was created, then the clone no longer runs.

  This can be fixed by marking the parent virtual machine of a linked clone as a template. You typically must have write access to a virtual machine to clone it. A virtual machine that is designated as a clone template can be cloned by users who do not have write access to the template virtual machine. To protect linked clones, you cannot delete a template virtual machine. You cannot delete snapshots of the template.

- **Clean up disks after shutting down this virtual machine** - Automatically cleans up the virtual hard disk when the virtual machine is shutdown. This option shrinks and defragments the virtual hard disk each time the virtual machine is shutdown.

  If you power off, suspend, restart, or reset the virtual machine, then the automated disk cleanup will not run.

  This feature will only run on virtual machines that have VMware Tools installed.

  The first time you shut down the virtual machine after enabling this feature, you will be prompted to accept the cleanup of the disks on the virtual machine. This will be the case each time you shut down unless you select the **Do not show this message again** option.

  After the cleanup starts, the progress of the cleanup appears on the left side of the Workstation Pro status bar. You can terminate the cleanup task by closing the virtual machine tab and clicking Yes. After the cleanup finishes, a note appears in the message log, and on the right side of the Workstation Pro status bar, that reports the amount of disk space reclaimed.

- **Enable VBS (Virtualization Based Security) support** - Only available for virtual machines that use hardware version 14 or later. This feature provides technical support for the Microsoft VBS feature. You can then turn on and configure the Microsoft VBS feature in one of the following supported Windows guest operating systems:

  - Windows 10, version 1703 and later, Enterprise, 64-bit

  - Windows Sever 2016, version 1607 and later. To use Windows 2016, version 1607 as the guest operating system, you will need to apply all Microsoft updates for VBS to function VBS reinforces the security of Microsoft Hyper-V. When you turn on VBS, Workstation Pro will also enable the following settings:

    - UEFI

    - Secure boot

    - Intel VT-x/EPT

    - IOMMU (IO memory management unit)

With the VBS feature enabled, the **Firmware type** section will become grayed out as UEFI will automatically have been enabled. This is shown in Figure 10-35.

Figure 10-35. *VBS enabled*

If you haven't configured VBS, then you will be able to configure the Firmware type as shown in Figure 10-36.

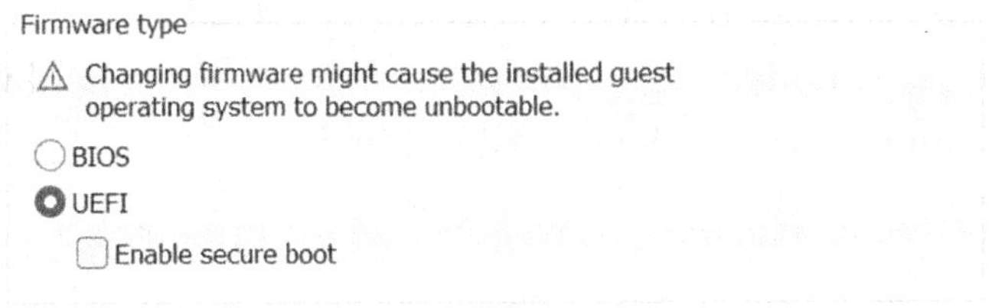

Firmware type

⚠ Changing firmware might cause the installed guest
operating system to become unbootable.

○ BIOS
● UEFI

☐ Enable secure boot

Figure 10-36. *Firmware type configuration*

As the warning states, beware of changing the firmware type as you can prevent the virtual machine from booting. You can choose from either **BIOS** or **UEFI** by clicking the corresponding radio button.

With UEFI enabled, you can also check the **Enable secure boot** box to switch on the secure boot feature.

Finally on the **Advanced** configuration options screen is the file locations section. The file locations cannot be changed and are for information purposes only.

You will see details of the location of the configuration files and, if the virtual machine is powered on, the location of the log file. If the virtual machine is powered off, then the log file box will state **Not powered on**.

In the next section, we are going to look at installing and configuring the virtual printer feature.

Virtual Printer

The Virtual Printer feature enables you to print from a virtual machine to any printer that is available on the host machine. The big advantage is that you do not need to install any additional drivers on the virtual machine for the feature to work.

When the Workstation Pro Virtual Printer feature is enabled, a virtual serial port is created and configured that is used to communicate with printers connected to the host machine.

As a little bit of history, before Workstation Pro version, the virtual printing functionality was part of VMware Tools. Now the virtual printing functionality is delivered as a separate application.

Before you install VMware Virtual Printer on a virtual machine, you must add a virtual printer device to the virtual machine.

How to install the virtual printer device was discussed in Chapter 7.

With the virtual printer added to the virtual machine's virtual hardware, you can now Install the virtual printer following the steps described:

1. Select the virtual machine you want to add the printer to.

2. Now click the **VM** menu and then select the option for **Install Virtual Printer**.

3. This is shown in Figure 10-37.

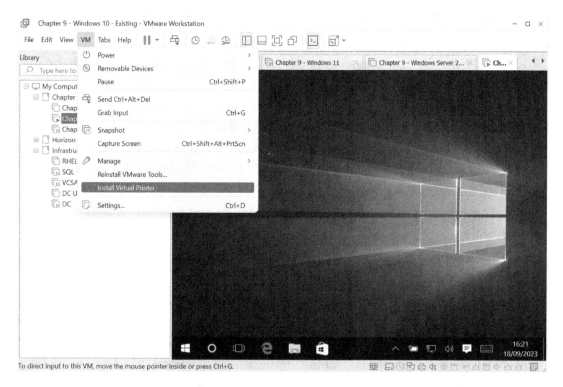

***Figure 10-37.** Install Virtual Printer*

4. You will now see a pop-up message on the virtual machine stating that a DVD drive D: containing the Virtual Printer has been attached. This DVD drive contains the Virtual Printer application that we will install.

5. Click the message to select the action to perform.

6. This is shown in Figure 10-38.

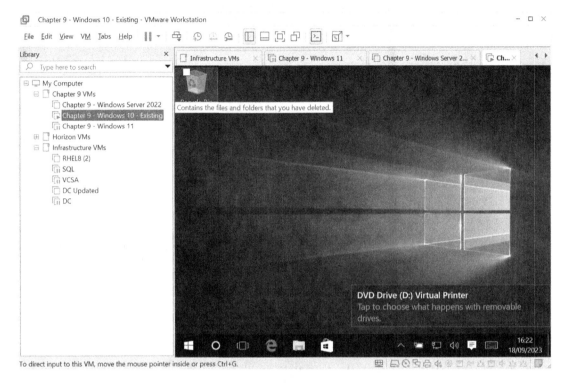

Figure 10-38. *Virtual Printer DVD attached*

7. Alternatively, you can open a File Explorer window and navigate
    to the D: DVD drive.

8. You will then see the **Virtual-Printer-1.1.2-19075060.exe** file as
    shown in Figure 10-39.

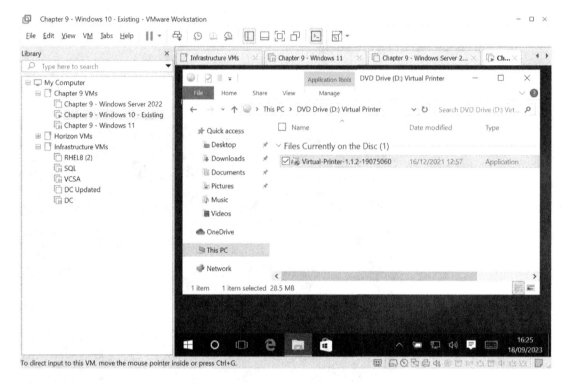

Figure 10-39. *Virtual Printer Installer application*

9. Double click to launch the installer.

10. You will see a User Account Control warning message appear. Click the **Yes** button to allow the app to make changes to the virtual machine.

11. This is shown in Figure 10-40.

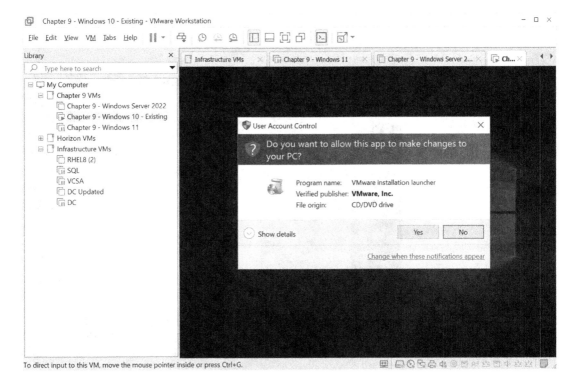

Figure 10-40. *User Account Control warning message*

12. The Virtual Printer installer will now be launched.

13. You will see the **Welcome to the VMware Virtual Printer Setup Wizard** screen as shown in Figure 10-41.

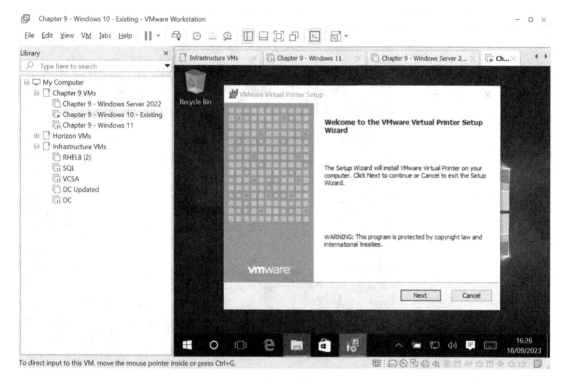

Figure 10-41. *Welcome to the VMware Virtual Printer Setup Wizard*

14. Click **Next** to continue.

15. You will now see the **Destination Folder** screen as shown in Figure 10-42.

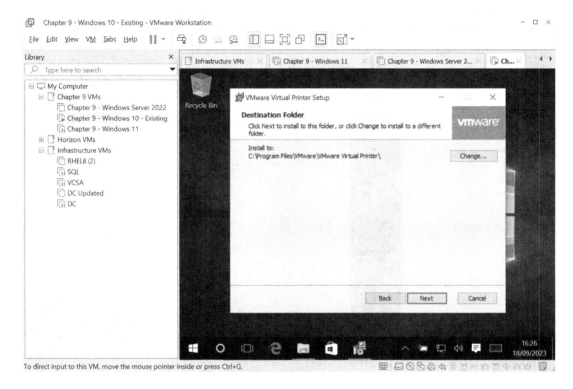

Figure 10-42. *Destination Folder configuration*

16. You can either accept the default folder location or click the
    Change... button and create a new folder or select a different
    folder. In this example we are going to use the default folder
    setting.

17. Click **Next** to continue.

18. You will see the Ready to install VMware Virtual Printer screen as
    shown in Figure 10-43.

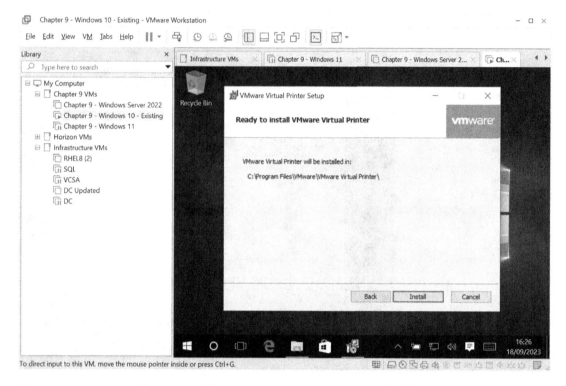

Figure 10-43. *Ready to install VMware Virtual Printer screen*

19.   Click the **Install** button.

20.   You will see the status bar appear showing the progress of the installation.

21.   This is shown in Figure 10-44.

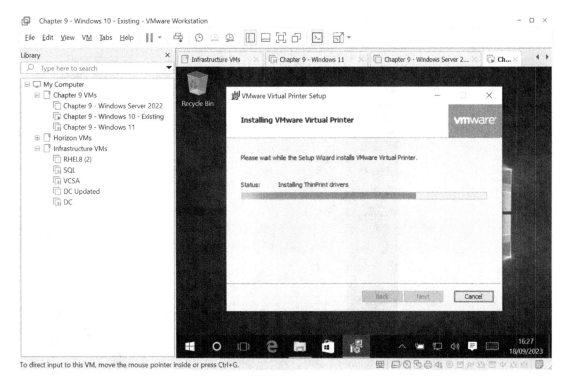

Figure 10-44. *Installation status*

22. Once the installation has finished, you will see the Completed
    the VMware Virtual Printer Setup Wizard screen as shown in
    Figure 10-45.

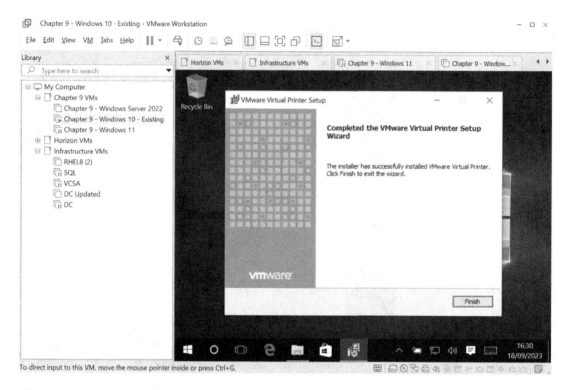

Figure 10-45. *Installation completed*

23. Next you will see a pop-up box stating that you need to restart the virtual machine for the configuration changes to take effect.

24. Click the **Yes** button.

25. This is shown in Figure 10-46.

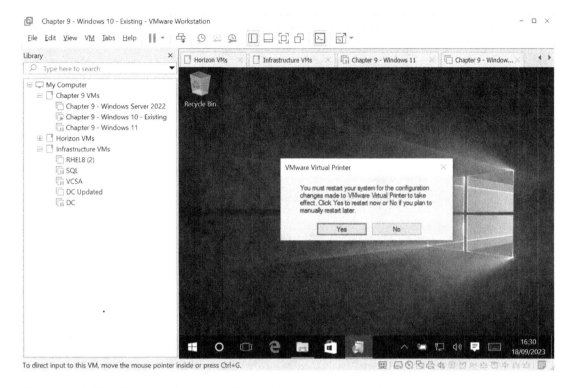

Figure 10-46. *Restart the virtual machine*

Once restarted you can check to see if the printer is able to be added to the virtual machine.

26.   Log in to the virtual machine.

27.   Press the Windows key and then type **Printers** into the search bar.

28.   You will see the **Printers & Scanners** systems settings option appear. Now click to launch the Printers & Scanners configuration screen.

29.   Click the + button to Add a printer or scanner.

30.   You should then see the printer you want to add appear in the list. In this example we have a network printer, the HP OfficeJet Pro 9010 series printer as shown in Figure 10-47.

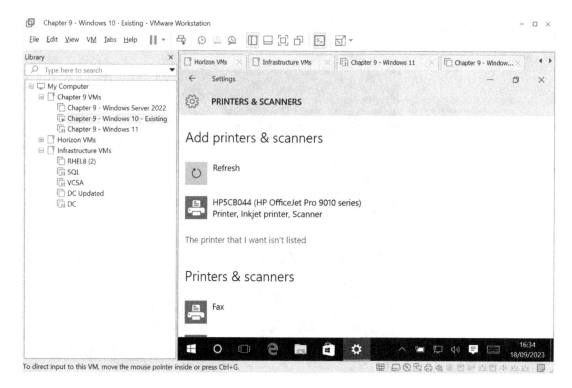

Figure 10-47. *Adding a printer*

31.   Click to add the printer.

32.   Once successfully added, you will see the printer appear on the list of available printers as shown in Figure 10-48.

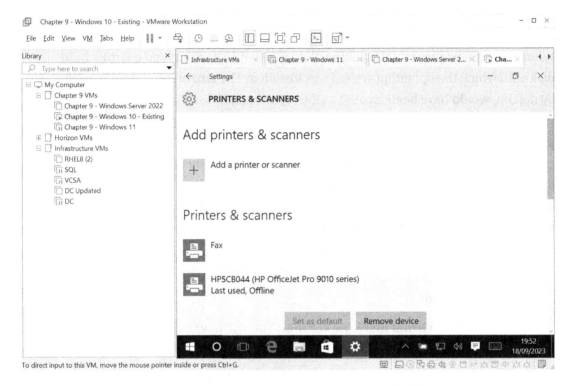

Figure 10-48. *Printer successfully added*

We have now completed our review and discussion around configuring virtual machine options.

In the next section we are going to look at how to add and configure new and additional virtual hardware to a virtual machine.

Adding New Hardware

In the previous section, we looked at the virtual hardware that is provisioned by default when you create a new virtual machine and some of the options available to configure some of these virtual hardware components.

You also have the option to add additional devices to the virtual machine by either adding a brand-new device or a second or third device such as extra network cards or hard disks (up to the maximum number of supported devices for that device type).

There are also options to add new devices such as a Trusted Platform Module.

The first option we are going to look at is to add additional virtual hard disks.

Hard Disk

When you created the virtual machine, then you would have created a virtual hard disk onto which the operating system was installed. The size of this virtual hard disk, by default, would have been created as the recommended size when using the typical virtual machine creation process. However, you may have changed this size if you used the custom creation method.

Once the virtual machine was created and before you finished the creation there was the option to click the **Customize Hardware** button whereby you could add additional hardware, but in this example, we are going to add a virtual hard disk after the virtual machine has been created and configured.

To do this follow the steps described:

1. Select the virtual machine you want to add the additional virtual hard disk to.

2. Click **Edit virtual machine settings**. You will now see the **Virtual Machine Settings** screen and the **Hardware** tab.

3. From the bottom of the screen, click the **Add...** button.

4. You will now see the **Add Hardware Wizard** screen where you will see a list of the virtual hardware that you can add. This is shown in Figure 10-49.

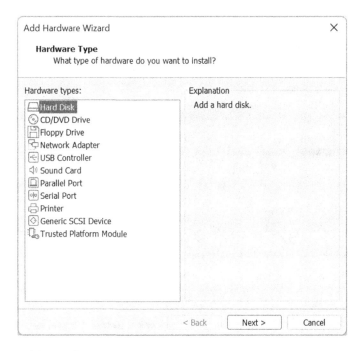

Figure 10-49. *Add Hardware Wizard - Hard Disk*

5. Select the option for **Hard Disk** from the **Hardware types** section.

6. Click **Next >**.

7. You will see the **Select a Disk Type** screen.

8. From the **Virtual disk type** list, click the radio button to select the type of virtual hard disk you want to add.

9. In this example we are going to select the **NVMe (Recommended)** option, so click the corresponding radio button.

10. This is shown in Figure 10-50.

Figure 10-50. *Add Hardware Wizard - Select Hard Disk Type*

11. Click **Next >**.

12. You will see the **Select a Disk** screen.

13. You have the three options as presented when you created the
     virtual machine:

     - **Create a new virtual disk** - Creates a brand-new hard disk. In
       this example this would be a second virtual hard disk.

     - **Use an existing virtual disk** - Allows you to select a virtual disk
       that has already been created.

     - **Use a physical disk** - Allows you to select a physical local disk.

14. For this example, we are going to create a new and empty virtual
     hard disk that is going to be used as a D: drive or data drive, so
     click the radio button for Create a new virtual disk as shown in
     Figure 10-51.

Figure 10-51. *Add Hardware Wizard - Select a Disk*

15.   Click **Next >**.

16.   You will see the **Specify Disk Capacity** screen.

17.   In the **Maximum disk size (GB)** box, type in the size in GB
that you want for this new virtual hard disk. You will see the
recommended size already configured; however, as this is a
second virtual hard disk, then you can create a different size that
meets the use case.

18.   Click the radio button for **Split virtual disk into multiple files**.

19.   This is shown in Figure 10-52.

Figure 10-52. *Add Hardware Wizard - Specify Disk Capacity*

20.   Click **Next >**.

21.   You will see the **Specify Disk File** screen. This is where you name the file that will be the new virtual hard disk.

By default, it will share the name of the virtual machine but will be appended with a hyphen and a number. In this case **-0**. If you create another new virtual hard disk for this virtual machine, then it will be appended with **-1** and so on as you create additional virtual hard disks.

You could also rename the new virtual hard disk with a completely new name, but beware of doing that and then not associating the virtual hard disk with the virtual machine.

This is shown in Figure 10-53.

Figure 10-53. *Add Hardware Wizard - Specify Disk File*

22. Click **Finish**.

23. The new virtual hard disk will appear in the hardware list for the
     virtual machine as shown highlighted in Figure 10-54.

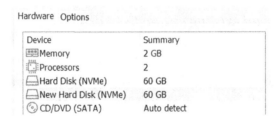

Figure 10-54. *New Virtual Hard Disk successfully added*

The other option for adding an additional virtual hard disk is to use
an existing disk. It may be the case that this was a data disk that was
attached to a different virtual machine; however, you now want this
virtual hard disk to be attached to a different virtual machine.

To do this follow the steps described:

24. Select the **Use an existing virtual hard disk** option from the
    Select a disk screen.

25. You would then see the **Select an Existing Disk** screen as shown
    in Figure 10-55.

Figure 10-55. *Adding an existing virtual hard disk*

26. Enter the details to the existing disk file or click the **Browse...**
    button, and then from the **Browse for Existing Disk**, navigate to
    the location of the virtual hard disk file you want to use.

27. Click **Finish** once you have completed the configuration.

    The final option for adding an additional virtual hard disk is to
    select a physical disk.

    To do this follow the steps described:

28. Select the **Use a physical disk** option from the **Select a**
    disk screen.

29. Click **Next >**

30. You will see the UAC warning message. Click **Yes** to continue.

31. You will now see the **Select a Physical Disk** configuration screen as shown in Figure 10-56.

Figure 10-56. *Select a Physical Disk*

32. From the **Device** drop-down menu, select the physical drive you want to use.

33. Then, in the **Usage** section, select either **Use entire disk** or **Use individual partitions**.

34. If you select **Use entire disk** and click **Next >**, you will see the **Specify Disk File** screen; however, this time the virtual disk file will store the partition information as you are using a physical disk.

35.   This is shown in Figure 10-57.

Figure 10-57.   *Select a Physical Disk - Specify Disk File*

36.   Click **Finish** once you have completed the configuration.

If you chose the **Use individual partitions** option from the **Select a Physical Disk** screen, then you would see the **Select Physical Disk Partitions** screen as shown in Figure 10-58.

Figure 10-58. *Select Physical Disk Partitions screen*

37.   Click to select partition and then click **Next >**.

38.   Now specify the file name and click **Finish**.

We have now discussed the different options for adding additional hard disks to the virtual machine. In the next section we are going to look at how to add a CD or DVD drive.

CD and DVD Drive

As part of the default virtual machine creation, a CD or DVD drive is already added and is typically used to install the operating system. However, if you want to add a second drive, or add a drive if the virtual machine does not already have one, then follow the steps described:

1.   Select the virtual machine you want to add the additional virtual hard disk to.

2.   Click **Edit virtual machine settings**. You will now see the **Virtual Machine Settings** screen and the **Hardware** tab.

3. From the bottom of the screen, click the **Add…** button.

4. You will now see the **Add Hardware Wizard** screen where you will see a list of the virtual hardware.

5. Click on **CD/DVD Drive** as shown in Figure 10-59.

Figure 10-59. *Add a CD/DVD Drive*

6. Click **Finish**.

7. You will return to the **Virtual Machine Settings** screen and the **Hardware** tab where you will see an entry for **New CD/DVD (SATA)** has been added to the hardware inventory for the virtual machine.

8. You can then configure the **Device status** and set the device as **Connected** or to **Connect at power on**.

9. You can also configure a physical drive or select to use an ISO image file.

10.   This is shown in Figure 10-60.

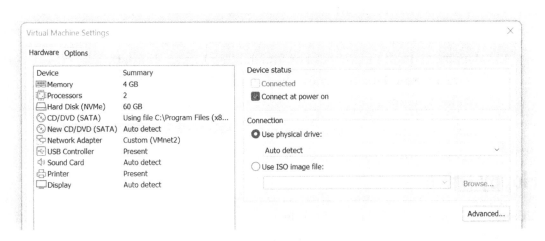

Figure 10-60. *New CD/DVD Drive successfully added*

11.   If you click the **Advanced...** button, you will see the **CD/DVD Advanced Settings** screen as shown in Figure 10-61.

Figure 10-61. *CD/DVD Advanced Settings screen*

12.   On the Advanced Settings screen, you can configure the Virtual device node which is essentially the type of interface used. You can choose from **SATA**, **SCSI**, or **IDE**.

315

Then, on the enabled interface, you can select the node. In this case we have a SATA drive which is configured as device 0 on channel 0.

13. Finally, you will see a check box for enabling **Legacy emulation** if you are experiencing issues when connecting the drive to the virtual machine.

Next is the option to add a floppy drive.

Floppy Drive

Although it is unlikely that you need this feature, Workstation Pro supports a number of legacy features. In this case the ability to add a floppy drive to a virtual machine.

1. Select the virtual machine you want to add the additional virtual hard disk to.

2. Click **Edit virtual machine settings**. You will now see the **Virtual Machine Settings** screen and the **Hardware** tab.

3. From the bottom of the screen, click the **Add...** button.

4. You will now see the **Add Hardware Wizard** screen where you will see a list of the virtual hardware.

5. Click on **Floppy Drive** as shown in Figure 10-62.

Figure 10-62. *Adding a Floppy Drive*

6. Click **Finish**.

7. You will return to the **Virtual Machine Settings** screen and the **Hardware** tab where you will see an entry for **Floppy Drive** has been added to the hardware inventory for the virtual machine.

8. You can then configure the **Device status** and set the device as **Connected** or to **Connect at power on**.

9. You can also configure the virtual machine to use a physical drive, or you can select to use a floppy image file.

10. This is shown in Figure 10-63.

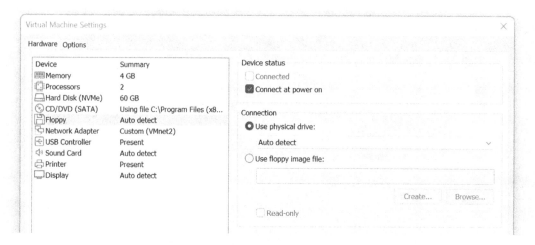

Figure 10-63. *Configuring a Floppy Drive*

Next is the option to add a network adapter.

Network Adapter

The next hardware component to add is a network adapter. When the virtual machine was created, a network adapter is created by default; however, you may need to add additional adapters to allow the virtual machine to connect to different network.

To add an additional network card, follow the steps described:

1. Select the virtual machine you want to add the additional virtual hard disk to.

2. Click **Edit virtual machine settings**. You will now see the **Virtual Machine Settings** screen and the **Hardware** tab.

3. From the bottom of the screen, click the **Add…** button.

4. You will now see the **Add Hardware Wizard** screen where you will see a list of the virtual hardware.

5. Click on **Network Adapter** as shown in Figure 10-64.

Figure 10-64. *Configuring a Floppy Drive*

6. Click **Finish**.

7. You will return to the **Virtual Machine Settings** screen and the **Hardware** tab where you will see an entry for **Network Adapter 2** has been added to the hardware inventory for the virtual machine.

8. You can then configure the **Device status** and set the device as **Connected** or to **Connect at power on**.

9. Next you can configure the network connection depending on what you want to connect the virtual machine to. Either a Bridged, NAT, Host-only, or Custom network connection as well as configuring LAN segments.

10. This is shown in Figure 10-65.

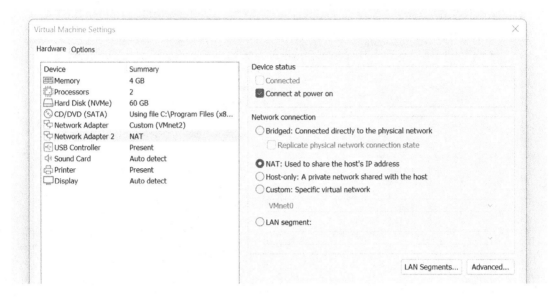

Figure 10-65. *Configuring a Network Adapter*

Next is the option to add a USB controller.

USB Controller

By default, a USB controller will have been installed as part of the initial virtual machine build.

Therefore, when you try to add one, and as the virtual machine only supports a single USB controller, when you try to add an additional USB controller you will be unable to.

When you click the **Add…** button on the **Add Hardware Wizard** screen, you will see a message in the explanation section that states **Maximum limit reached**.

This is shown in Figure 10-66.

Figure 10-66. *USB controller maximum limit reached*

If the virtual machine currently does not have a USB controller, then you will be able to add one and configure it.

Next is the option for sound cards.

Sound Card

As with USB controller, a sound card will have also been installed as part of the initial virtual machine build.

Therefore, when you try to add one, and as the virtual machine only supports a single sound card, when you try to add an additional sound card, you will be unable to.

When you click the **Add...** button on the **Add Hardware Wizard** screen, you will see a message in the explanation section that states **Maximum limit reached**.

This is shown in Figure 10-67.

Figure 10-67. *Sound card maximum limit reached*

If the virtual machine currently does not have a sound card configured, then you will be able to add one and configure it.

Parallel Port

Another legacy support feature is the ability to add a parallel port to a virtual machine.

To add a parallel port, follow the steps described:

1. Select the virtual machine you want to add the additional virtual hard disk to.

2. Click **Edit virtual machine settings**. You will now see the **Virtual Machine Settings** screen and the **Hardware** tab.

3. From the bottom of the screen, click the **Add…** button.

4. You will now see the **Add Hardware Wizard** screen where you will
    see a list of the virtual hardware.

5. Click on **Parallel Port** as shown in Figure 10-68.

Figure 10-68. *Add a parallel port*

6. Click **Finish**.

7. You will return to the **Virtual Machine Settings** screen and the
    Hardware tab where you will see an entry for **Parallel Port** has
    been added to the hardware inventory for the virtual machine.

8. You can then configure the **Device status** and set the device as
    Connected or to **Connect at power on**.

9. Next you can configure the connection to use a physical parallel
    port and also the option to use an output file with the ability to
    browse to the location of where you want to save the file to.

10. This is shown in Figure 10-69.

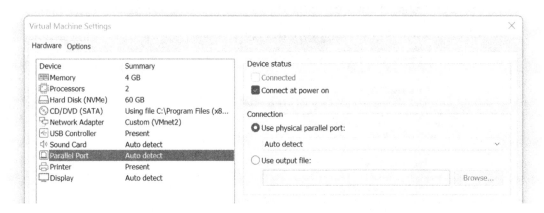

Figure 10-69. *Configuring the parallel port*

Next is the option to add a serial port.

Serial Port

To follow on from adding legacy support to a virtual machine as well as the parallel port, you can also add a serial port.

To add a serial port, follow the steps described:

1. Select the virtual machine you want to add the additional virtual hard disk to.

2. Click **Edit virtual machine settings**. You will now see the **Virtual Machine Settings** screen and the **Hardware** tab.

3. From the bottom of the screen, click the **Add...** button.

4. You will now see the **Add Hardware Wizard** screen where you will see a list of the virtual hardware.

5. Click on **Serial Port** as shown in Figure 10-70.

Figure 10-70. Adding a serial port

6. Click **Finish**.

7. You will return to the **Virtual Machine Settings** screen and the **Hardware** tab where you will see an entry for **Serial Port 2** has been added to the hardware inventory for the virtual machine.

8. You can then configure the **Device status** and set the device as **Connected** or to **Connect at power on**.

9. Next you can configure the connection to use a physical serial port and also the option to use an output file with the ability to browse to the location of where you want to save the file to.

10. A final connection option is the **Use named pipe** option. You have the following options:

    • This end is server.

    • This end is client.

- The other end is a virtual machine.

- The other end is an application.

11. The final option is for **Yield CPU on poll**. This enables the virtual machine to use the serial port in polled mode. Check the box if you want to enable this feature.

12. The serial port configuration is shown in Figure 10-71.

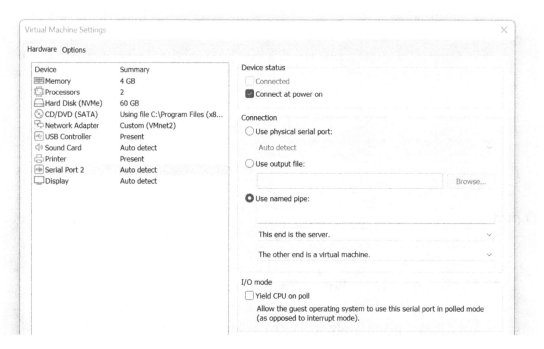

Figure 10-71. *Configuring a serial port*

Next is the option to add a printer.

Printer

A printer will have been installed as part of the initial virtual machine build.

Therefore, when you try to add one, and as the virtual machine only supports a single sound card, when you try to add an additional printer you will be unable to.

When you click the **Add...** button on the **Add Hardware Wizard** screen, you will see a message in the explanation section that states **Maximum limit reached**.

This is shown in Figure 10-72.

Figure 10-72. *Adding a printer*

If the virtual machine currently does not have a printer installed, then you will be able to add one and configure it. Before you do, you will need to ensure that the virtual printer is installed first. We discussed this earlier on in this chapter.

Next is the addition of a SCSI device.

Generic SCSI Device

You can add a generic SCSI device to a virtual machine to enable you to map virtual SCSI devices from a virtual machine to a physical generic SCSI device that is connected to the host machine.

Up to 60 generic SCSI devices are supported on a virtual machine.

To add a generic SCSI device, follow the steps described:

1. Select the virtual machine you want to add the additional virtual hard disk to.

2. Click **Edit virtual machine settings**. You will now see the **Virtual Machine Settings** screen and the **Hardware** tab.

3. From the bottom of the screen, click the **Add...** button.

4. You will now see the **Add Hardware Wizard** screen where you will
   see a list of the virtual hardware.

5. Click on **Generic SCSI device** as shown in Figure 10-73.

Figure 10-73. *Adding a generic SCSI device*

6. Click **Finish**.

7. You will return to the **Virtual Machine Settings** screen and the
   Hardware tab where you will see an entry for **Generic SCSI (SCSI
   0:0)** has been added to the hardware inventory for the virtual
   machine.

   The SCSI 0:0 refers to the controller and device ID, so in this case
   the controller has an ID of 0.

   If we added another SCSI controller, then it will appear as 1:0 with
   the controller having the ID of 1.

8. You can then configure the **Device status** and set the device as
   Connected or to **Connect at power on**.

9. Next is the drop-down for **Physical SCSI device to connect to**
   which will require you to click the **Administrator privileges** link
   in order to list the physical SCSI devices. The settings are shown in
   Figure 10-74.

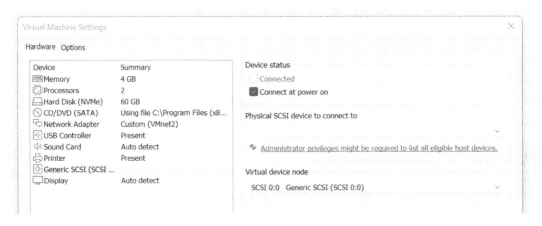

Figure 10-74. *Configuring a generic SCSI device*

10. Click the **Administrator privileges** link.

11. You will see the **User Account Control** (UAC) warning box appear
    to allow Workstation Pro to make changes to the device.

12. Click **Yes** to continue.

13. The UAC warning message is shown in Figure 10-75.

***Figure 10-75.** UAC warning message*

14.   You will now see the physical SCSI devices listed as shown in
        Figure 10-76.

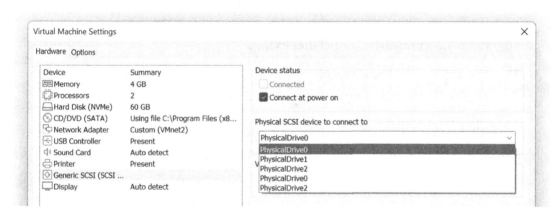

***Figure 10-76.** Physical SCSI device list*

15.   Select the SCSI device from the list.

16.   Next, select the **Virtual device node** from the drop-down list.

17.   This is shown in Figure 10-77.

Figure 10-77. *Virtual SCSI device node*

The final hardware option is for adding a Trusted Platform Module (TPM).

Trusted Platform Module

To increase the security of a virtual machine, you can add a virtual crypto processor that is equipped with Trusted Platform Module (TPM) technology.

It is worth noting that having a TPM capability will be a requirement for some of the latest operating system such as Windows 11 and Windows Server 2022.

There are a couple of prerequisites for using a TPM:

- An encrypted virtual machine

- Minimum of hardware compatibility version 14

- UEFI firmware

To add a Trusted Platform Module, follow the steps described:

1. Select the virtual machine you want to add the TPM to.

2. Click **Edit virtual machine settings**. You will now see the **Virtual Machine Settings** screen and the **Hardware** tab.

3. From the bottom of the screen, click the **Add...** button.

4. You will now see the **Add Hardware Wizard** screen where you will see a list of the virtual hardware.

5. Click on **Trusted Platform Module**. You will only be able to add the TPM so long as the prerequisites have been met.

   If they have not been met, then you will see a message prompting you to complete those first. You also won't be able to click the **Finish** button to add the device.

6. The TPM screen is shown in Figure 10-78.

Figure 10-78. *Adding a Trusted Platform Module*

Once successfully added, you will see the screen shown in Figure 10-79.

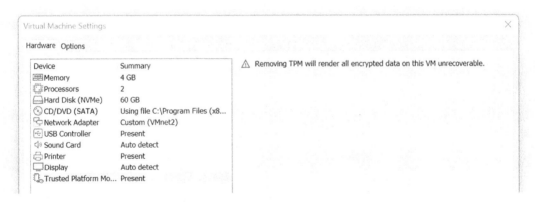

Figure 10-79. *Trusted Platform Module successfully added*

We have now covered the adding of new virtual hardware to a virtual machine.

Summary

In this chapter we started by looking at the configurable options that can be enabled for individual virtual machines. From power settings to some of the more advanced settings such as debugging and configuring firmware types.

We then looked at how to install and configure printing from a virtual machine by using the virtual printer feature that is delivered as an additional application for Workstation Pro.

Finally, we looked at how to add new and additional virtual hardware to a virtual machine. Adding virtual hardware such as additional network adapters and additional hard disks.

CHAPTER 11

Managing and Working with Existing Virtual Machines

In this chapter we are going to look at how to manage your existing virtual machines.

Where we previously focused more on the configuration side of building and creating virtual machines, and how to configure the various virtual machine features, in this chapter we are going to look at the ongoing management of those virtual machines and the tasks that you can perform on them.

For example, we are going to look at tasks such as how to clone a virtual machine and how to configure the order in which virtual machines are powered on. We will also look at removing virtual machines from the inventory and deleting the associated virtual hard disk files.

We will start with the Auto Start feature.

Configure Auto Start for Virtual Machines

In this section we are going to look at how you can configure specific virtual machines to automatically power on in the background as the host machine boots.

This is used as an automation process so that if you have multiple virtual machines that you know you are going to be using straight away, then Auto Start powers them on without you having to power on each one manually.

It is also worth mentioning that virtual machines configured for Auto Start will power on when the host machine boots and not when you launch Workstation Pro.

© Peter von Oven 2023
P. von Oven, *Learning VMware Workstation for Windows*, https://doi.org/10.1007/978-1-4842-9969-2_11

The only word of warning is that you have enough resources on the host machine in order to run all the virtual machines you start. Having said that it is likely that you will have had all the machines powered on at the same time in any case, but it is worth highlighting.

To configure Auto Start, follow the steps described.

1. The first thing you need to do is enable the VMware AutoStart service in the Services console.

2. Press the Windows key, and then from the **Run** dialog box, type **services.msc** in the **Open** field and then click **OK**.

3. You will see the Services management console as shown in Figure 11-1.

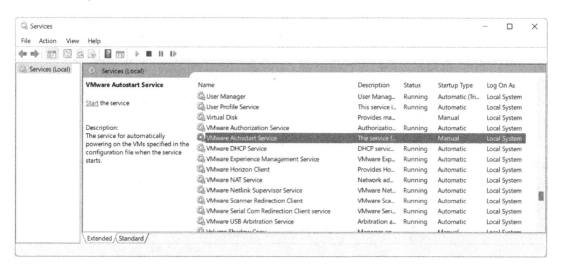

Figure 11-1. *Configuring Auto Start VMs*

4. Scroll down to the entry for **VMware Autostart Service** and double click to open the properties.

5. In the **Startup type** section, in the drop-down menu, select the option for **Automatic**. This means that the service will launch and run when the host machine boots.

6. This is shown in Figure 11-2.

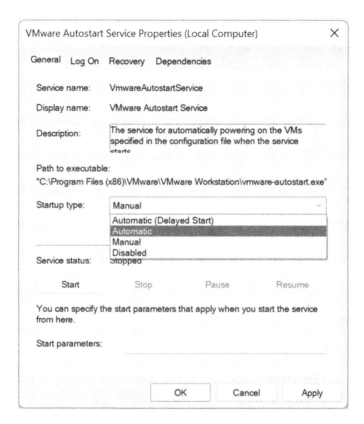

Figure 11-2. *Configuring the Auto Start Service*

7. The next step is to update the account that this service used to log on with. This will be the same account that you log on with to run the virtual machines in Workstation Pro.

8. Click the **Log On** tab.

9. Click the radio button for **This account**.

10. Now click the **Browse...** button

11. You will see the **Select User** screen.

12. In the **Enter the object name to select** box, start to type in the username for the account that you want to use. In this case PvO.

13. Now click the **Check Names** button.

14. The username will be checked and if valid will appear in the box and will be underlined as shown in Figure 11-3.

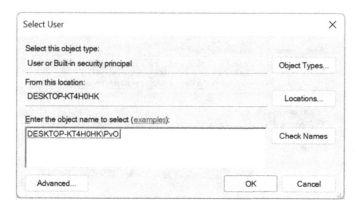

Figure 11-3. *Select User for Auto Start Log On Service*

15. Click **OK**.

16. You will return to the Log On box.

17. Now, in the **Password** box, type in the password for the account/ username you entered.

18. Then type the password in again in the **Confirm password** box.

19. This is shown in Figure 11-4.

Figure 11-4. *Entering Log On details*

20. Click **Apply** and then click **OK**.

21. You will return to the Service management console screen.

22. Now right click **VMware Autostart Service**, and from the contextual menu, select **Start**.

23. This is shown in Figure 11-5.

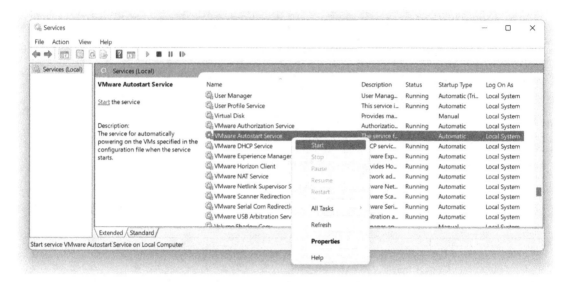

Figure 11-5. *Starting the Auto Start Service*

24. You will now see that the **VMware Autostart Service** is running as shown in Figure 11-6.

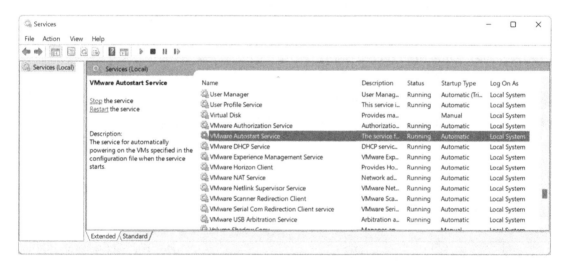

Figure 11-6. *Auto Start Service running*

You can now return to Workstation Pro and configure which virtual machines you want to configure auto start for.

25. Launch Workstation Pro.

26. Right click My Computer, and from the contextual menu, click
     Configure Auto Start VMs as shown in Figure 11-7.

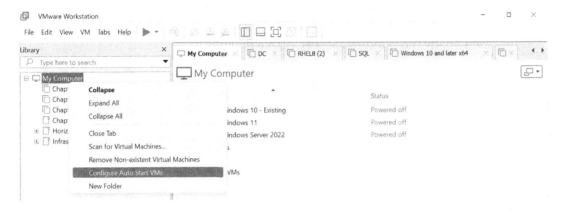

Figure 11-7. *Configuring Auto Start VMs*

27. You will now see the **Configure VM Power Actions** screen as
     shown in Figure 11-8.

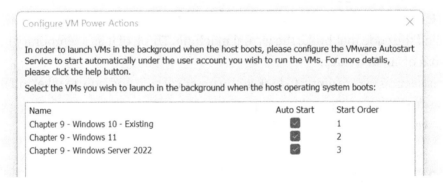

Figure 11-8. *Configure VM Power Actions screen*

Virtual machines in a folder will not be available to configure for auto start. They
need to be under My Computer.

---

28. To enable Auto Start for a specific virtual machine, check the box
     next to it.

29. You will also see another configurable column for Start Order. This allows you to select in which order the virtual machines power on. In the example shown in Figure 11-8, the Windows 10 virtual machine is first followed by the Windows 11 virtual machine and then finally the Windows Server virtual machine.

30. To change the start order, simply click the relevant box and then type in the number to represent the order in which you want that virtual machine to start.

In the next section, we are going to discuss snapshots.

Snapshots

In Chapter 4, we had a deep dive into what snapshots are and how they work. As a quick reminder, a snapshot is the process of saving the current state of a virtual machine which then allows you to roll back to that captured state at any given time.

Typically, this is used on development when you want to try a new piece of code and perhaps it doesn't go quite to plan. You can then roll back to the previous state of before you applied the code that broke the virtual machine. Think of it as a temporary back up or a get-out of jail free card.

In this section we are going to look at the practical side and how to take and manage snapshots for your virtual machines.

First, we are going to look at taking a snapshot of a virtual machine.

Taking a Snapshot

In this section we are going to create or take a snapshot using the Windows 10 virtual machine we created previously.

To take the snapshot, follow the steps described:

1. Click the virtual machine for which you want to take a snapshot of, in this example the Windows 10 virtual machine, right click, and from the contextual menu, click **Snapshot** to expand the Snapshot menu and then click **Take Snapshot…**.

2. This is shown in Figure 11-9.

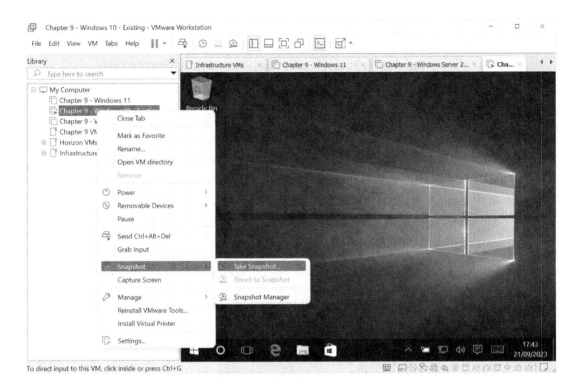

Figure 11-9. *Taking a Snapshot menu*

3. You will now see the **Take Snapshot** screen as shown in Figure 11-10.

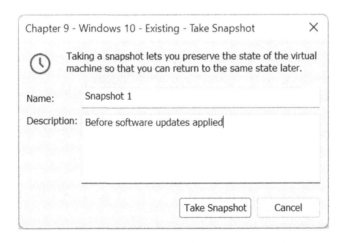

Figure 11-10. *Take Snapshot screen*

4. In the **Name** box, type in a name for this snapshot. By default, as this is the first snapshot created for this particular virtual machine, it is called **Snapshot 1**. You can edit this box and provide your own name if you want to.

5. Next, in the **Description** box, you can optionally add some text describing what this snapshot is. In this example we called it **Before software updates applied** as we are creating this point in time copy of the virtual machine before we apply software updates and patches. If the patches break the virtual machine, then we are able to roll back to before they were applied and return to a working virtual machine.

6. Click the **Take Snapshot** button to create the snapshot.

7. You will briefly see a progress bar before returning to the virtual machine.

8. If you click the **Snapshot** menu again, you will see the Figure 11-11 showing the snapshot has been created.

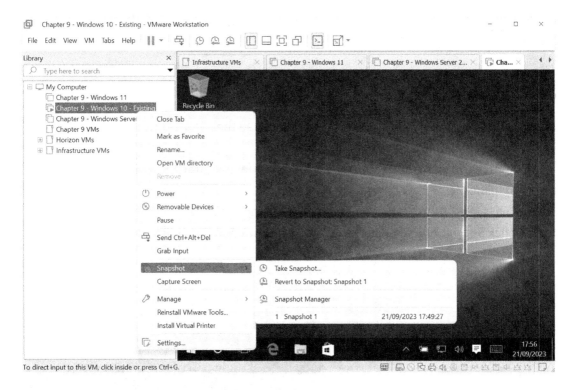

Figure 11-11. *Snapshot successfully created*

Now you have created snapshots, you will be able to see these in File Explorer alongside the virtual machine files as shown in Figure 11-12.

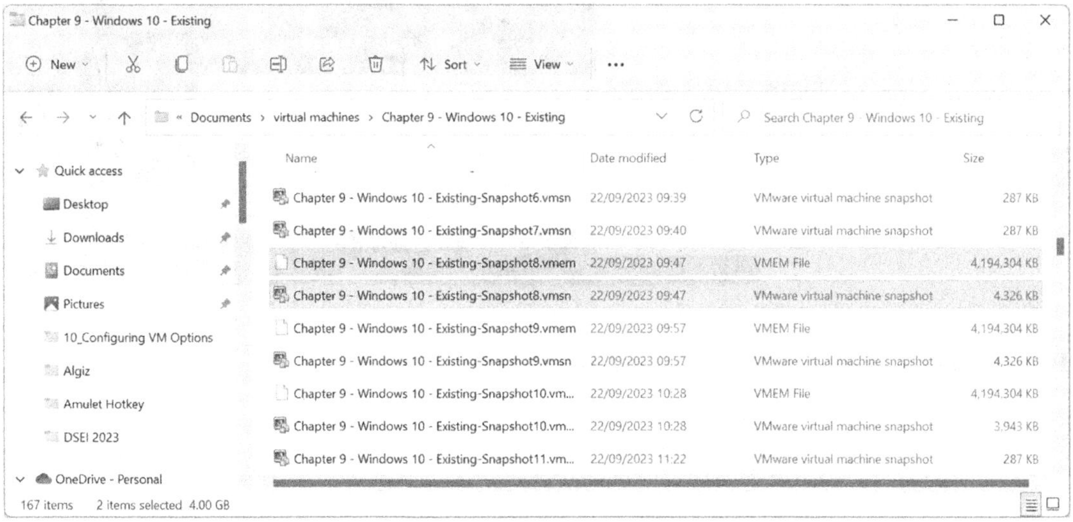

Figure 11-12. *Snapshots as viewed in File Explorer*

Now that we have our first snapshots, next we are going to look at the Snapshot Manager.

Snapshot Manager

In this section we are going to look at how to manage the snapshots that you have created using the Snapshot Manager.

To launch the Snapshot Manager, click the virtual machine for which you want to take a snapshot of.

In this example the Windows 10 virtual machine, right click and, from the contextual menu, click **Snapshot** to expand the Snapshot menu and then click **Snapshot Manager.**

This **is** shown in Figure **11-13**.

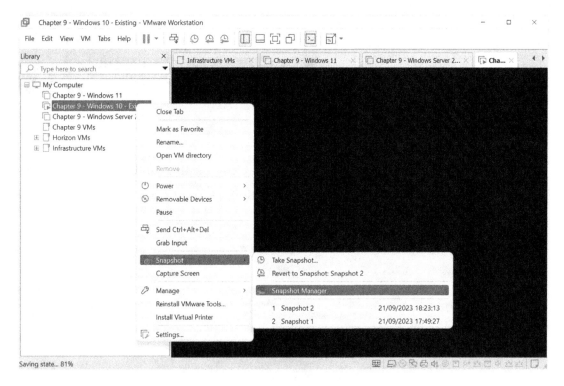

Figure 11-13. *Launching Snapshot Manager*

You will now see the **Snapshot Manager** as shown in Figure 11-14.

Figure 11-14. Snapshot Manager

The first thing you will see is the map of the snapshots with **You Are Here** highlighted. This is the current state of the virtual machine.

You will also see that two snapshots exist. **Snapshot 1** was taken first, followed by **Snapshot 2** which then takes us to the current state.

You can click any of the snapshots to take you to the state of the virtual machine at the point in time when the snapshot was taken.

For this example, click **Snapshot 1**.

You will now see the details of this snapshot displayed, along with a number of other options and actions that you can perform on the snapshot. This is shown in Figure 11-15.

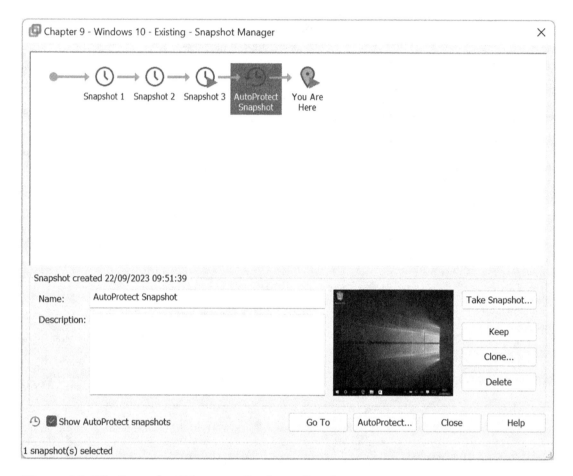

Figure 11-15. *Snapshot Manager for Snapshot 1*

As you can see, the date and time of when the snapshot was created is displayed, along with the name and description that you configured. You could also see a thumbnail screenshot of the virtual machine when the snapshot was taken. This would also depend on the view being displayed at the time the snapshot was taken too.

You also have a number of additional options. The first of these is the **Show AutoProtect snapshots** check box. When enabled you will also see displayed any snapshots that were created as part of the AutoProtect feature that we discussed in Chapter 10.

The next button you see is the **Go To** button. This will take you back to a specific snapshot. For example, if you highlight **Snapshot 1** and click **Go To**, you will see the message shown in Figure 11-16.

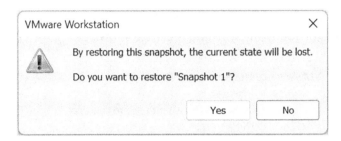

Figure 11-16. *Go To a Specific Snapshot - Snapshot 1*

If you click the **Yes** button, then Snapshot 1 will be restored, and you will lose the current state. The current state effectively becomes the state of Snapshot 1.

You can also double click the Snapshot icon which will also take you to the message shown in Figure 11-14.

Next is the **AutoProtect...** button. If you click this button, then you will be automatically taken to the **Options** page for the selected virtual machine and the **AutoProtect** feature as shown in Figure 11-17.

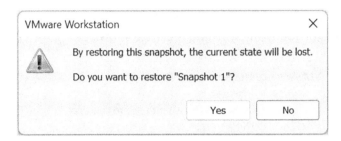

Figure 11-17. *AutoProtect configuration screen*

We discussed the **AutoProtect** feature, how it works, and how to configure it in Chapter 10.

Next is the **Close** button. This simply closes the Snapshot Manager. Likewise, when you click the **Help** button, it takes you to the help page on the Internet for VMware Workstation Pro.

The **Delete** button, unsurprisingly, deletes the snapshot. When you click the delete button, you will see the following warning message shown in Figure 11-18.

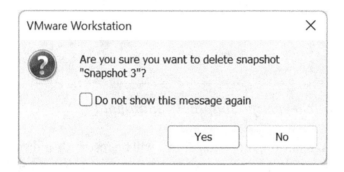

Figure 11-18. *Deleting a snapshot warning message*

Click **Yes** to delete the snapshot, or no to return to the Snapshot Manager. You also have the option to check the box so that you no longer see the warning message when you delete a snapshot.

With the **Clone…** button, you are able to take a clone of a snapshot or a virtual machine that is powered off. We will look at the cloning process later in this chapter.

The **Keep** button will only be available when you have the AutoProtect feature enabled and applies only to snapshots that have been taken by the AutoProtect feature. You will only be able to click it when you highlight one of the AutoProtect Snapshots if you want to keep that particular snapshot.

Lastly you have the **Take Snapshot…** button. Clicking this will create a new snapshot for the selected virtual machine.

In the next section, we are going to look at how to export the virtual machine as an OVF template.

Export to OVF

The Export to OVF feature allows you to export a virtual machine as an OVF file that can then be used to import the virtual machine complete with the setup and configuration you created. This is useful if you want to use the OVF as a template for an operating system gold build.

To export a virtual machine as an OVF, follow the steps described:

1. Click and highlight the virtual machine that you want to export as an OVF.

2. Right click and select **Export to OVF...**

3. This is shown in Figure 11-19.

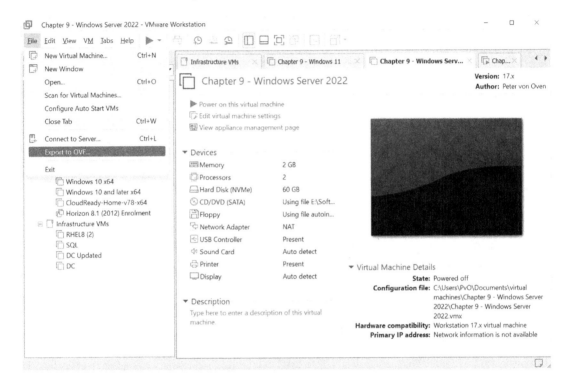

Figure 11-19. *Exporting a Virtual Machine to an OVF*

4. You will now see a file explorer window where you can navigate to the location of where you want to save the OVF file to. The File name box will have been populated automatically with the name of the virtual machine as it appears in the library pane. This is shown in Figure 11-20.

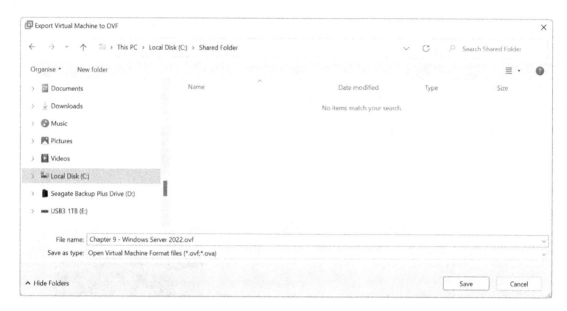

Figure 11-20. *Saving the OVF file*

5. Click **Save**.

6. You will see the progress bar as shown in Figure 11-21.

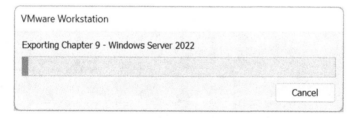

Figure 11-21. *Saving the OVF file progress bar*

Once the export has successfully completed, you will see the following as shown in Figure 11-22.

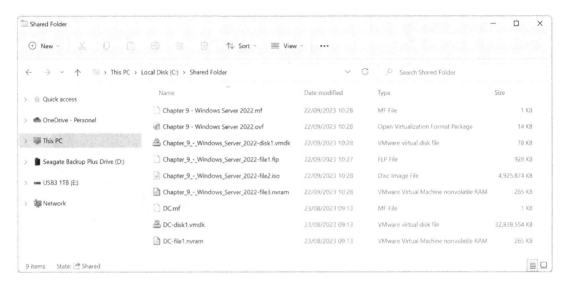

Figure 11-22. *OVF successfully exported*

In the next section, we are going to look at how to clone a virtual machine.

Cloning a Virtual Machine

In this section we are going to look at how to create a clone of an existing virtual machine. This is useful if you want to make an exact copy of a virtual machine that you have already spent time on building and configuring. This could be used for creating things like gold images.

To clone a virtual machine, follow the steps described:

1. Select the virtual machine that you want to create a clone of, right click it, and then move your mouse to **Manage**.

2. From the menu that pops up to the side, click **Clone…**.

3. This is shown in Figure 11-23.

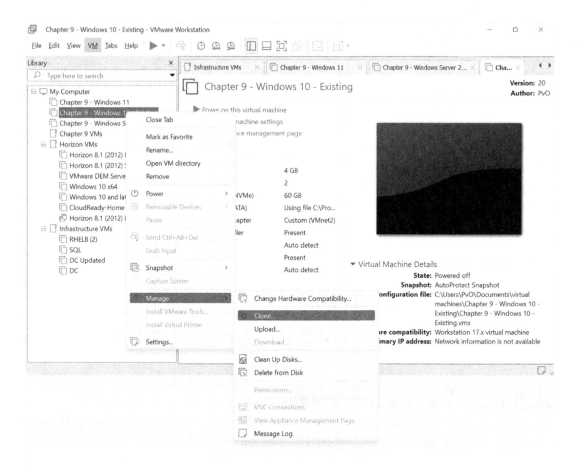

Figure 11-23. *Cloning a virtual machine*

4. You will now see the **Welcome to the Clone Virtual Machine Wizard** screen.

5. This is shown in Figure 11-24.

Figure 11-24. Welcome to the Clone Virtual Machine Wizard

6. Click **Next >** to continue.

7. You will now see the Close Source screen where you can select the state from which you want to create the clone from.

8. In the **Clone from** section, you have the choice of two options which are selected by clicking the corresponding radio button.

    The first option is **The current state in the virtual machine** which will create a linked clone using the current virtual machine state.

    The second option is to create a clone from **An existing snapshot**. You then have the drop-down menu from which to select the snapshot from.

9. In this example click the radio button for **The current state in the virtual machine**.

10. This is shown in Figure 11-25.

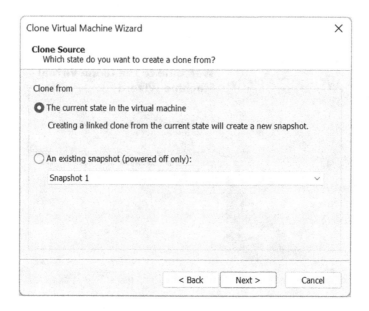

Figure 11-25. *Selecting the clone source*

11. Click the **Next >** button. You will see the **Clone Type** screen shown in Figure 11-26.

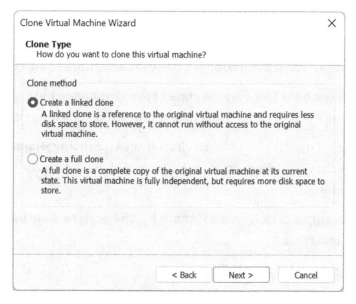

Figure 11-26. *Selecting the Clone Type*

12. In the **Clone method** you can select what type of clone is going
    to be created. You can **Create a linked clone** which creates
    deltas of any changes to the virtual machine but references the
    original virtual machine, or you can **Create a full clone** which is a
    complete copy of the virtual machine in its current state.

13. In this example click the radio button for **Create a Linked clone**
    and click **Next >**.

14. You will see the **Name of the New Virtual Machine** screen as
    shown in Figure 11-27.

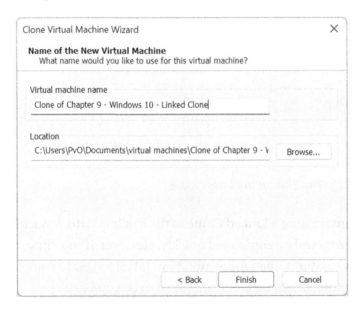

Figure 11-27. *Name the clone*

15. In the **Virtual machine name** box, by default, you will see the
    existing name of the virtual machine. As this is a clone, you need
    to give it a unique name. In this example we have added the words
    Linked Clone to the name so as to identify the clone.

16. The **Location** box, by default, will be set to the default folder name
    set in the Workstation Pro preferences. We will leave this as is, but
    you can change it if required.

17. Now click **Finish**.

18. You will see the **Cloning Virtual Machine** screen as shown in Figure 11-28.

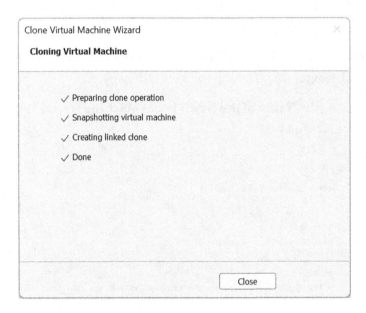

Figure 11-28. *Cloning the virtual machine*

As we are creating a Linked Clone of the original virtual machine, this process will be completed quickly. However, if you chose the full clone options, then this would have taken longer to complete as the entire virtual hard disk will need to be copied.

19. Click the **Close** button to complete the cloning process.

20. You will now see the new cloned virtual machine appear in the library pane as shown in Figure 11-29.

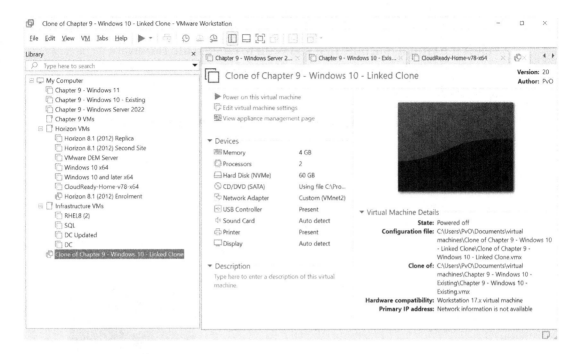

Figure 11-29. *Virtual Machine successfully cloned*

In the next section, we are going to look at how to change the Hardware Compatibility version.

Changing the Hardware Compatibility Version

In this section we are going to look at how to change the current version of the Hardware Compatibility for a virtual machine.

You may want to do this if you upgrade the version of Workstation Pro, and with that new version, the supported hardware has changed to support additional devices and resource maximums.

Equally if you create a virtual machine with the latest version of Workstation Pro and the latest Hardware Compatibility version, you might want to roll it back to an older version to test with older virtual machines that are running older versions.

To change the Hardware Compatibility version, follow the steps described:

1. Select the virtual machine that you want to change the Hardware
    Compatibility for, right click it, and then move your mouse
    to **Manage**.

2. From the menu that pops up to the side, click **Change Hardware
    Compatibility...**

3. This is shown in Figure 11-30.

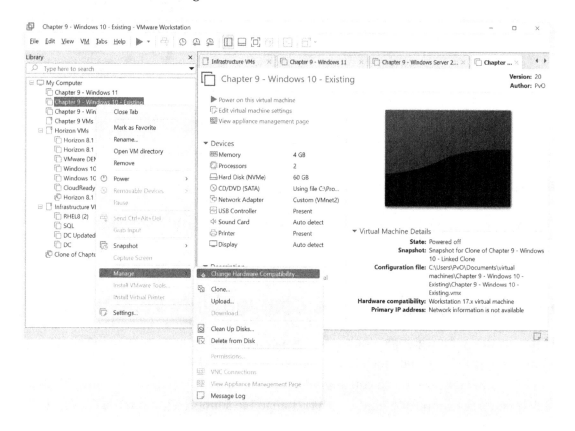

Figure 11-30. *Change the Hardware Compatibility Version*

4. You will now see the **Welcome to the Change Hardware
    Compatibility Wizard** screen as shown in Figure 11-31.

Figure 11-31. *Welcome to the Change Hardware Compatibility Wizard*

5. Click **Next >**.

6. You will see the **Choose the Virtual Machine Hardware Compatibility** screen.

7. From the **Hardware compatibility** drop-down menu, select the compatibility version you want to change to.

    By default, the current version has been selected. You will know this as the Next > button will remain grayed out until you select a different version from the current version.

    In this example, from the drop-down menu, select the option for **Workstation 16.2.x** as shown in Figure 11-32.

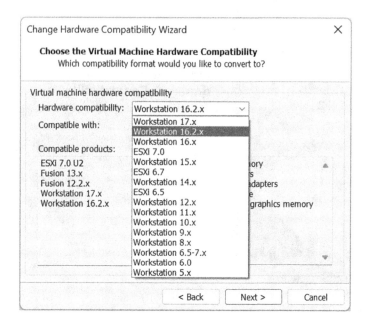

Figure 11-32. *Select the New Hardware Compatibility Version*

8. You will see the **Clone before Converting** screen in Figure 11-33.

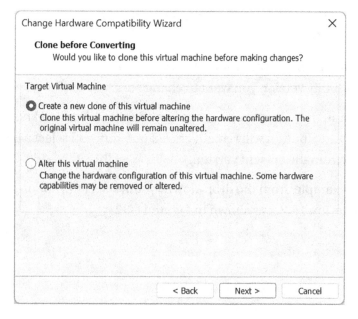

Figure 11-33. *Select the New Hardware Compatibility Version*

9. On this screen you can select, by clicking the corresponding radio button, from two options:

   a. **Create a new clone of this virtual machine** will first of all create a clone of the selected virtual machine and then will change the hardware configuration. Basically, you will have a new machine that is a copy of the selected virtual machine but running a different hardware version.

   b. **Alter this virtual machine** will just change the hardware configuration without creating a clone first. With this option it is recommended to take a snapshot first just in case the new hardware version causes any issues.

   We are going to look at both options.

10. If you select the option for **Create a new clone of this virtual machine** and then click **Next >**, you will see the **Name the Clone** screen.

11. In the Virtual machine name box, type in a name for this cloned version of the virtual machine. In this example we have called it **Chapter 11 - Windows 10 - Hardware Compatibility**.

12. Then in the Location box, either type in the folder location of where the cloned virtual machine is going to be saved to or click the **Browse...** button and navigate to the folder location. By default, as you entered the virtual machine name, the box would have been populated with the default location.

13. This is shown in Figure 11-34.

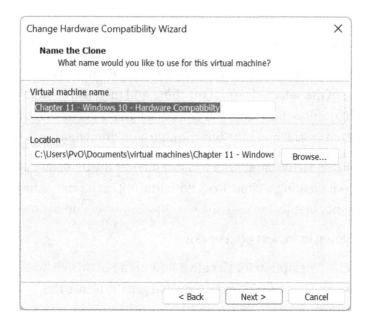

Figure 11-34. *Name the Clone for Changing Hardware Compatibility*

14.   Click **Next >**.

15.   You will now see the **Review Changes** screen as shown in Figure 11-35.

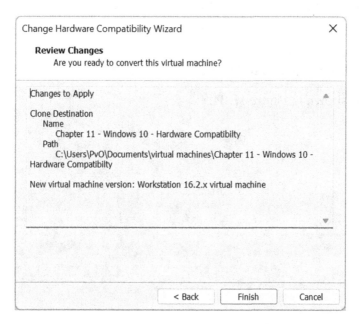

Figure 11-35. *Review Changes screen*

16. Click **Finish**.

17. You will see the progress bar showing the cloning process and
     its status.

18. This is shown in Figure 11-36.

Figure 11-36. *Cloning progress*

19. Once the cloning process has successfully completed, then you
     will see the **Converting Virtual Machine** screen which shows
     each of the tasks that have been completed.

They should all have a tick next to them as shown in Figure 11-37.

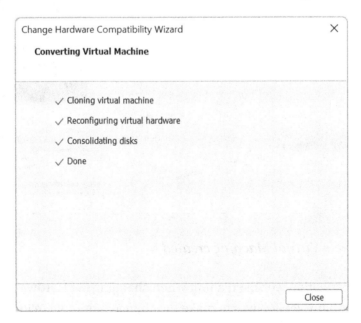

Figure 11-37. *Converting Virtual Machine successfully completed*

20. Click **Close**.

21. If you now look at the Workstation Pro main screen, you will see
    that the newly cloned machine will appear in the library pane.

    You will also see that there is a new link showing in the virtual
    machine view under the virtual machine name. This link is for
    Upgrade this virtual machine.

    The virtual machine has detected that it is running an older
    Hardware Compatibility version, and so if you click this link, it will
    launch the **Change Hardware Compatibility Wizard**.

    This is shown in Figure 11-38.

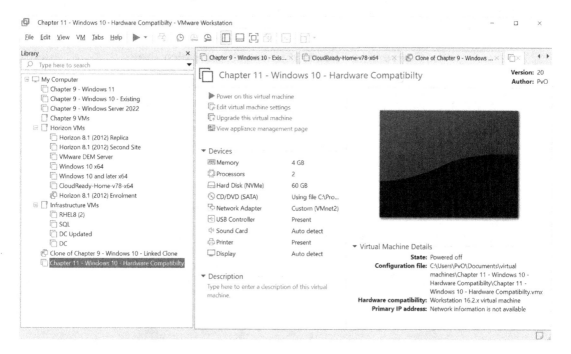

Figure 11-38. *New Virtual Machine created*

The other option we talked about when changing the Hardware
Compatibility version was to make the changes without creating
a clone.

Let's look at that process from the **Clone Before
Converting** screen.

22. Click the radio button for **Alter this virtual machine**.

23. This is shown in Figure 11-39.

Figure 11-39. *Alter this virtual machine screen*

24. You will now see the **Review Changes** screen shown in
     Figure 11-40.

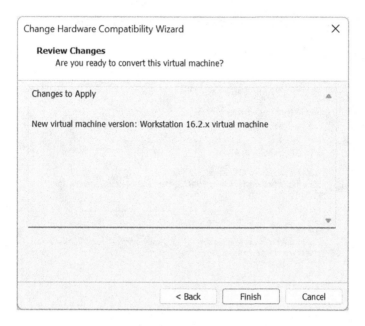

Figure 11-40. *Review Changes*

25.   Click **Finish**.

26.   You will see the Converting Virtual Machine screen as shown in
       Figure 11-41.

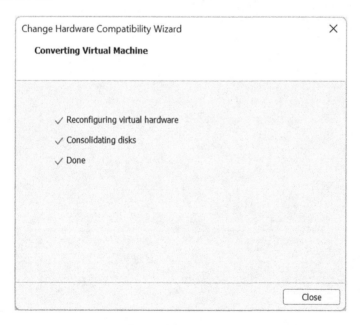

Figure 11-41. *Converting Virtual Machine completed*

27. Once the process has successfully completed, then you will see the **Converting Virtual Machine** screen which shows each of the tasks that have been completed. In this case one less task as we have not created a clone.

28. Click **Close** to complete the process.

You return to the Workstation Pro main screen. This time, however, you won't see a new cloned virtual machine as the existing virtual machine has been altered.

What you will see though is the new link showing in the virtual machine view under the virtual machine name. This link is for **Upgrade this virtual machine** as Workstation Pro has realized that this virtual machine is no longer running the latest Hardware Compatibility version.

Next, we are going to look at cleaning virtual hard disks.

Clean Up Disk

Deleting files from virtual machines does not mean that the disk space the files occupied is immediately made available to the host machine.

By running the Clean Up Disk feature, if a virtual machines virtual hard disk has any free space, then that space will now immediately be made available to the hard drive on host machine.

To run the Clean Up Disk feature, follow the steps described:

1. In the library pane, click and select the virtual machine that you want to run the Clean Up Disk utility for.

2. Right click and then move your mouse to **Manage**, and from the menu that pops up to the side, click **Clean Up Disks... as** shown in Figure 11-42.

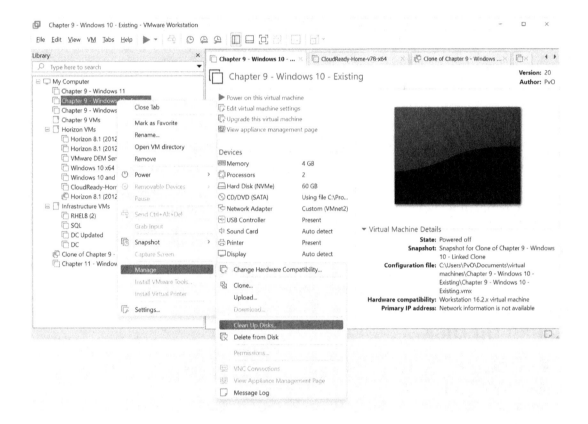

Figure 11-42. *Launching Disk Cleanup*

3. You will now see the virtual machine calculate the disk space that
    could be reclaimed as shown in Figure 11-43.

Figure 11-43. *Calculating reclaimable disk space*

4. Once the estimation process has completed, you will see the results as shown in Figure 11-44.

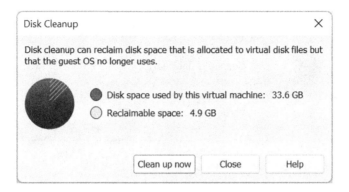

Figure 11-44. *Results of reclaimable disk space*

5. To action the cleanup process, click the **Clean up now** button.

6. You will see the **Cleaning up disks...** progress bar as shown in Figure 11-45.

Figure 11-45. *Cleaning up disks progress*

7. Once the process has completed, you will see the **Disk Cleanup is finished** message as shown in Figure 11-46.

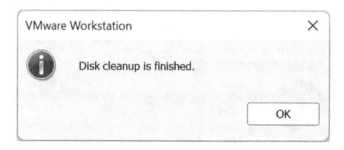

Figure 11-46. *Cleanup successfully completed*

In the next section, we are going to look at how to disable the scoreboard files that we discussed in Chapter 9 when we created virtual machines and looked at what files were created that make up a virtual machine.

Disabling Scoreboard Files

The scoreboard files in Workstation Pro contain performance statistics that can be used by VMware vRealize for monitoring purposes.

Unless you are using this feature, then you likely don't need the scoreboard files, and so as to save disk space, you can disable them.

To disable the scoreboard files from being created, follow the steps described:

1. Open a File Explorer session.

2. Navigate to the location of the VMX file for the selected virtual machine. In this example the **Chapter 9 - Windows 10** virtual machine. This is shown in Figure 11-47.

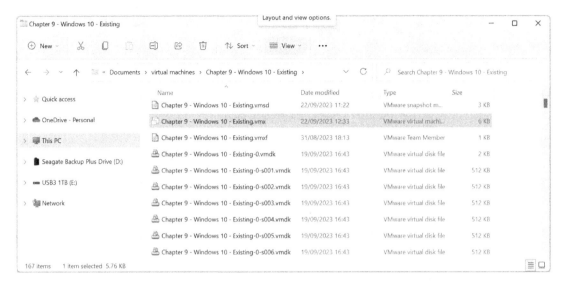

Figure 11-47. *Navigate the VMX file*

3. Right click and select **Open with**.

4. Select **Notepad**.

5. The VMX file will now open in Notepad allowing you to make changes.

You might want to make a backup copy of the VMX file before making any changes.

---

6. Scroll down to the bottom of the open VMX file and add the following line:

    vmx.scoreboard.enabled = "FALSE"

7. The VMX file with the newline added is shown in Figure 11-48.

Figure 11-48. *Navigate the VMX file*

8. Now save the updated file and exit Notepad.

You have now disabled the scoreboard file creation.

In the next section, we are going to look at how to configure a MAC address manually.

Configuring MAC Addresses

When you power on a virtual machine, it is assigned a MAC (Media Access Control) address for each network card that is configured. This is no different to having a physical machine which will also have a MAC address for each network card it is configured with.

Virtual machines are given the same MAC address each time they are powered on. However, there are some cases where that is not the case. For example, if you move the virtual machine configuration file (VMX) or you make any changes to the network settings or virtual machine IS (UUID). The MAC address will also change if you move the virtual machine to a different host machine or move the virtual machine to a new location on the same host machine.

There may be use cases whereby you don't want the virtual machine to have its MAC address changed. Maybe it is down to software licensing being tied to a certain MAC address, or you have security rules in place that lock down access based on a MAC address.

You could of course avoid doing any of these things in order to preserve a virtual machine's MAC address, but luckily, as with other VMware solutions, Workstation Pro allows you to manually assign a MAC address which is a far better solution.

To configure a manual MAC address for a virtual machine involves editing the VMX configuration file. Follow the steps described to manually configure a MAC address:

1. Open a File Explorer session.

2. Navigate to the location of the VMX file for the selected virtual machine. In this example the **Chapter 9 - Windows 11** virtual machine.

3. Right click and select **Open with**.

4. Select **Notepad**.

5. The VMX file will now open in Notepad allowing you to make changes.

6. The first task is to remove the information that is currently configured for the MAC address currently being used.

   In this example the virtual machine has a single network card called **Ethernet0**. If you have multiple network cards, then these will be listed as Ethernet1, Ethernet2, and so on. You can, if required, change the MAC address for all network cards. Just repeat the process for each numbered card.

7. Scroll down until you find the following lines:

   ethernet0.generatedAddress

   ethernet0.generatedAddressOffset

   Now delete these lines from the VMX file as shown in Figure 11-49.

Figure 11-49. *Removing current network settings for MAC address*

8. You also need to remove the line:

   ethernet0.addressType

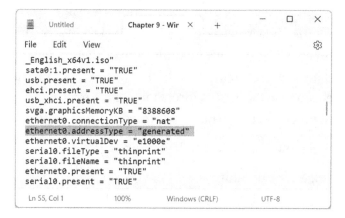

Figure 11-50. *Removing current network settings for address type*

You can now add the new manually created MAC address.

9. Scroll down until you find the lines that start with **UUID** as shown
    in Figure 11-51.

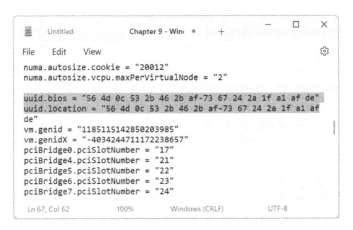

Figure 11-51. *Locating the UUID section of the VMX file*

10. Above the first UUID line, add the following line:

    ethernet0.address = 00:50:56:XX:YY:ZZ

11. The 00:50:56 are the values that identify this as a VMware virtual
    MAC address and shouldn't be changed. The other values should
    be configured as the following:

    XX must contain a valid hexadecimal number between 00h
    and 3Fh.

    YY must contain valid hexadecimal numbers between 00h
    and FFh.

    ZZ must contain valid hexadecimal numbers between 00h
    and FFh.

12. Virtual machines do not support arbitrary MAC addresses, and
    the values entered for XX:YY:ZZ must be unique among your
    hard-coded addresses to avoid conflict between the automatically
    assigned MAC addresses and the manually assigned addresses.

13. An example of this new configuration is shown in Figure 11-52.

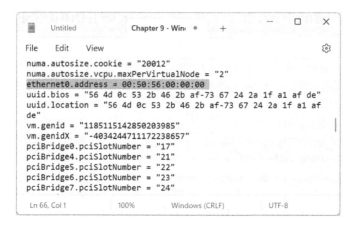

Figure 11-52. *Adding a manual MAC address*

14. Now save the updated file and exit Notepad.

You have now configured a manual MAC address for the specified virtual machine. In the next section, we are going to look at deleting a virtual machine.

Deleting a Virtual Machine

In this section we are going to delete a virtual machine.

You can delete the virtual machines entry in the library; however, that just removes it from the inventory. If you want to delete it fully, then you need to remove all the associated files that get created such as the virtual disk files and configuration files.

To permanently delete the virtual machine, follow the steps described:

1. In the library pane, click and select the virtual machine that you want to permanently delete.

2. Right click and then move your mouse to **Manage**, and from the menu that pops up to the side, click **Delete from Disk as** shown in Figure 11-53.

Figure 11-53. *Permanently delete a virtual machine*

3.   You will now see a warning box stating that the action you are
     about to take is irreversible and that the virtual machine selected
     will be permanently deleted.

4. This is shown in Figure 11-54.

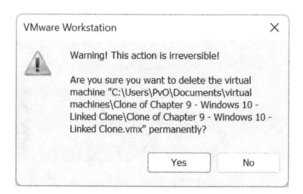

Figure 11-54. *Warning box for deleting a virtual machine*

5. Click **Yes** to confirm you want to permanently delete the selected virtual machine.

6. The virtual machine and all its files will now be deleted.

In the next section, we are going to look at how you can connect to VMware virtual infrastructure to upload and download virtual machines, as well as manage them.

Connecting to VMware Infrastructure

In this section we are going to look at the ability for Workstation Pro to connect to remote infrastructure, namely, vSphere.

The use case for this is when you use Workstation Pro for development and testing. You may need to download a virtual machine from the datacenter to a local device running Workstation Pro in order to complete development work.

It also works the other way around too in that you can build virtual machines locally using Workstation Pro and then upload them to the virtual infrastructure platform.

In this section we are going to connect to the virtual infrastructure and then look at how to upload and download virtual machines.

Connect to Server

First, we are going to look at how to connect to the vSphere infrastructure.

To do this follow the steps described:

1. From the **File** menu, click **Connect to Server...** as shown in Figure 11-55.

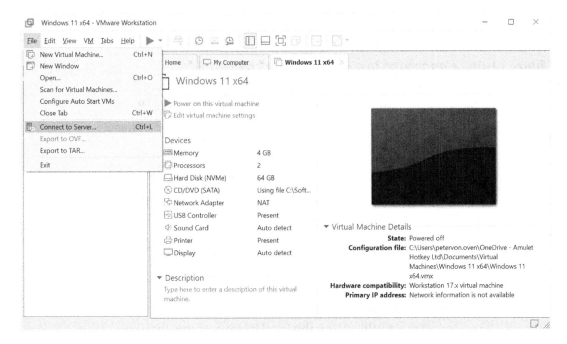

Figure 11-55. *Connecting to a server*

2. You will now see the **Connect to Server** screen as shown in Figure 11-56.

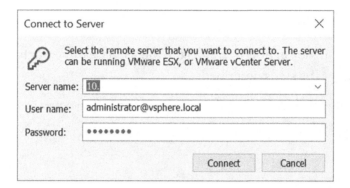

Figure 11-56. *Connecting to a aerver - enter credentials*

3. In the **Server name** box, type in the server's name or the IP address of the server you want to connect to. This can be either a VMware ESXi host server or a VMware vCenter Server.

4. Then, in the **User name** box, type in the name of the user you want to log in as. In this case as it is a vCenter, we are using the "standard" administrator@vsphere.local user account.

5. Finally, enter the password for the account in the **Password** box.

6. Click **Connect**.

7. If you see a certificate warning, then accept this and continue. If you install the certificate on the local host machine, then you won't see the certificate warning again.

8. Once connected you will see the virtual machine hosted on the vSphere infrastructure appear in the library pane as shown in Figure 11-57.

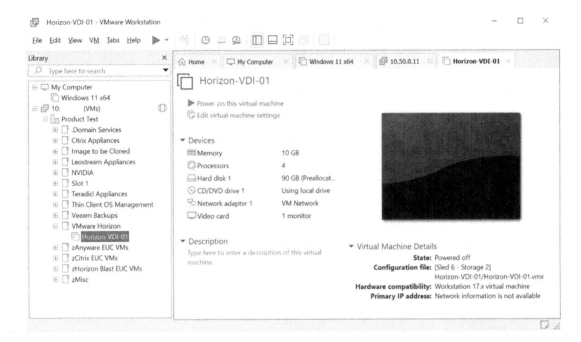

Figure 11-57. *Library pane now showing vSphere inventory*

You will now, depending on permissions, have access to the virtual machines running on the vSphere infrastructure.

In the next section, we are going to look at how to download a virtual machine from the vSphere infrastructure onto the local host machine and run the virtual machine locally on Workstation Pro.

Downloading a Virtual Machine

The next thing we are going to look at is how to download a virtual machine that is currently hosted on the vSphere platform to the local host running Workstation Pro.

To do this follow the steps described:

1. With the vSphere infrastructure connected, following the process followed in the previous sections, in the library pane, navigate to the virtual machine you want to download.

2. Right click and then move your mouse to **Manage**, and from the
    menu that pops up to the side, click **Download...** as shown in
    Figure 11-58.

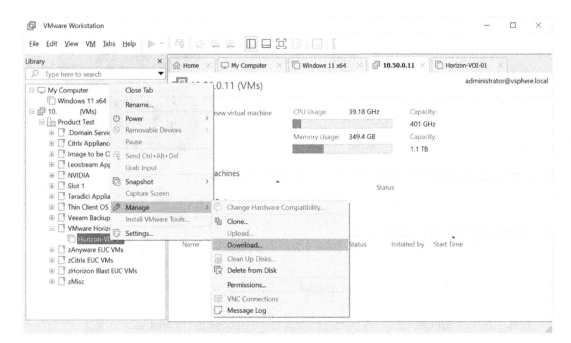

Figure 11-58. *Downloading a virtual machine*

3. You will now see the **Download Virtual Machine** screen and the
    Store the New Virtual Machine option as shown in Figure 11-59.

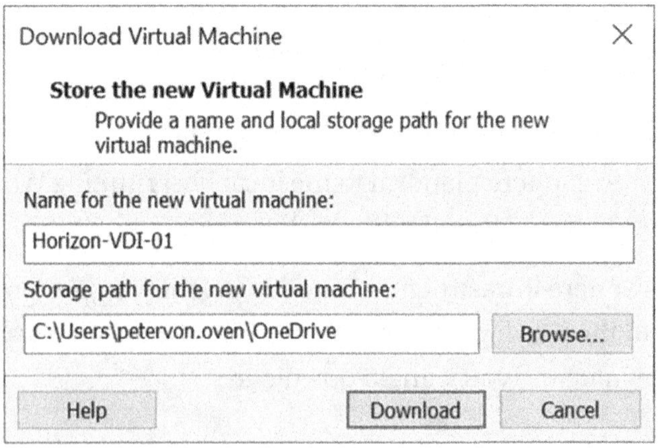

Figure 11-59. *Configuring the storage for the new virtual machine*

4. In the **Name for the new virtual machine** box, type in a name for this virtual machine when it is running on Workstation Pro.

5. Then in the **Storage path for the new virtual machine**, enter the path to where you want to store the virtual machine files. You also have the option to click the **Browse...** button, and navigate to the locations.

6. Now click the **Download** button.

7. You will see the download start and the progress bar as shown in Figure 11-60.

Figure 11-60. *Downloading the virtual machine*

8. Once the download has been completed, you will see that the virtual machine is visible and available in the library pane of Workstation Pro.

9. This is shown in Figure 11-61.

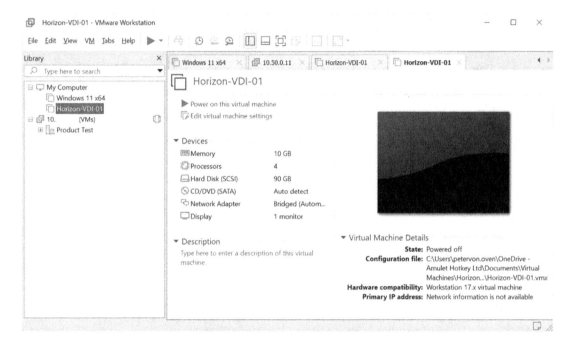

Figure 11-61. *Virtual machine successfully downloaded*

In the next section, we are going to look at how to upload a virtual machine from Workstation Pro to the vSphere infrastructure.

Uploading Virtual Machines

In this section we are going to do the reverse of what we covered in the previous section and upload a virtual machine from Workstation Pro to the vSphere infrastructure.

To do this follow the steps described:

1. With the vSphere infrastructure connected, following the process followed in the previous sections, in the library pane, navigate to the virtual machine you want to upload.

2. Right click and then move your mouse to **Manage**, and from the menu that pops up to the side, click **Upload...** as shown in Figure 11-62.

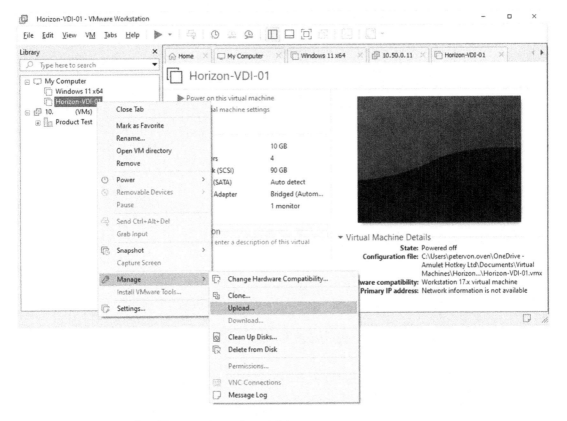

Figure 11-62. *Uploading a virtual machine*

3. You will now see the **Select a Destination Server** screen.

4. In the **Destination Server** section, you will see an entry for **Other VMware vSphere Server** and as we are connected to the vSphere infrastructure, the name of the vCenter Server.

5. In this example we will start by selecting **Other VMware vSphere Server** and work through the process for if you are not connected.

6. This is shown in Figure 11-63.

Figure 11-63. *Selecting the Destination Server*

7. Click **Next >**.

8. You will now see the **New Server Connection** screen where
    you can enter the credentials to log on to the server you want to
    connect to.

9. In the **Hostname or IP Address** box, type in the server's name or
    the IP address of the server you want to connect to. This can be
    either a VMware ESXi host server or a VMware vCenter Server.

10. Then, in the **User name** box, type in the name of the user you
    want to log in as. In this case as it is a vCenter we are using the
    "standard" administrator@vsphere.local user account.

11. Finally, enter the password for the account in the **Password** box.

12. This is shown in Figure 11-64.

Figure 11-64. *New Server Connection*

13. Click **Next >**.

14. Click **Next >**.

15. The connection will now be made, and you will see the **Select a Destination Location**. In the **Folder** section you will see the folders on vCenter.

16. This is shown in Figure 11-65.

Figure 11-65. *Destination folders*

17. Select a destination folder and then click **Next >**.

18. Next you will see the next **Select a Destination Location** screen, this time to select a resource to run the uploaded virtual machine.

19. In the **Name** box, enter a name for the virtual machine.

20. In the **Host** box, from the drop-down menu, select the host on which you want this uploaded virtual machine to run.

21. Finally, in the **Datastore** section, select the datastore where the uploaded virtual machine files will be stored.

22. This is shown in Figure 11-66.

Figure 11-66. Destination resources

    23.   Click **Finish**.

The virtual machine will now be uploaded to the vSphere platform and will be available to run on the selected vSphere host.

Summary

In this chapter we have looked at some of the additional tasks that can be performed such as configuring virtual machine to start automatically, creating snapshots, and connecting to vSphere infrastructure. We also looked at cloning and deleting virtual machines.

CHAPTER 12

Installing VMware vSphere

One of the more popular uses for Workstation Pro, when it comes to development and learning, is to install VMware ESXi and vCenter Server running as virtual machine hosted by Workstation Pro. We touched on this back in Chapter 1 when we discussed nested environments.

In fact, all my previously written books on VMware Horizon, App Volumes, and Dynamic Environment Manager have been installed as virtual machines running on VMware Workstation Pro.

That includes the hypervisor and all the supporting infrastructure and is shown as an example configuration in Figure 12-1.

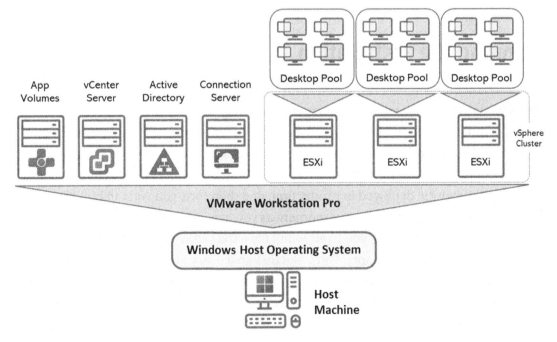

Figure 12-1. *Example vSphere Architecture with Horizon on Workstation Pro*

© Peter von Oven 2023
P. von Oven, *Learning VMware Workstation for Windows*, https://doi.org/10.1007/978-1-4842-9969-2_12

One of the key reasons to do this is that it is much cheaper and easier for me to personally install my demo lab on one physical machine rather than having to build an entire datacenter comprising of multiple physical machines.

In this chapter we are going to walk through the process and steps to install VMware vSphere infrastructure as virtual machines hosted by Workstation Pro. Before we do it, it is just worth noting that this isn't a vSphere installation guide, and as such we are not going to cover that side in any great detail. Instead, we will concentrate on the configuration nuances in getting vSphere up and running on Workstation Pro.

As an example, in this chapter we are going to create a 3-node vSphere cluster that will also host a vSAN cluster using those 3 nodes, a vCenter Server, a Domain Controller, and finally a Windows Desktop VM to act as the management console and software repository for the installation software required. As the domain controller and desktop VM are standard VMs, the building of those was covered in Chapter 9.

We will also include an example network setup and the configuration of additional virtual hard disks for the vSAN cluster to show as an example of what you can do with Workstation Pro. If your host machine is powerful enough, you may even be able to deploy VMware VCF!

Planning the Installation

Before starting any physical installation and configuration tasks, it is worth planning what your infrastructure will look like, in the same way as you would for any other infrastructure deployment. Even though this may be for testing and learning, it is still good to get in the habit of doing this.

This could be especially important as you are building a development infrastructure that will ultimately be deployed in production, and therefore, you want to build it as close to mirror your production environment as you can.

However, having said that you likely won't have the same resources available in Workstation Pro, such as memory, CPU, and disk space as you would when using the production systems. That will likely not be a problem as you are more than likely testing how things work, and how they are configured rather than measuring performance. It's all about the functionality.

Example CPU and Memory Requirements

When it comes to CPU considerations, you need to look at the virtual machine minimum CPU requirements. While we can configure most virtual machines with limited CPU resources, knowing that this is for testing and development and in production more CPU will be available, there may be virtual machines that won't even install and deploy with limited CPU.

If you remember back in Chapter 6, where we discussed virtual CPUs, if you try to configure more virtual processors than the host machine can support, then the virtual machine will fail to power on.

You also need to think about the amount of memory required and not to overcommit too much. The result of this would be poor performing virtual machines and, even worse, virtual machines that don't even power on.

Network Requirements

The key component is networking, and obviously vSphere has a number of different networks that it utilizes for management, vMotion, and vSAN, for example. Therefore, these network requirements need to be taken into consideration when deploying vSphere on Workstation Pro, and the network configuration needs to be set up to reflect this.

Figure 12-2 shows an example network configuration that also includes the other solution components such as a Domain Controller.

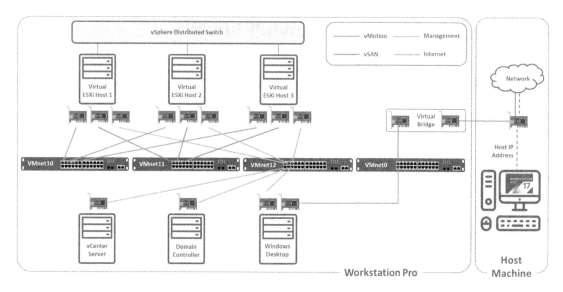

Figure 12-2. *Example vSphere networking in Workstation Pro*

Just to recap, in the example configuration, we have a basic 3-node vSphere cluster, complete with a vCenter Server and an Active Directory Domain Controller.

We have also added a Windows desktop that is used as a management console as well as being the conduit for connecting to the external network and/or the Internet. This is for downloading software and updates for the virtual machines as well as running things like the vSphere Client.

For the ESXi hosts, we have created three networks and have configured them as host-only networks, so they are all internal to Workstation Pro and therefore have no external connections. These are configured as shown in the table in Figure 12-3.

Network	Use Case	IP Address Range
VMnet0	Bridge connection for external/internet access	Same as host
VMnet10	vMotion network	10.0.10.xxx
VMnet11	vSAN network	10.0.11.xxx
VMnet12	Management Network	10.0.12.xxx

Figure 12-3. *Example network configuration*

In this example you will see that we have configured a single network card for each of the three ESXi host servers. If you wanted to test things like NIC teaming and creating port groups with multiple uplinks, that too is easy to configure with an example shown in Figure 12-4.

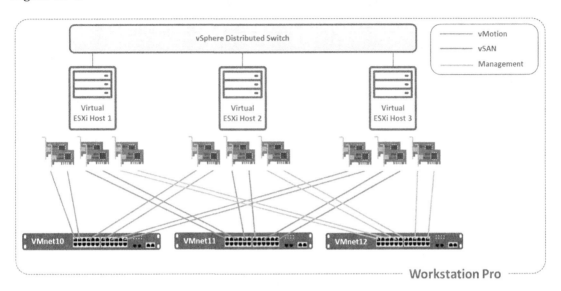

Figure 12-4. *Example vSphere networking for multiple network cards*

All you need to configure is the additional network cards for the virtual ESXi hosts and then connect them to the corresponding network.

Although this book is not about vSphere, it is worth just showing an example of the end-to-end networking, configured to be all internal to VMware Workstation Pro, as shown in Figure 12-5.

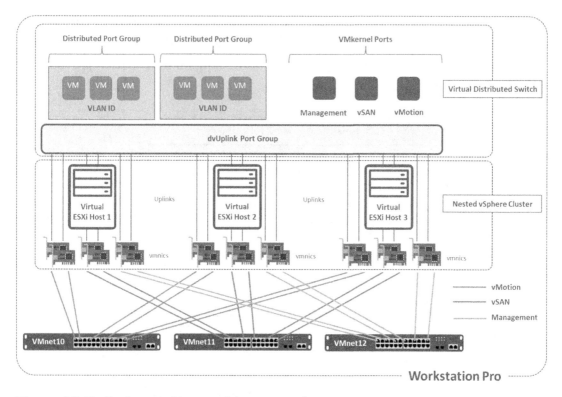

Figure 12-5. *End-to-end networking example*

In the next section of this chapter, we are going to start the practical tasks. The first of these is to create the virtual machine.

Building and Configuring the VM for VMware ESXi

The first step of the process is to create the virtual machine, or machines, in this example, that are going to be the ESXi host servers. We also need to build and configure the networking elements too.

We are going to start with the network first and configure the virtual networks that will be used for our vSphere environment.

Configuring the Network

To configure the networking for the example environment, follow the steps described:

1. Launch VMware Workstation Pro.

2. From the menu, click **Edit** and then select the option for **Virtual Network Editor**. You will see the Virtual Network Editor launch as shown in Figure 12-6.

Figure 12-6. *Virtual Network Editor*

3. Before you can start editing settings, you need to click on the **Change Settings** button.

4. You will see the User Account Control (UAC) message appear as shown in Figure 12-7.

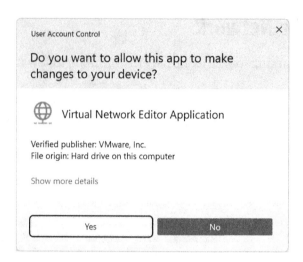

Figure 12-7. *Usae Account Control warning*

5.   Click **Yes** to accept and allow configuration changes. You will now be able to change the network settings.

6.   Click the **Add Network...** button.

7.   You will see the **Add a Virtual Network** dialog box as shown in Figure 12-8.

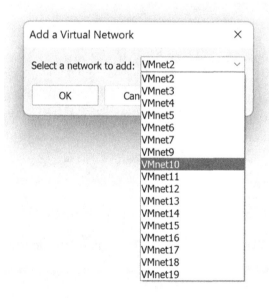

Figure 12-8. *Adding a new virtual network*

8. Click the **Select a network to add** drop-down and select the
    network you want to add. In this example we are going to add the
    VMnet10 network, so select this from the list. You will now see this
    has been added as shown in Figure 12-9.

Figure 12-9. *VMnet10 network selected to be added*

9. Click **OK**. In Figure 12-10, you will see that VMnet10 has been
    successfully added.

Figure 12-10. *VMnet10 network successfully added*

10. Ensure that the **Host-only** radio button has been selected.

11. Uncheck the box for **Use local DHCP service to distribute IP address to VMs**.

12. In the **Subnet IP** box, enter the IP address for the subnet you want to use for this network. In this example we are using 192.168.10.0.

13. Ensure that the **Subnet mask** is set to 255.255.255.0.

14. Click **Apply,** and finally, click **OK.**

15. The next step is to rename the network to something that describes what it is used for. Click on the entry for **VMnet10** and then click the **Rename Network...** button. You will see the **Rename a Virtual Network** dialog box as shown in Figure 12-11.

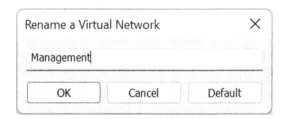

Figure 12-11. *Renaming a Virtual Network*

⊕ Virtual Network Editor   ✕

Name	Type	External Connection	Host Connection	DHCP	Subnet Address
VMnet0	Bridged	Microsoft Wi-Fi Direct Virtua...	-	-	-
VMnet1	Host-only	-	Connected	Enabled	192.168.119.0
VMnet8	NAT	NAT	Connected	Enabled	192.168.180.0
Manage...	Host-only	-	Connected	-	192.168.10.0
vSAN	Host-only	-	Connected	-	192.168.11.0
vMotion	Host-only	-	Connected	-	192.168.12.0

[Add Network...]   [Remove Network]   [Rename Network...]

VMnet Information

○ Bridged (connect VMs directly to the external network)

   Bridged to: Microsoft Wi-Fi Direct Virtual Adapter #4   ⌄   [Automatic Settings...]

○ NAT (shared host's IP address with VMs)   NAT Settings...

● Host-only (connect VMs internally in a private network)

☑ Connect a host virtual adapter to this network
   Host virtual adapter name: VMware Network Adapter VMnet12

☐ Use local DHCP service to distribute IP address to VMs   DHCP Settings...

Subnet IP: [192 . 168 . 12 . 0]   Subnet mask: [255 . 255 . 255 . 0]

[Restore Defaults] [Import...] [Export...] [OK] [Cancel] [Apply] [Help]

Figure 12-12. New network for management successfully added

You have now successfully configured the network for VMnet10 which is going to be used for the vMotion network for the ESXi host servers.

The next step is to repeat this process to create the remaining two networks for VMnet 11 (vSAN) and VMnet 12 (vMotion), ensuring that you give them the appropriate subnet IP addresses for the relevant network.

Once completed the network configuration will look like the example shown in Figure 12-11.

You could also create additional networks if required, if you want to use separate networks for VM traffic; however, in this example we will just use the management network as we are testing the infrastructure and don't have any clients attached.

The next step is to create the virtual machine configuration.

Configuring the Virtual Machines

In the next section of this chapter, we are going to configure the virtual machines that are going to be running in the example environment. This is the three ESXi host servers that will be running vSAN.

For the vSAN configuration, we are going to use ESA (Express Storage Architecture) that doesn't require separate cache and capacity drives. We are going to build the following configuration using 100GB capacity drives (Figure 12-13).

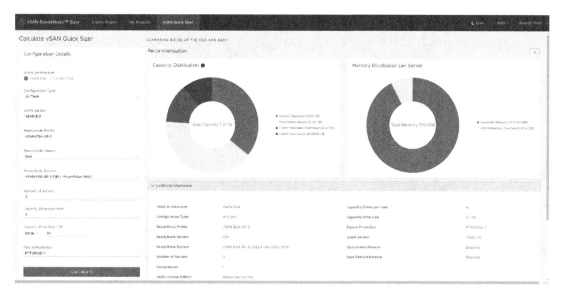

Figure 12-13. *vSAN sizing tool*

We are going to focus on the configuration of the vSphere elements (ESXi and vCenter Server) in this section, as the other components are just a standard Windows Server (Domain Controller in this example) and Windows Desktop (used as a management PC in this example) VMs that we discussed the building and configuration of in Chapter 9.

Creating a Virtual Machine for ESXi

At this stage we are just building the virtual hardware configuration for the virtual machine that will be the ESXi host server, so CPU, memory, and disk. ESXi will be installed in the next section.

When creating new virtual machines, as we have seen before, you can use the **Typical (recommended)** option in the **New Virtual Machine Wizard;** however, as we are going to add and configure this virtual machine beyond the standard configuration settings, we are going to use the **Custom (advanced)** option instead but use some of the same settings as would be used for the typical option.

To build the virtual machine for ESXi, follow the steps described:

1. Launch VMware Workstation Pro.

2. Click on the **File** menu, and then from the menu options, click on **New Virtual Machine...** as shown in Figure 12-14.

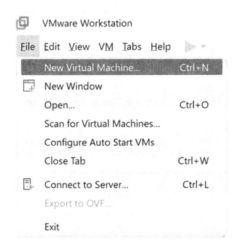

Figure 12-14. *Create a New Virtual Machine menu option*

3. You will see the **Welcome to the New Virtual Machine Wizard** launch as shown in Figure 12-15.

Figure 12-15. *Welcome to the New Virtual Machine Wizard*

4. Click the radio button for **Custom (advanced)**, and then click the
   Next > button.

5. You will see the **Choose the Virtual Machine Hardware
   Compatibility** screen as shown in Figure 12-16.

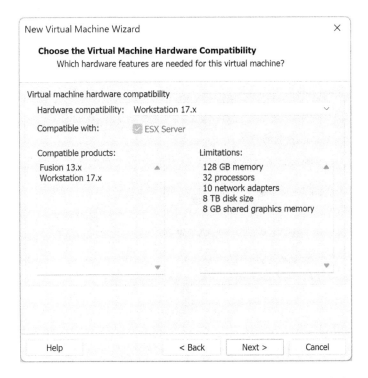

Figure 12-16. *Choose the Virtual Machine Hardware Compatibility*

6. From the **Hardware compatibility** drop-down, select the option
    for the virtual machine hardware compatibility. In this example
    we have left the default setting of **Workstation 17.x;** however, if
    you are installing an older version of ESXi, then you can select that
    from the list of options that are displayed.

    You will also see that the option **Compatible with ESX Server** has
    already been selected and cannot be deselected.

    Finally, on this screen you will see the **Compatible products**
    section and the maximum virtual hardware configuration limits.

7. Click **Next >** to continue. You will see the **Guest Operating System
    Installation** screen as show in Figure 12-17.

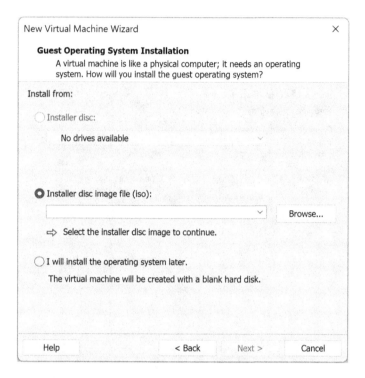

Figure 12-17. *Guest Operating System Installation*

8. Click the radio button for **Installer disc image file (iso)**, and then click the **Browse...** button.

9. You will see the **Browse for ISO Image** screen as shown in Figure 12-18.

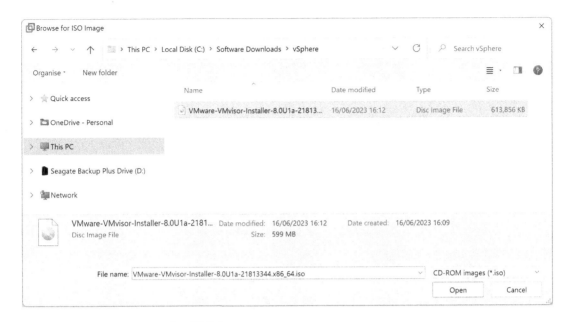

Figure 12-18. *Browse for ISO Image*

10. Navigate to the location of the ESXi installation media. In this
    example this has been downloaded and saved in a folder called
    Software Downloads.

11. Click and highlight the disc image file and then click **Open**.

12. You will return to the **Guest Operating System Installation**
    screen where you will now see the details of the selected ISO
    image and its folder path entered.

    You may also see a warning message stating that the OS type
    cannot be detected as shown in Figure 12-19.

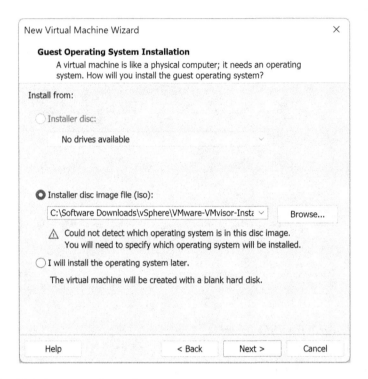

Figure 12-19. *ISO image selected*

13.   Click **Next >** to continue. You will see the **Select a Guest Operating System** screen as shown in Figure 12-20.

Figure 12-20. *ISO image selected*

14. Click the radio button for **VMware ESX,** and then in the **Version** drop-down, select the version from those listed. In this example we can only select VMware ESXi 7 as version 8 is not yet listed in this version of VMware Workstation.

15. Click **Next >** to continue.

16. You will see the **Name the Virtual Machine** screen as shown in Figure 12-21.

Figure 12-21. *ISO image selected*

17. In the **Virtual machine name** box, type in the name for this
     virtual machine. In this example, as this is the first host server to
     be built, it has been called **ESXi Host 001**.

18. In the **Location** box, you will see that the path and name of the
     virtual machine has been added. This is the default folder location
     for storing virtual machines. You can, if you need to, click the
     Browse... button and choose an alternative folder location.

19. Now click on **Next >**.

20. You will see the **Processor Configuration** screen as shown in
     Figure 12-22.

Figure 12-22. *Processor Configuration screen*

21. In the **Number of processors** box, from the drop-down, select the number of processors for this virtual machine. In this example we have selected a single CPU.

22. Then, in the **Number of cores per processor**, from the drop-down, select the number of cores for this virtual machine's CPU. In this example we have selected two cores. This configuration is the same as if you selected the typical build configuration.

23. Click **Next >** to continue.

24. You will now see the **Memory for the Virtual Machine** screen. In this example the memory has been configured as per the recommended minimum of 4GB as you can see in Figure 12-23.

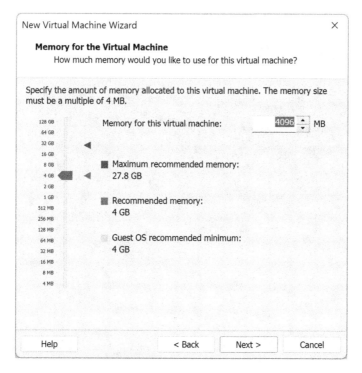

Figure 12-23. *Memory Configuration screen*

25.   Click **Next >** to continue.

26.   The next screen is for configuring the Network Type. Click the radio button for Use host-only networking.

In this example we are just configuring an internal network within VMware Workstation with no access to the host or an external network. This is shown in Figure 12-24.

Figure 12-24. *Memory Configuration screen*

27. Click **Next >**. You will see the **Select IO Controllers** screen
    (Figure 12-25).

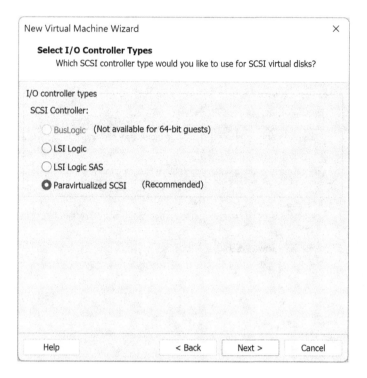

Figure 12-25. *I/O Controller Configuration screen*

28. Click the radio button for **Paravirtualized SCSI** and then
     click **Next >**.

29. You will now see the **Select a Disk Type** screen as shown in
     Figure 12-26.

Figure 12-26. Select a Disk Type Configuration screen

30. Click the radio button to select **SCSI (Recommended)** and then click **Next >**.

31. The next screen is to **Select a Disk**.

32. Click the radio button to select the option for **Create a new virtual disk** as shown in Figure 12-27.

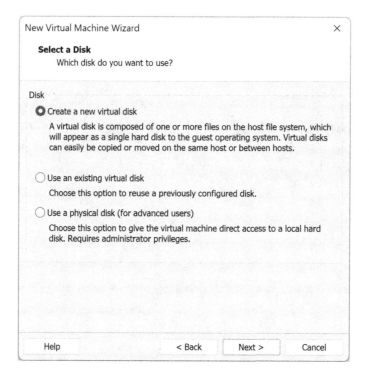

Figure 12-27. *Create a new virtual disk configuration screen*

33. Click **Next >** to continue. You will see the **Specify Disk Capacity** screen shown in Figure 12-28.

Figure 12-28. *Specify Disk Capacity configuration screen*

34. In the **Maximum disk size (GB)** box, leave the default size recommended for VMware ESXi and ensure that the radio button for **Split virtual disk into multiple files** is selected.

35. Click **Next >** to continue.

36. You will now see the **Specify Disk File** screen. This is where you provide the name for the disk file. By default, the virtual disk file will be named using the same as the default virtual machine name based on the type of guest OS. In this example, as we are creating several ESXi hosts, we have added a number, 001, to the name and as shown in Figure 12-29.

Figure 12-29. *Specify Disk File name*

37.   Click **Next >** to continue.

38.   You have now successfully configured the settings required to
      configure the basic virtual machine which will be displayed in the
      Ready to Create Virtual Machine screen shown in Figure 12-30.

Figure 12-30. *Ready to Create Virtual Machine*

In this example we need to create some additional virtual hardware in the form of additional network cards for the different networks required, and also additional hard drives as we are going to create a vSAN cluster.

39. Click the **Customize Hardware...** button.

40. You will now see the **Hardware** screen.

41. The first thing we are going to add is the additional network cards. If you click on **Network Adapter**, you will see that the first network adapter has already been created and by default is connected to a host-only network. Before creating the additional network cards, we are going to connect the first adapter to the correct network. In this case the management network.

42. Click the radio button for **Custom**, and then from the drop-down list of networks, select the **Management (Host-only)** network as shown in Figure 12-31.

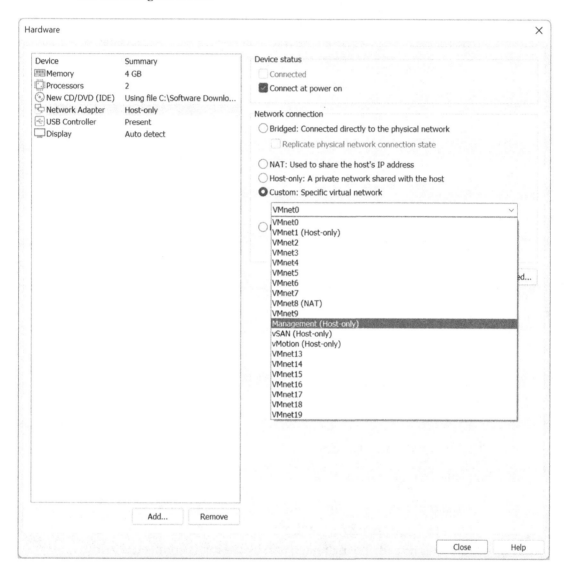

Figure 12-31. Connecting to the management network

43. The next step is to create additional network adapters to connect to the other networks.

44.   Click the **Add...** button.

45.   You will see the **Add Hardware Wizard** screen as shown in Figure 12-32.

Figure 12-32. *Add New Hardware Wizard - Network Adapter*

46.   Click on **Network Adapter** and then click **Finish**.

47.   You will return to the **Hardware** screen where you will see that **Network Adapter 2** has now been created.

48.   Click to highlight and select **Network Adapter 2** to configure its settings.

49.   In the **Network connection** section, click the radio button for **Custom**, and then from the drop-down list of networks, click to select the **vSAN (Host-only)** network as shown in Figure 12-33.

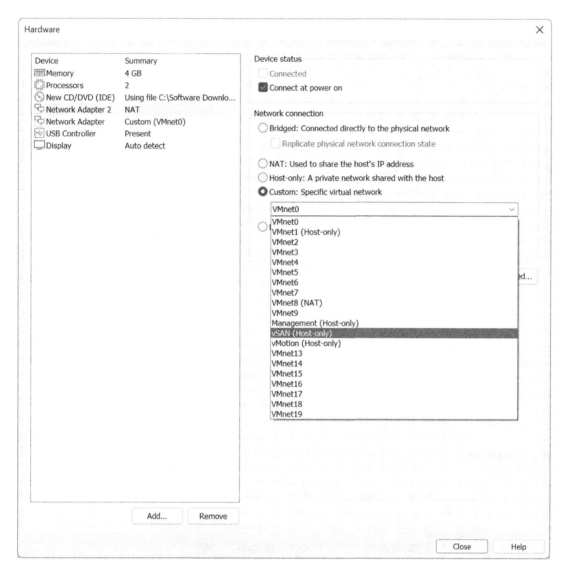

Figure 12-33. *Configuring new Network Adapter 2*

50. Now click the **Add...** button again.

51. You will see the **Add Hardware Wizard** screen.

52. Click and select the option for **Network Adapter** as shown in
     Figure 12-33.

Figure 12-34. *Configuring new Network Adapter 2*

53. Click **Finish**.

54. You will return to the **Hardware** screen where you will see that **Network Adapter 3** has now been created.

55. Click to highlight and select **Network Adapter 3** to configure its settings.

56. In the **Network connection** section, click the radio button for **Custom**, and then from the drop-down list of networks, click to select the **vSAN (Host-only)** network as shown in Figure 12-35.

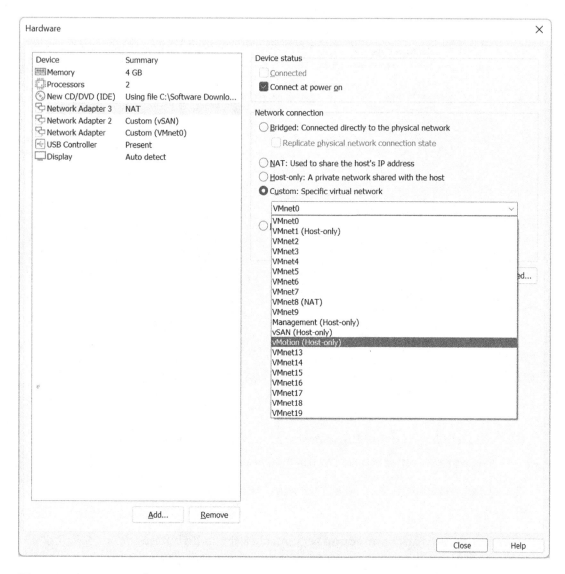

Figure 12-35. *Configuring new Network Adapter 3*

57. Now click **Close**.

58. You will return to the **Ready to Create Virtual Machine** screen as shown is Figure 12-36.

Figure 12-36. *Ready to Create Virtual Machine*

As part of the customizing virtual machine hardware, we also need to add additional virtual hard disks; however, as you may have seen when adding the network adapters, there is no option to add hard disks from this configuration screen. This option is available once the initial virtual machine has been created.

59. Click **Finish**.

60. You will return to the main Workstation screen as shown in Figure 12-37.

Figure 12-37. *ESXi-001 successfully created*

The next step is to add additional virtual hard disks. To do this follow the steps described:

61. Click to select the guest virtual machine to add the virtual hard disks to, in this case **ESXi Host 001**, and then click on **Edit virtual machine settings**.

62. You will see the Virtual Machine Settings screen as shown in Figure 12-38.

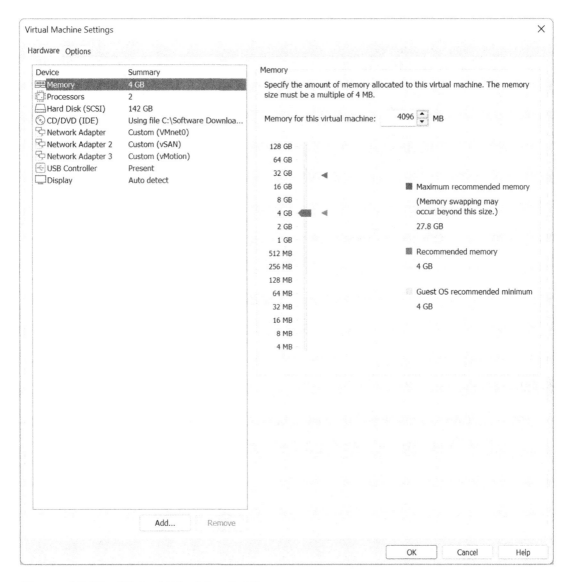

Figure 12-38. *Virtual Machine Settings screen*

63. Click the **Add...** button.

64. You will see the **Add Hardware Wizard** screen as shown in
     Figure 12-39.

Figure 12-39. *Hardware Type selection*

65. Click on Hard Disk and then click **Next >**. You will see the **Select a Disk Type** screen as shown in Figure 12-40.

Figure 12-40. *Selecting a Disk Type*

66.   Click the radio button for **SCSI** and then click **Next >**.

67.   You will see the **Select a Disk** screen shown in Figure 12-41.

Figure 12-41. *Selecting a Disk Type*

68. Click the radio button for **Create a new virtual disk** and then
     click **Next >**.

69. You will see the **Specify Disk Capacity** screen.

70. In the **Maximum disk size (GB)** box, enter the size of disk you
     want to create. In this example we have just created a 100GB
     virtual hard disk.

71. Click the radio button for **Split virtual disk into multiple files** as
     shown in Figure 12-42.

Figure 12-42. *Specifying the Disk Capacity*

72. Click **Next >** to continue.

73. Enter a disk name in the box. In this example the file is called **ESXi Host-001-1** as shown in Figure 12-43.

Figure 12-43. *Specifying the Disk File*

74. Click **Finish**.

75. You will return to the Virtual Machine Settings screen.

76. Click **OK**.

77. Repeat the adding virtual hard disks process to create the
     other three virtual hard disks or whatever number the vSAN
     requirement is.

78. Once finished, click **OK** in the Virtual Machine Settings screen.
     You will return to the VMware Workstation main screen.

As we are running vSAN, then the minimum number of hosts required is three.
Therefore, you need to repeat the process to create another two ESXi host servers to
make up the other nodes of the cluster. Do this by following exactly the same process,
building a new virtual machine for the ESXi host, and then adding the additional
networking and hard disks required.

Finally, you will have something that looks like the following screenshot with the
three ESXi host servers built and configured as shown in Figure 12-44.

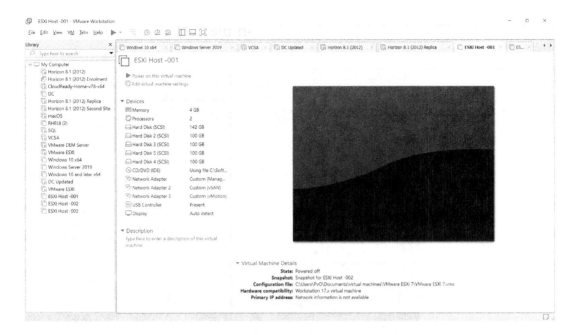

Figure 12-44. *Specifying the Disk File*

Note that the virtual hardware has been created and configured; the next step is to start installing the software.

Installing the VMware ESXi Software

In this section we are going to install the VMware ESXi hypervisor software on the virtual machines that we created in the previous section.

As we have mentioned previously, this isn't an ESXi installation guide, and so we will cover this at a very high level from a VMware Workstation Pro perspective.

To install VMware ESXi, follow the steps described:

1. From the Library pane in Workstation Pro, click on **ESXi Host-001**.

2. Now click on **Power on this virtual machine**.

3. You will see the virtual machine will power on, and as it is connected to the installation media via ISO images, then the ESXi installer will launch as shown in Figure 12-45.

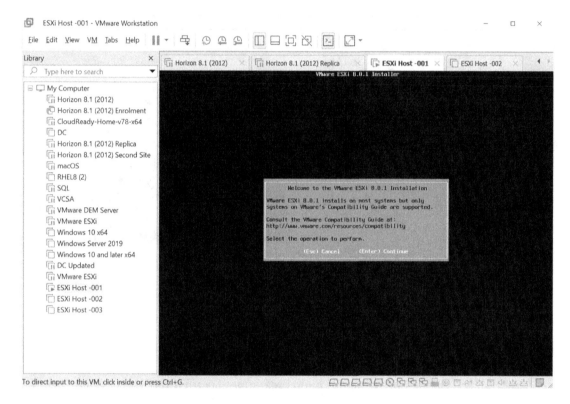

Figure 12-45. *VM powered on and ESXi installer launched*

4. With the focus on the VM, press **Enter** to continue.

5. On the **End-User License Agreement** screen, press **F11** to accept the terms of the license and continue.

6. The VM will then scan for the available hardware before showing the **Select a Disk to Install or Upgrade** screen.

    On this screen you will see the five virtual hard disks that we created in the previous section. Select the first disk on the list, labelled **mpx.vmhba0:C0:T0:L0** and with a configured size of 142GB. This is the disk that is going to be used for the ESXi host operating system or hypervisor.

    The selected disk will be highlighted in yellow as shown in Figure 12-46.

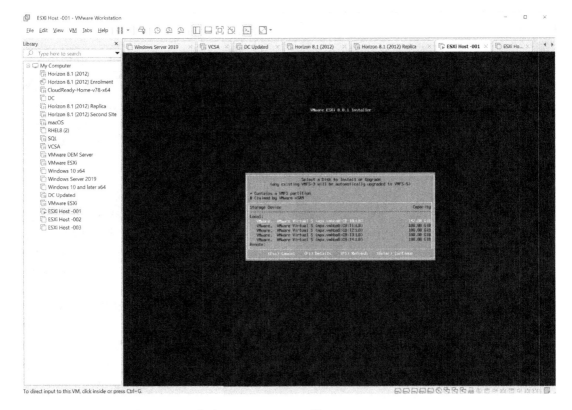

Figure 12-46. *Selecting a disk for ESXi installation*

7. Press **Enter** to continue.

8. You will see the keyboard layout configuration screen.

9. Select the language you want to use which will now show highlighted in yellow. In this example we have selected **United Kingdom** as shown in Figure 12-47.

Figure 12-47. *Selecting language for the keyboard layout*

10. Now enter a root password followed by typing in the password a
     second time to confirm.

11. Press **Enter** to continue.

12. You will see the installation confirmation screen. Press **F11** to start
     the installation.

13. You will now see ESXi 8 being installed.

14. Once you see the **Installation Complete** screen, press **Enter** to
     reboot and start ESXi. Once rebooted ESXi will load, and you will
     see the console as shown in Figure 12-48.

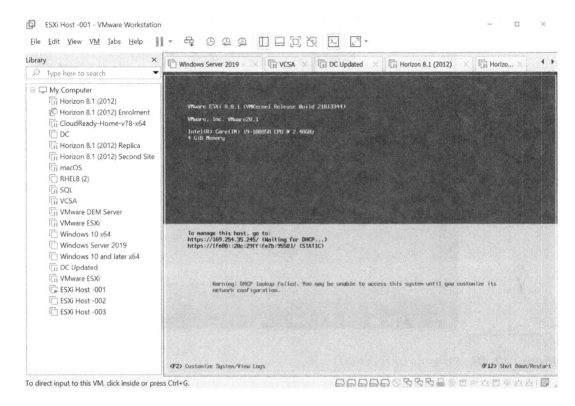

Figure 12-48. *Selecting language for the keyboard layout*

The next step is to configure the ESXi console for networking.

This would be done in exactly the same way as you would do for any other ESXi host server you were installing and configuring. So, logging in and then configuring the management network using the network adapter that was configured as the management network and a fixed IP address from the configured subnet for the management network.

Once you have completed this, then repeat the process for the remaining two host servers. You will now have your three ESXi host servers built and configured, ready for creating the cluster once vCenter has been installed and configured.

If, using one of the Windows VMs created back in Chapter 9, you connect to the management network, power the VM on, and launch a browser and connect to one of the ESXi hosts, you will be able to see the configuration as shown in Figure 12-49.

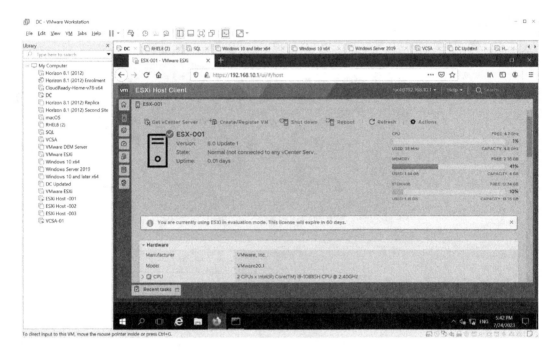

Figure 12-49. *Console of ESXi-001*

Figure 12-50 shows the networking configuration.

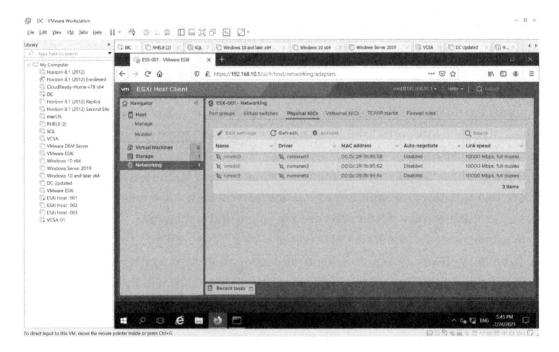

Figure 12-50. *Console of ESXi-001 - Networking Configuration*

And finally Figure 12-51 shows the storage configuration with the local 142GB datastore on which ESXi is installed and the four 100GB disks that were created as examples for building a vSAN cluster.

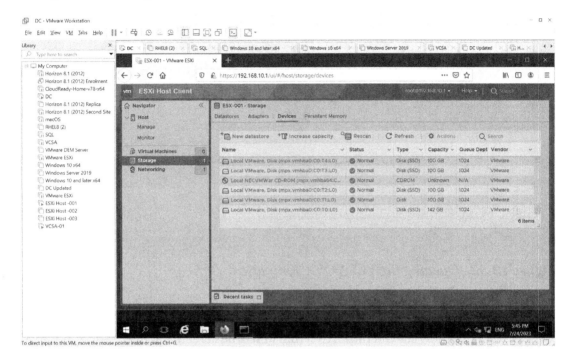

Figure 12-51. *Console of ESXi-001 - Storage Configuration*

Installing VMware vCenter Server Software

Now that the host servers have been installed and configured, then the next step is to install the vCenter Server to enable management of the ESXi hosts and to configure any other additional features such as vSAN.

To install vCenter Server as a VM running in VMware Workstation Pro, follow the steps described:

1. From the Workstation Pro main screen, click on the **File** menu, and then from the menu options, click **Open.** In the Open dialog box that is now displayed, navigate to the folder location that contains the VCSA OVA file as shown in Figure 12-52.

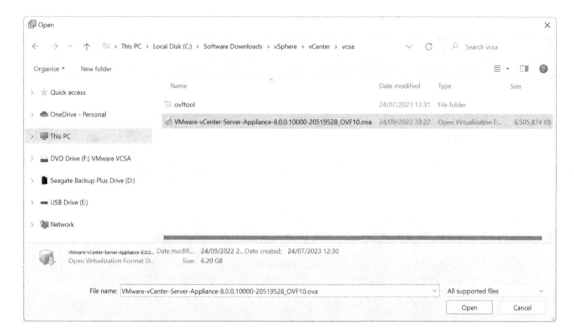

Figure 12-52. *Opening the VCSA OVA Template*

2. Click **Open**.

3. You will now see the **Import Virtual Machine** screen and the
    End-User License Agreement page.

4. Check the **I accept the terms** box and then click **Next >** as shown
    in Figure 12-53.

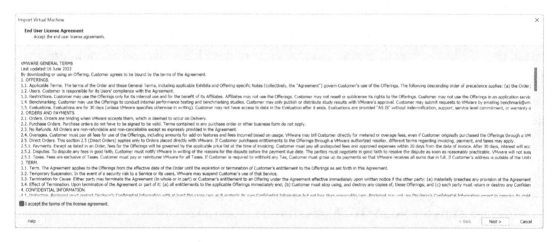

Figure 12-53. *End-User License Agreement*

5. The next screen is to provide a name for the VCSA. In this example it is called **VCSA-01**, and for the storage path, we have left it as default as shown in Figure 12-54.

Figure 12-54. *Configuring VM name for VCSA*

6. Click **Next** > to continue and then complete the configuration of the vCenter Server. We are not going to detail the configuration as this is the same as it would be for any other vCenter Server installation regardless of this running as a VM in Workstation Pro.

7. Once completed you will see the import process and its progress as shown in Figure 12-55.

Figure 12-55. *Progress of VCSA Import Process*

8. Once the import process has successfully completed, you will see vCenter Server is running as shown in Figure 12-56.

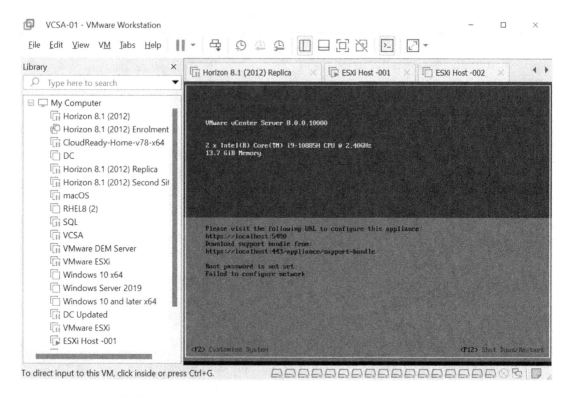

Figure 12-56. *VCSA Running in Workstation Pro*

You have now successfully deployed a vCenter Server appliance to manage the ESXi host servers.

Summary

In this chapter we have started by discussing the requirements for building a vSphere environment using VMware Workstation Pro.

Rather than making this chapter a vSphere configuration chapter, which would be a whole book in its own right, we have shown you the basics of how to go about building a vSphere environment using a simple 3-node cluster that has the additional virtual disk requirements for running vSAN and the appropriate networks for vSAN and vMotion.

This is just the bare minimum to get up and running and to give you an idea on how to approach creating a vSphere environment using Workstation Pro.

CHAPTER 13

Upgrading and Updating Workstation Pro

In this chapter we are going to discuss the process for upgrading to a newer version of Workstation Pro. We are going to approach the upgrade as two specific different types of upgrade depending on availability from VMware. Firstly, as an update, or point release, to the version of the software you are currently running. By this we mean the version will be the same version number, that is, version 16; however, the point release will be updated. For example, you might be running 16.2.1 currently, and the latest updated version available for download is 16.2.5. A point release will typically add a couple of minor features or bug fixes.

The second is a full upgrade to a new version. For example, upgrading from version 16 to version 17 as we will work through in this chapter. We will start with looking at the update process, and in this example, we are updating from version 16.2.1 to version 16.2.5.

Updating to a New Release

If you already know that there is an update for Workstation Pro, then you can go straight ahead and download it on to your host machine ready for installation. This is particularly useful if you don't have Internet access, so you can download the updated version as an offline version. We will cover the actual installation of an update later in this section.

If you haven't already downloaded a new update, then Workstation Pro can automatically check for updates. Of course, you will need to be connected to the Internet to do it this way as Workstation Pro will need to communicate with an update server hosted by VMware. Ensure you have the following address unblocked:

```
https://softwareupdate.vmware.com/cds
```

© Peter von Oven 2023
P. von Oven, *Learning VMware Workstation for Windows*, https://doi.org/10.1007/978-1-4842-9969-2_13

To check for updates, first ensure that Workstation Pro is running. Then click the **Help** menu, and then from the options shown, click **Software Updates** as shown in the following screenshot in Figure 13-1.

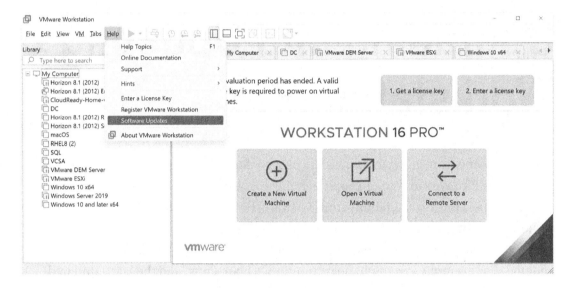

Figure 13-1. *Workstation Pro - Selecting Software Updates*

You will see the following **Software Updates** screen that states there are no updated pending as shown in the following screenshot in Figure 13-2.

Figure 13-2. *Software Updates screen*

Click the **Check for Updates** button.

You will now see that Workstation Pro is now connecting to the VMware hosted update server to check for any updates as shown in Figure 13-3.

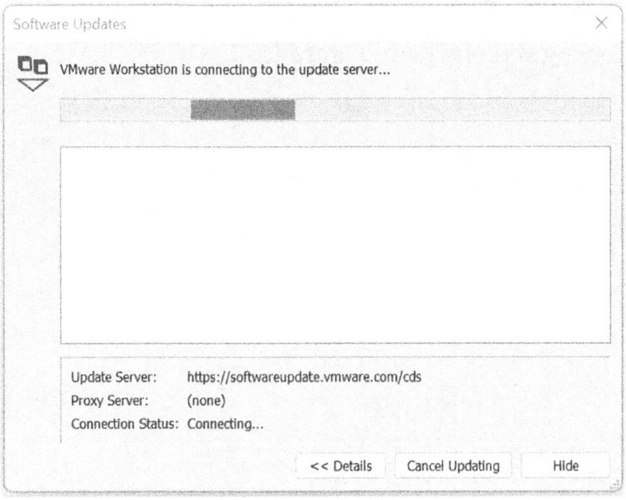

Figure 13-3. *Checking for new updates*

As a completely new version is now available, then you will see the following screenshot in Figure 13-4. Note that depending on when you upgrade, there may well be a newer version than that shown in these examples, or no new version at all.

Figure 13-4. *Displaying the available upgrade*

As this section is about updating the current version, then we are going to ignore the Workstation Pro 17 upgrade and click the **Cancel** button.

You will now see that the Software Updates screen shows the update to version 16.2.5 as shown in the following screenshot in Figure 13-5.

Figure 13-5. *Displaying the available updates*

Click the **Download and Install** button. You will see the following as the updated version is downloaded (Figure 13-6).

Figure 13-6. *Downloading the latest update*

The downloaded update is saved to the following location as shown in Figure 13-7.

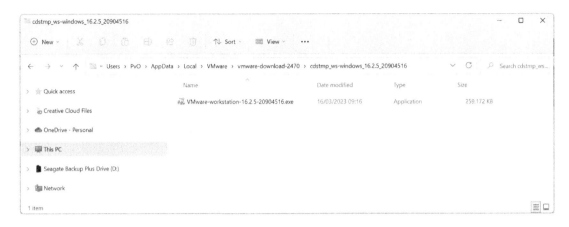

Figure 13-7. *Downloading the latest update*

As you can see, the folder location for the downloaded update is

C:\Users\<username>\AppData\Local\VMware\vmware-download-2470

You need not worry about launching the update installer as it is automatically launched once the download has completed.

As it launches, you will likely see two User Account Control (UAC) message windows pop up warning you about whether you want this app to be able to make changes to your device. One will be for the Workstation Pro installer, and the other one will be for the VMware CDS Update Launcher.

Click the **Yes** button on both messages to allow the Workstation installer to make the changes required.

The installer will now launch, and you will see the Welcome to the VMware Workstation Pro Setup Wizard screen as shown in the following screenshot in Figure 13-8.

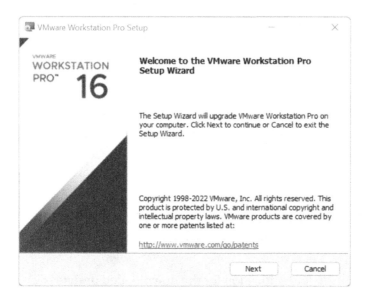

Figure 13-8. *Welcome to the Setup Wizard for update installation*

Click the **Next** button to continue.

One thing to be aware of. As you have used the update feature from a running instance of Workstation Pro, it is likely that it is still running. If that is the case, then you will see the following message pop-up shown in Figure 13-9.

Figure 13-9. *Warning message that Workstation is still running*

The vmware.exe it refers to is Workstation Pro. Click **OK** to close the warning message and then quit the running instance of Workstation Pro.

You can then go back and click the **Next** button again on the **Welcome to the VMware Workstation Pro Setup Wizard** screen. You will already be familiar with these screens as you would have seen them during the initial installation of Workstation Pro; however, you can change some of these configured features during the update if you want to. In this example we will go with the default settings. For details of these options and what they mean, refer to Chapter 7.

You will now see the **End-User License Agreement** screen as shown in Figure 13-10.

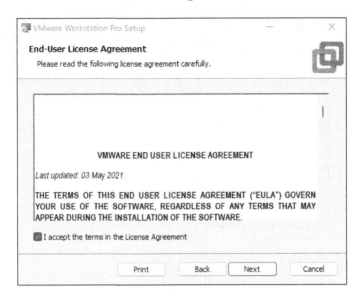

Figure 13-10. *End-User License Agreement*

Check the box for **I accept the terms in the License Agreement** and then click **Next**. You will see the **Custom Setup** screen as shown in Figure 13-11.

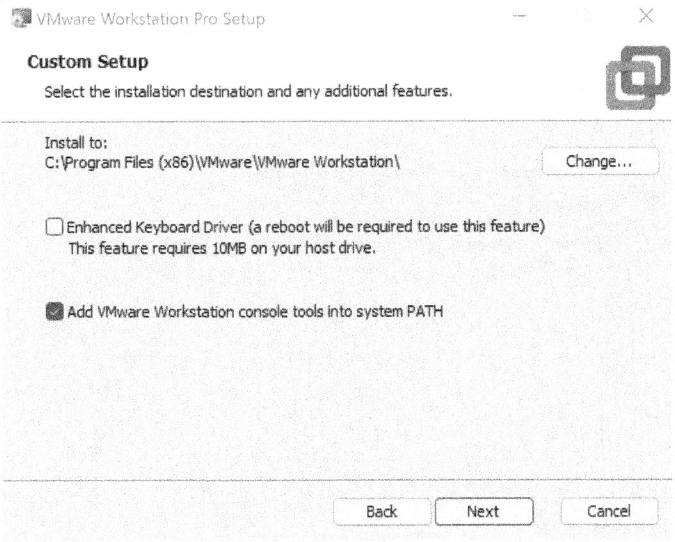

Figure 13-11. *Custom Setup*

Click **Next** to continue. You will see the **User Experience Settings** screen as shown in the following screenshot in Figure 13-12.

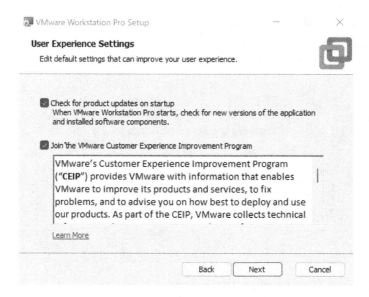

Figure 13-12. *User Experience Settings*

Click **Next** to continue. You will see the **Shortcuts** screen as shown in Figure 13-13.

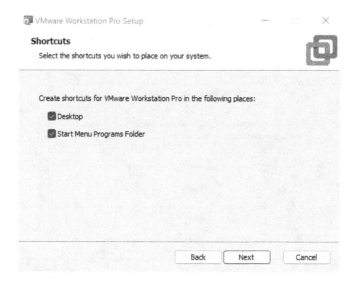

Figure 13-13. *Shortcuts*

Click **Next** to continue. You will see the **Ready to upgrade VMware Workstation Pro** screen as shown in Figure 13-14.

Figure 13-14. *Ready to Upgrade VMware Workstation Pro*

Click the **Upgrade** button to continue. You will see the upgrade process start and the progress and status as shown in the following screenshot in Figure 13-15.

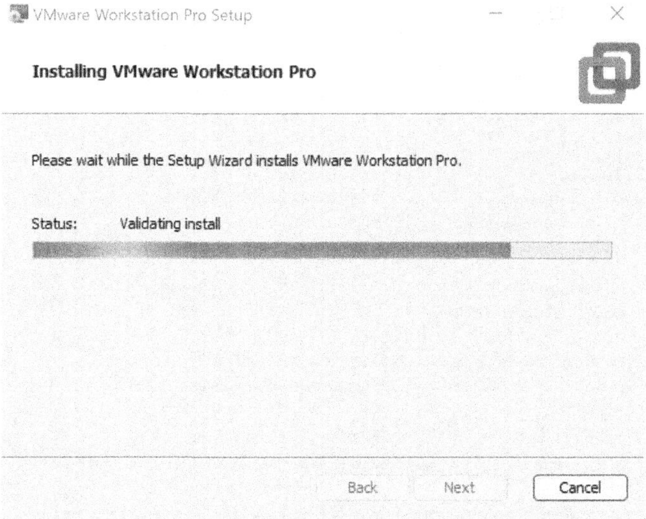

Figure 13-15. *Installation progress and status*

Once the upgrade has finished, you will see the **Completed the VMware Workstation Pro Setup Wizard** as shown in the following screenshot in Figure 13-16.

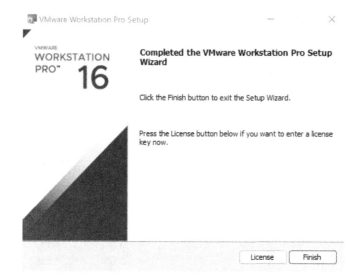

Figure 13-16. *Completed the VMware Workstation Pro Setup Wizard*

To check that Workstation Pro has been upgraded successfully, from the menu, click **Help** and then select **About VMware Workstation**. You will see that the **Version** is now showing as 16.2.5 as shown in Figure 13-17.

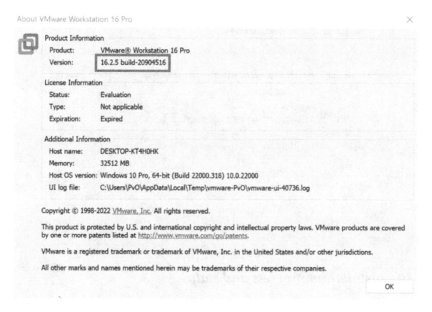

Figure 13-17. *About VMware Workstation showing new updated version*

Click **OK** to close the About VMware Workstation Pro screen.

We have now successfully updated VMware Workstation Pro from version 16.2.1 to version 16.2.5.

Even though the version of Workstation Pro has been updated, the process doesn't stop there. As part of the update, there is likely also going to be an update to the version of VMware Tools. This upgrade will affect all the virtual machines that you have configured and running and therefore all these virtual machines should be updated.

In the next section, we are going to discuss how to update VMware Tools.

Updating VMware Tools

In the section, following the update to Workstation Pro, we are going to update VMware Tools. To do this ensure that the virtual machine you are updating is powered on.

Click the **VM** menu and select **Reinstall VMware Tools...** as shown in Figure 13-18.

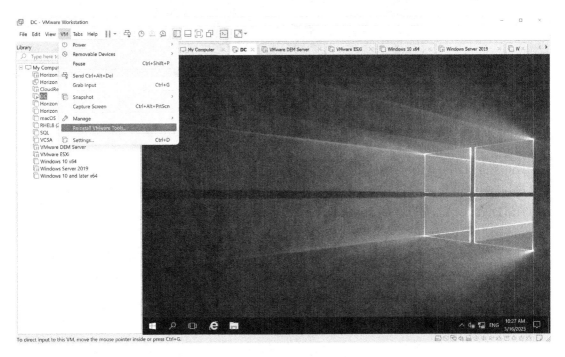

Figure 13-18. *About VMware Workstation showing new updated version*

You will see a yellow-colored box appear under the desktop of the running virtual machine. This is shown in the following screenshot in Figure 13-19.

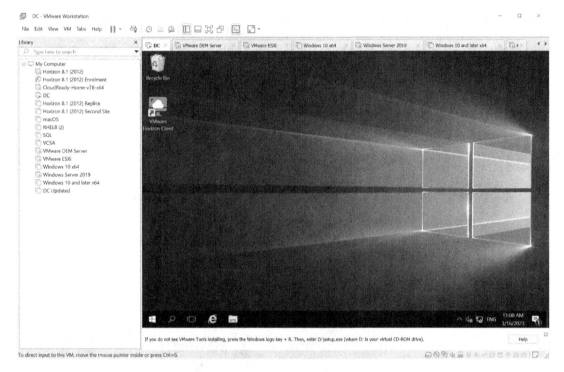

Figure 13-19. *About VMware Workstation showing new updated version*

This states that if the install of VMware tools does not start automatically, then you will need to launch it manually be opening a Run command and typing D:\setup.exe.

The D: drive CD-ROM will already have been mounted as an ISO to the virtual machine when you selected the Reinstall VMware Tools option.

The ISO image contains the updated version of VMware Tools, and for reference, the filename for VMware Tools is called **windows.iso** and can be found in the VMware Workstation folder as shown in the following screenshot in Figure 13-20.

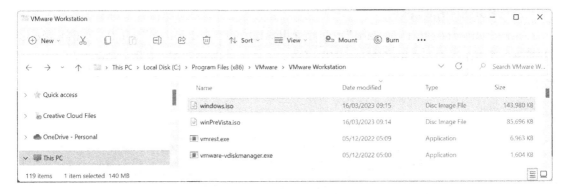

Figure 13-20. *VMware Tools Windows ISO file*

In the bottom right corner of the desktop of the virtual machine being updated, you will see the following message pop-up for the DVD Drive being mounted as shown in Figure 13-21.

Figure 13-21. *Pop-up message for DVD Drive containing VMware Tools ISO*

Click the box to select what to do.

You will now see the following box pop-up in the top right-hand corner of the desktop as shown in Figure 13-22.

Figure 13-22. *Pop-up message for DVD Drive containing VMware Tools ISO*

Click **Run setup64.exe**.

You will now see the VMware Tools installer launch, and you will see the **Welcome to the installation wizard for VMware Tools** screen as shown in the following screenshot in Figure 13-23.

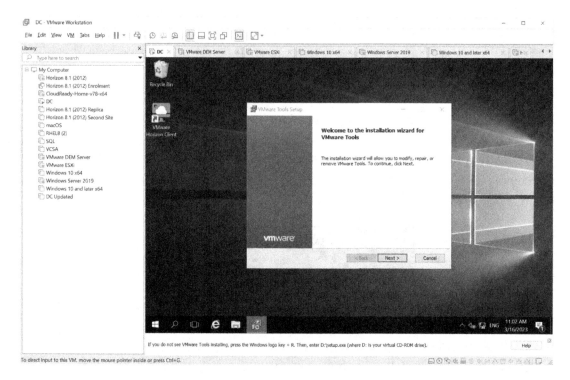

Figure 13-23. *VMware Tools Installation Wizard*

Click **Next >** to continue.

You will see the **Program Maintenance** screen as shown in the following screenshot in Figure 13-24.

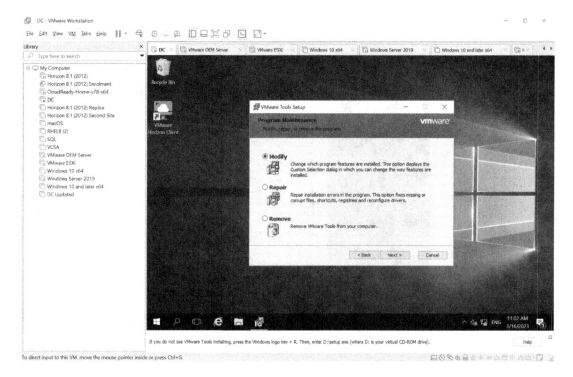

Figure 13-24. *VMware Tools Setup - Program Maintenance screen*

Click the radio button for **Modify**.

Now click **Next >** to continue.

The next screen is the **Custom Setup** screen where you can select what features of VMware Tools you want to be installed.

Updating the current version of VMware Tools also provides you with an opportunity to make changes to the currently installed features.

The **Custom Setup** screen is shown in the following screenshot in Figure 13-25.

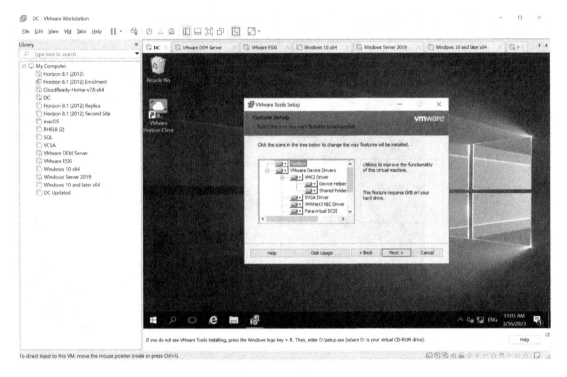

Figure 13-25. *VMware Tools Setup - Custom Setup screen*

In this example, we are going to accept the currently selected default features. Also, on this screen you can click the **Disk Usage** button if you want to check the amount of disk space that is being consumed. An example of this is shown in the following screenshot in Figure 13-26.

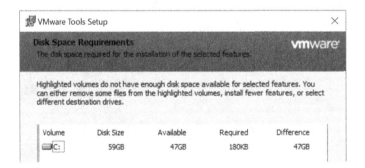

Figure 13-26. *VMware Tools Setup - Custom Setup screen*

Click **Next >** to continue.

You will now see the **Ready to change VMware Tools** screen as shown in Figure 13-27.

If you need to review any changes or to go back and change any of the configuration setting, then you can click the **< Back** button.

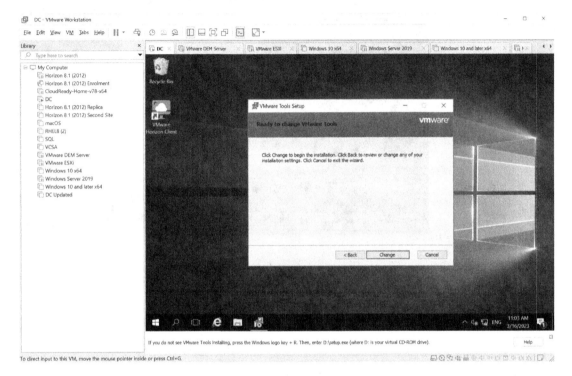

Figure 13-27. *VMware Tools Setup - Ready to Change screen*

Now click the **Change** button.

You will briefly see the status screen showing the progress of the update. Once the update has successfully completed, you will see the **Completed the VMware Tools Setup Wizard** as shown in the following screenshot in Figure 13-28.

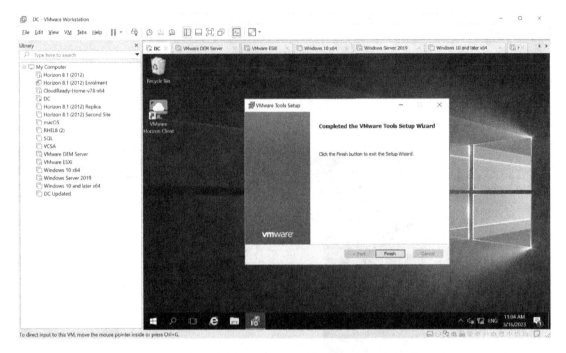

Figure 13-28. *VMware Tools Setup - Completed the Setup Wizard*

You have now successfully updated the version of VMware Tools for this virtual machine.

You will need to repeat this process for updating VMware Tools on all your virtual machines.

It's not just VMware Tools that may need updating. Depending on the version of update, it could also see a newer hardware compatibility for virtual machine hardware, although this is more likely with a completely new version.

We will discuss hardware compatibility updates at the end of the next section of this chapter, "Upgrading to a New Version."

Upgrading to a New Version

In the previous section, we discussed how to update to a new release of the same version. In that example we updated version 16.2.1 to version 16.2.5.

In this section we are going to discuss upgrading to a completely new version, and in this example, we will upgrade the 16.2.5 version to version 17.

There are a couple of ways to upgrade and acquire the new version. You may well have gone right ahead and purchased the new version and already have it downloaded on to your host machine. If that is the case, then you can skip to the "Performing the Upgrade" section.

The other way is to check for updates from your current version. To do this first ensure that Workstation Pro is running.

Now click the **Help** menu, and then from the options shown, click **Software Updates** as shown in the following screenshot in Figure 13-29.

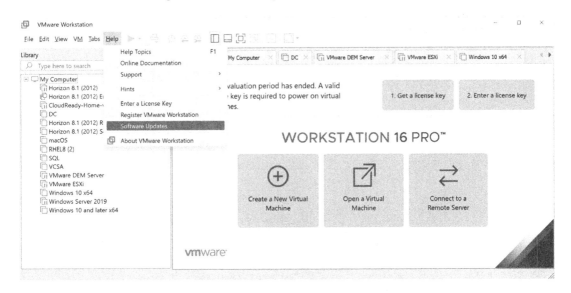

Figure 13-29. *Workstation Pro - Selecting Software Updates*

You will see the following **Software Updates** screen that states there are no updates pending as shown in the following screenshot in Figure 13-30.

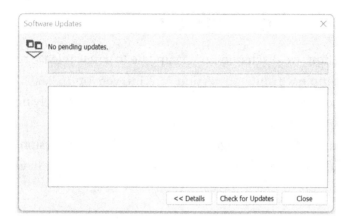

Figure 13-30. *Software Updates Screen.*

Click the **Check for Updates** button.

You will now see that Workstation Pro is now connecting to the VMware hosted update server to check for any updates as shown in Figure 13-31.

Figure 13-31. *Checking for New Updates*

As a completely new version is now available, then you will see the following screenshot in Figure 13-32.

Figure 13-32. *New version of VMware Workstation available*

You will see that you have three options via the three buttons at the bottom of the screen. You can be reminded later, you can skip this new version and continue using the current version, or if you click **Get More information**, you will be taken to the VMware website where you can purchase the new version as shown in the following screenshot in Figure 13-33.

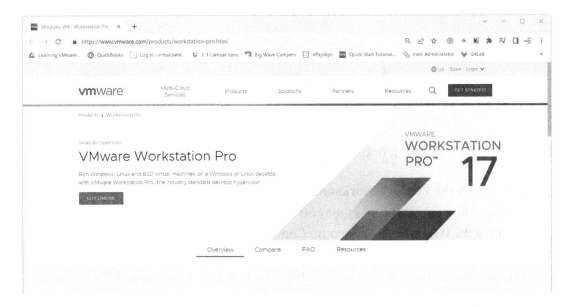

Figure 13-33. *VMware Workstation Pro page*

So now you have purchased and/or downloaded the new version of VMware Workstation Pro, you can start the upgrade process.

Performing the Upgrade

In this section we are going to upgrade our current version of VMware Workstation Pro. In this example version 16.2.5 to version 17. We are going to stick with the default configuration options, but if you want to understand more details on these options, then please refer to Chapter 7.

Ensure that Workstation Pro is not currently running before you start the upgrade process.

Navigate to the location of the newly downloaded version 17 installer. An example of this is shown in Figure 13-34.

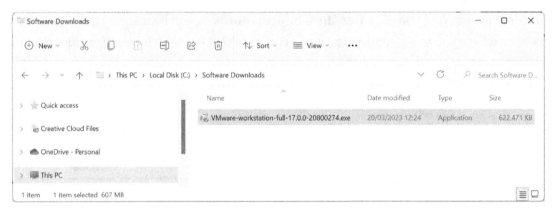

Figure 13-34. *VMware Workstation Pro new version*

Double click the **VMware-workstation-full-17.0.0-20800274.exe** file to launch the installer. Note that the last number may be different depending on the build.

If you see the Windows User Account Control (UAC) message appear, click **Yes** to accept, and continue.

You will now see the VMware Workstation Pro 17 splash screen appear as shown in the following screenshot in Figure 13-35.

Figure 13-35. *VMware Workstation Pro 17 splash screen*

You will also see the following VMware Product Installation message pop-up in the bottom right-hand corner of the desktop as shown in Figure 13-36.

Figure 13-36. *Preparing for VMware Workstation Pro 17 Installation*

You will now see the Welcome to the **VMware Workstation Pro Setup Wizard** screen as shown in the following screenshot in Figure 13-37.

Figure 13-37. *Welcome to VMware Workstation Pro Setup Wizard*

Click **Next** to continue. You will see the End-User License Agreement screen as shown in the following screenshot in Figure 13-38.

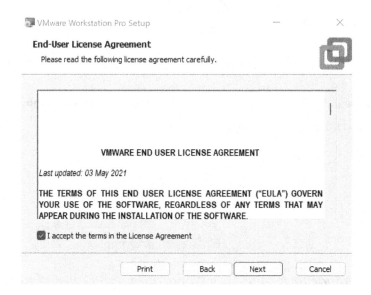

Figure 13-38. *End-User License screen*

Click **Next** to continue. You will see the **Custom Setup** screen as shown in Figure 13-39.

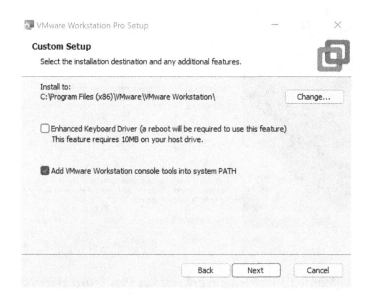

Figure 13-39. *Custom Setup screen*

Click **Next** to continue. You will see the **User Experience Settings** screen as shown in Figure 13-40.

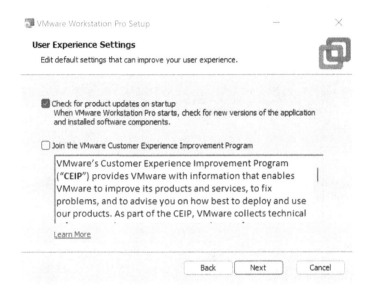

Figure 13-40. *User Experience Settings screen*

Click **Next** to continue. You will see the **Shortcuts** screen as shown in the following screenshot in Figure 13-41.

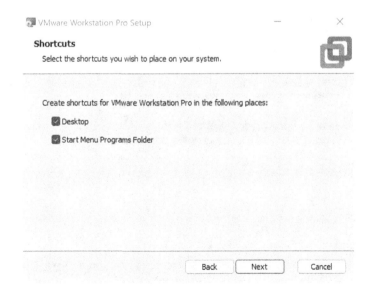

Figure 13-41. *User Experience Settings screen*

Click **Next** to continue. You will see the **Ready to Upgrade VMware Workstation Pro** screen as shown in the following screenshot in Figure 13-42.

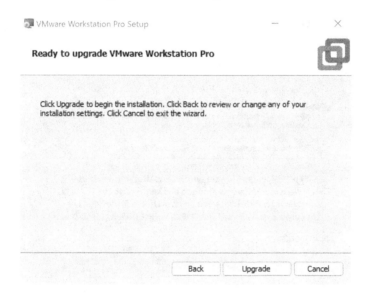

Figure 13-42. *Ready to Upgrade VMware Workstation Pro screen*

Click the **Upgrade** button. You will see the installation screen as shown in Figure 13-43.

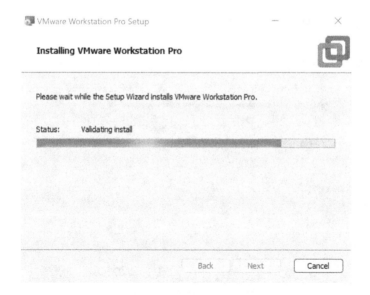

Figure 13-43. *Installing Upgrade VMware Workstation Pro screen*

As part of the install progress and status, you will see old drivers and files removed and then new drivers, files, and registry keys installed.

Once completed you will see the **Completed the VMware Workstation Pro Setup Wizard** screen as shown in the following screenshot in Figure 13-44.

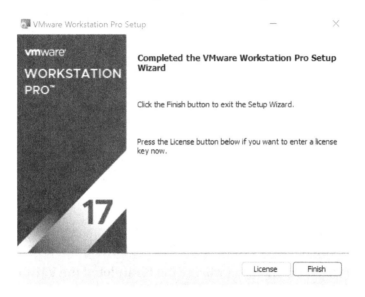

Figure 13-44. *Completed the VMware Workstation Pro Setup Wizard screen*

You will see that there are two buttons at the bottom of the screen. You can either quit the installer by clicking the **Finish** button, or you can click the **License** button to add a license key before you exit and complete the installation. If you opt not to add a license key, then Workstation Pro will default to a 30-day evaluation license. After 30 days you will no longer be able to power on virtual machines until you enter a new license key.

VMware Workstation Pro 17 will need a new license key. The Workstation Pro 16 license key will not work with version 17.

In this example we are going to add the license key for version 17, so click the License button.

You will now see the Enter License Key screen as shown in the following screenshot in Figure 13-45.

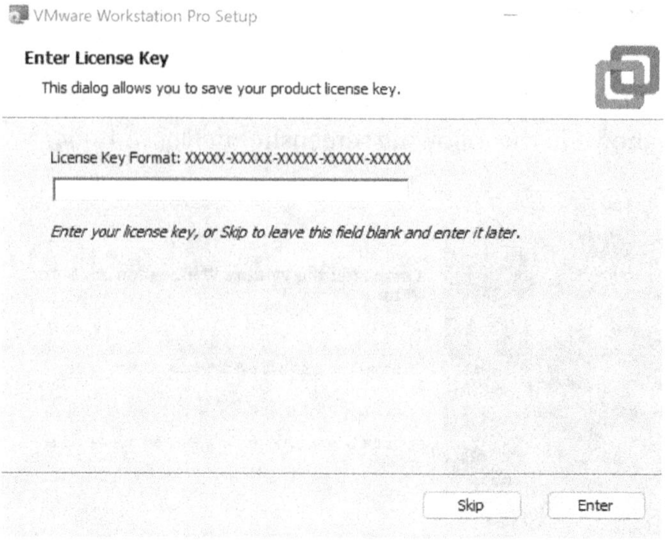

Figure 13-45. *Enter License Key screen*

Once you have entered your license key, click the **Enter** button. When the license has been successfully validated, then you will see the **Completed the VMware Workstation Pro Setup Wizard** screen as shown in the following screenshot in Figure 13-46.

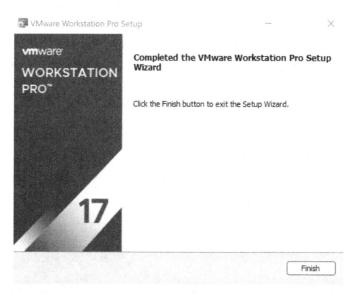

Figure 13-46. *Completed the VMware Workstation Pro Setup Wizard screen*

Click the **Finish** button.

You will now be prompted to restart your host machine as shown in the following screenshot in Figure 13-47.

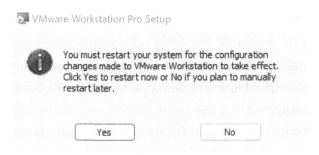

Figure 13-47. Restart host machine after installation

Click the **Yes** button to restart your host machine.

You have now successfully upgraded from Workstation Pro version 16.2.5 to Workstation Pro version 17.

Although we have just upgraded the Workstation Pro application itself, we now need to upgrade the version of VMware Tools running on the virtual machines, along with potentially changing the hardware compatibility so that you can take advantage of some of the new hardware features that may be available as part of this upgrade.

We have already discussed how to upgrade VMware Tools in the **Updating VMware Tools** section of this chapter, when we updated Workstation Pro to a new release so, please refer to that section on how to perform the upgrade task as it is no different.

Hardware Compatibility

In this section we are going to discuss how to change the hardware compatibility which allows you to take advantage of new hardware capabilities, expanded virtual machine capabilities, or enabling Workstation Pro to work with different generation of VMware solutions.

The hardware compatibility changes and updates apply to both Workstation Pro versions we have discussed throughout this chapter, so it may well be that there were some changes between updating from 16.2.1 to 16.2.5 as well as new features of version 17. In this discussion we will show both.

Before we start the process, you need to ensure that the virtual machine you want to change is powered off. It is also worth noting that changing the hardware compatibility is done on a per virtual machine basis which means you don't need to change all virtual machines. You could have a use case where you need to be running an older version of hardware.

To change the hardware compatibility, follow the steps described:

Click and select the virtual machine you want to change the hardware compatibility for, from the **Library** pane.

Then, from the menu, click **VM** and point to **Manage**. From the next level menu that appears to the right, click **Change Hardware Compatibility...** as shown in the following screenshot in Figure 13-48.

Figure 13-48. *Change the Hardware Compatibility*

You will now see the **Welcome to the Change Hardware Compatibility Wizard** screen. Depending on the version of Workstation Pro, you will see either of the two screenshots shown in Figure 13-49.

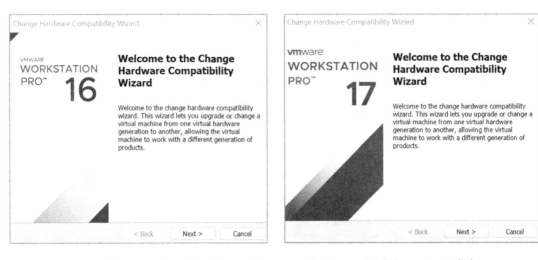

Figure 13-49. *Change the Hardware Compatibility - v16(L) and v17(R)*

Click **Next >** to continue.

You will now see the **Choose the Virtual Machine Hardware Compatibility** as shown in Figure 13-50.

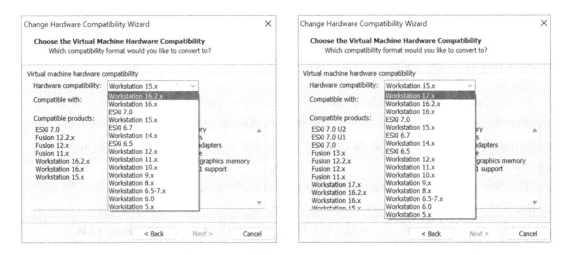

Figure 13-50. *Selecting the Hardware Compatibility - v16(L) and v17(R)*

From the **Hardware Compatibility** drop-down, select the version you want to be compatible with. Under the **Compatible products** field, you will see listed which versions of product your selected compatibility works with and then on the right hand side in the **Limitations** field, you will see the maximum hardware limits for your chosen compatibility. In this example we are running Workstation Pro 17 and are going to change the hardware compatibility to Workstation 17.x.

From the **Hardware Compatibility** drop-down, select **Workstation 17.x**.

Now click **Next >** to continue.

You will see the **Clone before Converting** screen which is the same regardless of the version and is shown in the following screenshot in Figure 13-51.

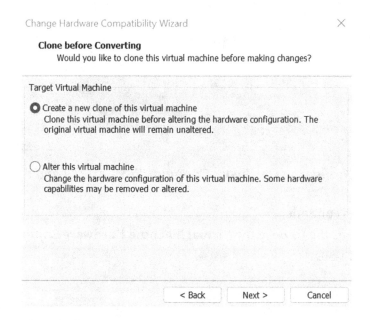

Figure 13-51. *Clone before Converting screen*

In the **Target Virtual Machine** field, there are two options. The first option will create a clone of the virtual machine and then make the changes on the clone leaving the original virtual machine in the same state so that you can go back to it should you need to.

The second option goes right ahead and makes the changes immediately without having a clone as a backup.

Lets work through the two examples. If we take the **Create a new clone of this virtual machine** option first and click the radio button to select it.

Now click the **Next >** button.

You will now see the **Name the Clone** screen as shown in Figure 13-52.

Figure 13-52. *Name the Clone screen.*

In the **Virtual machine name** box, type in a name for the clone. In this example we are cloning a virtual machine called DC so have simply called it DC Updated to reflect the update of the hardware compatibility. The original virtual machine will remain and will still be called DC.

Next, in the **Location** box, either leave the default path, in this case the default path configured for virtual machines in Workstation Pro, enter a new path, or click the **Browse...** button and select a new folder location.

Click **Next >** to continue.

You now see the **Review Changes** screen that summarizes all the changes that are about to be made as shown in the following screenshot in Figure 13-53.

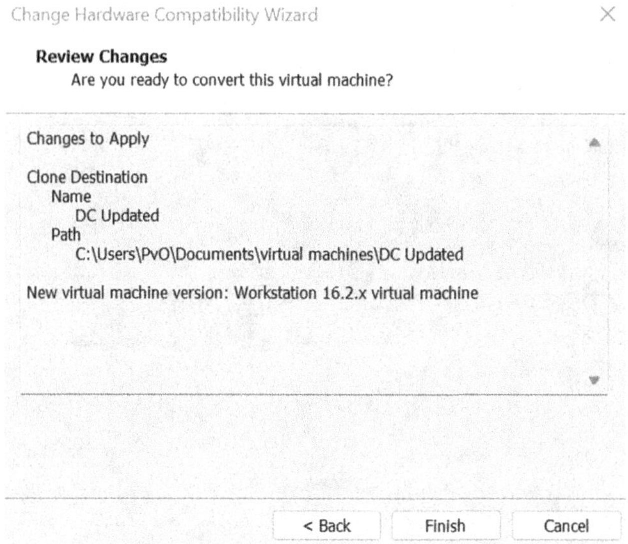

Figure 13-53. *Review Changes screen*

Click **Finish**. You will see the **Converting Virtual Machine** screen as the clone is created as shown in the following screenshot in Figure 13-54.

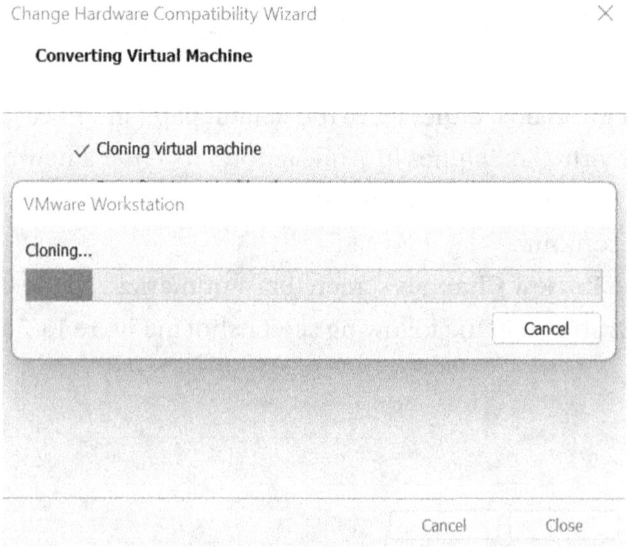

Figure 13-54. *Virtual Machine Cloning process*

Once completed you will see the following (Figure 13-55).

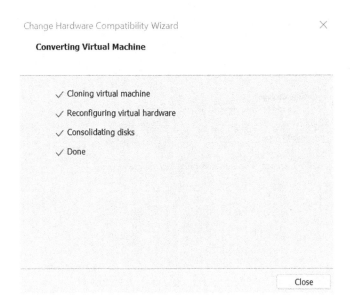

Figure 13-55. *Completed Cloning process*

Click **Close** to complete the process.

If we now look at the second option for Altering the virtual machine. To do this click the radio button for **Alter this virtual machine** as shown in Figure 13-56.

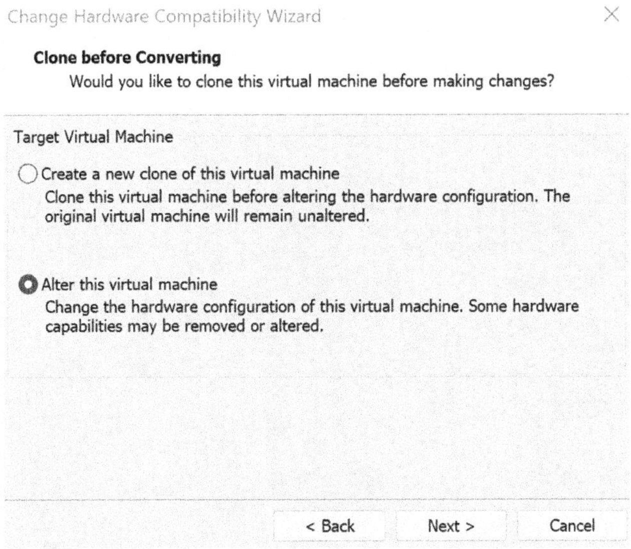

Figure 13-56. *Altering the virtual machine*

Click **Next >** to continue. You will see the **Review Changes** screen as shown in Figure 13-57.

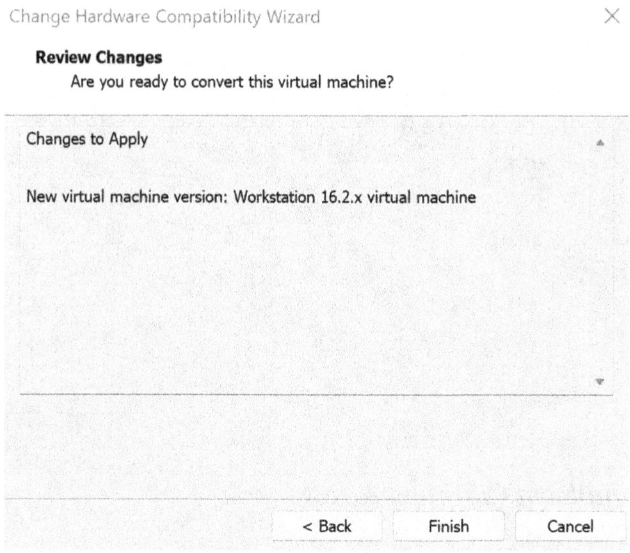

Figure 13-57. *Review Changes for altering the virtual machine*

Now click the **Finish** button as shown in Figure 13-58.

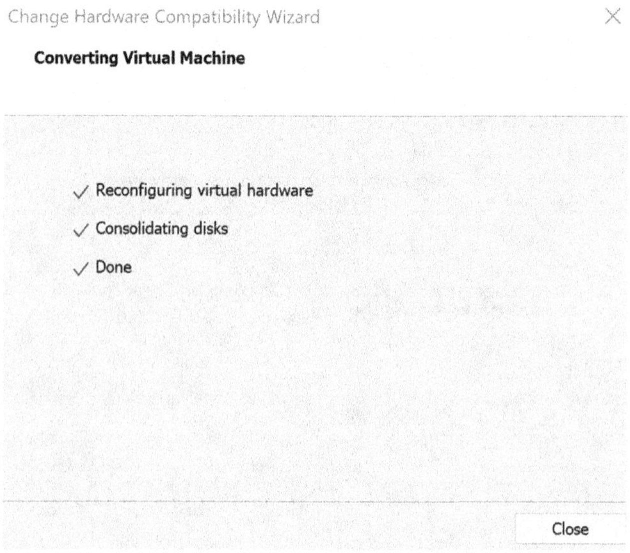

Figure 13-58. *Review Changes for altering the virtual machine*

Once you see all the tasks have been completed and have a tick next to them, you can click the **Close** button.

You have now successfully upgraded or updated the hardware compatibility of VMware Workstation Pro.

Summary

In this chapter, we have discussed how to update your current version to another release of the same version, and in this case, we updated Workstation Pro 16.2.1 to Workstation Pro 16.2.5. As part of the update, we also discussed how to update the VMware tools version that is running on the virtual machines hosted by Workstation Pro.

Next, we discussed the difference between the update and a full upgrade to a new version. In this example we took our Workstation Pro 16.2.1 instance and upgraded it to a completely new version, Workstation Pro 17. Again, as we did with the update, we updated the VMware tools version that is running on the virtual machines hosted by Workstation Pro. Also, in this example of a full version upgrade, we looked at upgrading the hardware compatibility to take advantage of any new hardware features in the new version as well as compatibility with other VMware hypervisor solutions.

Index

A

Access control
  change password, 277, 278
  configuring encryption, 276
  encryption, 276
  encryption successfully
    configured, 277
  feature, 276
  removing encryption, 278, 279
  TPM, 277
Appliance view, 283, 284
Application virtualization, 10
Autofit, 137, 138
  guest option, 138
  window option, 138
Autologin, 284–286
AutoProtect
  configuration, 274
  enable, 274
  feature, 274
  interval, 274
  Maximum AutoProtect
    snapshots, 274
Auto Start
  automatic, 336
  configuration, 337, 341
  configure VM Power Actions
    screen, 341
  enter log on details, 339
  power on, 335
  run, 340

  select user, Auto Start Log On
    service, 338
  services console, 336
  services management console, 336
  start, 340
  start order, 342
  Startup type section, 336
  VMware Autostart Service, 336
  warning, 336

B

BIOS, 291
Bridged networking options, 56, 57
BusLogic parallel, 43

C

Cache, 27, 404
CD/DVD drive, 313–316
  advanced configuration settings, 88, 89
  Auto detect option, 88
  Connect at power on option, 88
  Device status box, 88
  hardware settings, 88
  SATA, 88, 89
  settings, 88
  Troubleshooting section, 89
  Use ISO image file option, 88
  Use physical drive option, 88
Center guest option, 139

© Peter von Oven 2023
P. von Oven, *Learning VMware Workstation for Windows*, https://doi.org/10.1007/978-1-4842-9969-2

W, X, Y, Z

Printed in the United States
by Baker & Taylor Publisher Services